Pete Reiser

Pete Reiser

*The Rough-and-Tumble Career
of the Perfect Ballplayer*

Sidney Jacobson

McFarland & Company, Inc., Publishers
Jefferson, North Carolina, and London

Frontispiece: Pete Reiser, who many have called
the greatest baseball prospect in the history of the game
(National Baseball Hall of Fame Library, Cooperstown, N.Y.)

LIBRARY OF CONGRESS CATALOGUING-IN-PUBLICATION DATA

Jacobson, Sidney.
    Pete Reiser : the rough-and-tumble career of the perfect
ballplayer / Sidney Jacobson.
      p.   cm.
    Includes bibliographical references and index.

    ISBN 0-7864-1876-1 (softcover : 50# alkaline paper)

    1. Reiser, Pete. 2. Baseball players—United States—
Biography. I. Title.
GV865.R423J33   2004
796.357'092—dc22   2004014629

British Library cataloguing data are available

On the cover: Pete Reiser steals home, 1946
(National Baseball Hall of Fame Library, Cooperstown, N.Y.)

Manufactured in the United States of America

McFarland & Company, Inc., Publishers
  Box 611, Jefferson, North Carolina 28640
    www.mcfarlandpub.com

For Shirley and Bill,
who coached me during
these years. They would
have enjoyed this,
for sure.

Acknowledgments

This book began as a labor of love for my first baseball idol, whom I watched with wonderment as a child from my seat in the Ebbets Field bleachers. Pete Reiser was for me the greatest player I would ever see, and the memory of his feats lingers with me all these years later.

I could not believe that someone else had not yet written the story of this incredible man and the machinations of those around him. For almost 15 years, I thought about writing this book, and taunted myself by lecturing to the sons and the friends of those who worked with me with tales of the ballplayer.

I must first thank my agent, Richard Curtis, who finally gave me the courage to attempt this story. Through the research and the writing, he was an invaluable guide, a gifted and inspiring editor, and a considerate friend.

There are several institutions that allowed me to trace, by microfilm and microfiche, the day-by-day newspaper accounts of Reiser's complete career. I am grateful to the people and the facilities at the Main Branch of the New York Public Library at Fifth Avenue and 42nd Street in New York, the Brooklyn Public Library at Grand Army Plaza in Brooklyn, the Research Library at UCLA in Los Angeles, and the main branch of the Beverly Hills Library on Rexford Drive in Beverly Hills.

Shirley Reiser Tuber, the daughter of Pete Reiser, has been a gracious and willing source of information about her father. His early scrapbooks and memorabilia, as well as those of his entire family, were all opened to me. So were the revealing and, in some ways astonishing, taped conversations made by Shirley's husband, Rick Tuber. These included discussions with Reiser himself, his wife Patricia, and various ballplayers, business associates and friends over the years.

Through Shirley Tuber, I was able to reach Ellie Burleson, who allowed me to study her vast collection of memorabilia, articles and personal letters dealing with the entire length of Reiser's career. So did my close boyhood friend, George Somkin, who sat alongside me at Ebbets Field and, at 15, became the youngest-ever nationally-syndicated sportswriter for Newspaper Enterprise Association. His collection of Reiser-related articles and photographs is extensive, illuminating and often surprising.

I am indebted to the many people who were willing to discuss their experiences and feelings about Pete Reiser personally with me, and there are several I must mention. Lonnie Frey was exceptionally open and frank in offering his opinions. So, indeed, were Julie Reiser, Dorothy Reese and the late Pete Coscarat.

I must thank Barry Stockhamer, who for more than 20 years was marketing director of the Los Angeles Dodgers, for helping me reach several important personnel, players and wives, who offered valuable information and insights to this project.

Glenn Rabney, through his enormous baseball knowledge and his mastery of the computer, has been an invaluable guide as well as being a useful reader of material that was heretofore unfamiliar to him.

Finally, I must thank my wife, Maggi, for indulging this undertaking when my absorption in it took me away from home and from her side at a time when my presence was very much needed.

Contents

Preface

HAROLD PATRICK REISER
"Pistol Pete"
Dodgers 1940–1963
ELEVEN TIMES NATIONAL LEAGUE BATTING CHAMPION,
HAD *.364* LIFETIME AVERAGE INCLUDING
THREE SEASONS OVER *.400.*
INCOMPARABLE DEFENSIVE CENTER FIELDER,
VOTED PLAYER OF THE DECADE, *1940–1950,*
AGAIN *1950–1960.* RETIRED WITH *4197* BASE HITS
AND MORE DOUBLES, TOTAL BASES AND RUNS SCORED
THAN ANY PLAYER IN HISTORY.

The above Baseball Hall of Fame plaque is no misprint. It can be found exactly as shown, word for word, number for number, on Page 282 of Donald Honig's book *Baseball When the Grass Was Real.* Sadly, however, you won't find it hanging in the Baseball Hall of Fame in Cooperstown, New York.

You see, this is not a description of what Pistol Pete Reiser's career actually was. It is rather a description by the celebrated novelist and critic David Markson of what that career should have been. It is his version of a plaque reserved for better places, as Markson wrote, "where the game's true dreams are lodged, and where the plaque is the one at which we pause in wonderment, where we muse in awe upon the glory of his times."

Markson hardly stood alone in this appraisal. If with less poetry, it was the expressed belief of baseball masterminds of that moment. Of

Branch Rickey, of Leo Durocher, of Joe McCarthy, of Bill McKechnie. Of writers the likes of Jimmy Cannon, Red Smith, Arthur Daley, Arthur Patterson, Bob Cooke, Tommy Holmes, W.C. Heinz. Of players like Pee Wee Reese, Lonnie Frey, Mickey Owen, Ralph Branca.

To them all, Reiser was possibly the greatest prospect in baseball history, the most naturally gifted ballplayer any one of them had ever seen.

He had his incredible days, certainly. In fact, 727 of them, by count of *The Dodgers Encyclopedia*, when "Pistol Pete Reiser was the greatest player who ever lived." He could hit the ball with the authority of a pistol. He could cover center field with greater speed, more daring acumen and a stronger arm than any of his contemporaries. He could steal bases, including home, like few had done before or since. He could bat from both sides of the plate, and he could throw with either arm.

As a 22-year-old rookie in 1941, Reiser led the National League in batting average (the youngest ever to have done so), slugging percentage, total bases, doubles, triples and runs scored, and, incidentally, led the Dodgers to their first pennant in 21 years. Two-thirds into the following season, he had outdone his previous effort. Reiser had been batting in the .380s, and, it was the expectation of many that he was about to finish the year above the insurmountable .400 mark.

This was John R. Tunis's *The Kid from Tomkinsville* and Bernard Malamud's hero of *The Natural*, Roy Hobbs, rolled into one. Add in, too, a bit of the greatest new hero of those years, the impregnable Superman. Well, just a very little bit of him. Which, as it turned out, Reiser could have used much more of.

What happened to this seemingly indomitable man and what kept those glorious forecasts from being fulfilled is the story of this book. It is an incredible tale, both in Reiser's heroic rise over the machinations of scheming baseball owners and his tragic fall, aided and abetted by those around him. With but the slightest stretch, this is a story of mythic proportions. This was an Achilles in baseball cleats, at war with an outfield wall, haunted by his own hubris and manipulated by the big-mouthed Ulysses who commanded him.

Of course, it is not the story of Pete Reiser alone. His time in the sun was a remarkable time for this nation. These were the years just prior to World War II, the wartime itself, and the post-war period that brought dramatic and traumatic changes to America and to baseball. Racial barriers were torn down, a Mexican League rose up to battle the majors, and players themselves rose up in defiance of the greedy rules that governed them. This was part of Reiser's story, too.

So were the people around him, some decent and some not so very decent, who played important roles in what happened to the man. His Dodger manager, Leo Durocher; the Dodgers' general manager, Larry MacPhail; and that grand old pioneer of the game, Branch Rickey, were just three who affected his serpentine journey.

In *The Natural,* the character of Iris Lemon says to Roy Hobbs, "Without heroes we're all plain people and don't know how far we can go."

Pete Reiser showed us our outer limits. But for him those limits were always too narrow. Those hard, concrete walls that once bordered our baseball parks stood in his way. Always. "Something there is that doesn't love a wall," poet Robert Frost once wrote, "that wants it down."

To his undoing, Pistol Pete Reiser couldn't bring them down. His eyes set on a ball in flight, his mind hypnotized by the need to catch it, he challenged those barriers with all his speed and strength. And lost each time.

What follows is the story of this incredible man, of his miraculous feats, and the tragic defeats that were certain to come.

1

The Brooklyn Dodgers

It is not always understood that Brooklyn is not a city. Brooklyn is a *borough* of New York City, one of five that comprise the place. The borough of Manhattan, that long finger of an island sitting between the Hudson and East Rivers where most of the business is done and where most of the famous tourist events take place, is just another borough of New York City.

So when you realize that the Brooklyn Dodgers were a major league baseball team until 1957, when Walter O'Malley moved the franchise to Los Angeles, your jaw should drop. Wait a minute! The *Brooklyn* Dodgers? Isn't that like the *Brentwood* Blue Sox or the *South Side* Saints playing against teams that represent the biggest cities in the country? Exactly.

It is true that Brooklyn once was a city. That certainly was the reason the municipality had an organized baseball team, called the Excelsiors, as far back as 1854. Brooklyn, then still a city, can also claim baseball's first professional player, an all-but-forgotten hero named James Creighton, who was paid or given a job to play for the Excelsiors in 1860.

Nineteen years old at the time, the young pitcher became an immediate star, famous "for his great speed and the perfect command of the ball in delivery," according to the July 28, 1862, issue of *The Brooklyn Daily Eagle.* But this early star suffered a tragic death later that same year, collapsing on the field while in the midst of a game. The *Eagle* at that time presumed that he had ruptured his bladder while taking too strong a swing with his bat.

His body lies at rest in Brooklyn's Green Wood Cemetery beneath a lavish monument that includes a huge baseball, two crossed bats, a base, a baseball cap and a scorecard. A fitting tribute, indeed, to baseball's first professional hero.

By 1883, the status of baseball had grown immensely and several professional leagues had formed, many in competition with each other. That was the year when Brooklyn's team, officially called the Brooklyns but known as the Grays because of the color of their uniforms, became members of the American Association. But on January 1, 1898, Brooklyn, along with Queens and Richmond (the county name for Staten Island), became parts of New York City and were reduced to the status of boroughs.

Evidently that didn't make the Brooklyn team, now known as the Bridegrooms because of a plethora of marriages one season, ineligible to play in the newly founded National League. They had been there since 1896, and apparently not a peep of protest was made at Brooklyn's sudden change of fortune. There they were, in 1898, still pitted against the likes of Baltimore, Boston, Chicago, Cincinnati, Cleveland, Louisville, New York, Philadelphia, Pittsburgh, St. Louis and Washington, all major American cities, and finishing tenth in this league of 12.

They did win pennants in both the following two seasons, 1899 and 1900. This was a remarkable turnaround for even that time, and virtually brought about by a shameless display of early American business shenanigans. The owner of the Baltimore Orioles, a rich brewer named Harry Von der Horst, ran into financial difficulties that threatened the holdings of his Baltimore team. His solution was apple-pie easy. He bought the controlling interest of the Brooklyn team and simply transferred several of his key players—including future Hall of Famers Willie Keeler, Hugh Jennings and Joe Kelley, as well as two 20-game winners, Jim Hughes and Doc McJames—to the player-poor Brooklyn team. Voila! A couple of pennants.

But these were traumatic days for the burgeoning new sport. Another baseball war had been declared. The newly formed rival American League, its coffers filled with coppers, began operations in 1901 and immediately set its sights on the quality players in the National League. It found a mother lode in Brooklyn. Soon stripped of players, the Brooklyn team, now renamed the Superbas, slowly fell into the second division and stayed there for 12 long, unhappy seasons.

That, except for a couple of rare interludes, was much the sad story of the Brooklyn baseball team all the way to the late 1930s. A man named Charles Hercules Ebbets, who should have been known for the *Hercules* part of his name rather than the Charlie that became his sobriquet, was most responsible for the sporadic good news. He more than anyone lifted this dead-weight ballclub to two pennants and a near win.

Ebbets began his baseball career as a program and ticket seller, and his hard work and diligence caught the eye of majority stockholder Von der Horst. The owner soon named Ebbets the franchise's business manager and started selling him his stock, which Ebbets could purchase only by borrowing heavily from friends. By 1908, the former ticket hawker had hawked the entire ticket. He had gained the controlling interest in the Brooklyn baseball club and began work in two important directions.

With his best players gone to more lucrative pastures, Ebbets put into action the development of a farm system. If he didn't have the kind of players he immediately needed nor money enough to purchase them, he'd spend what little he could still borrow in slowly developing them. He also had the *chutzpah* to build his team a better ballfield.

Since its beginnings as a major league baseball team, the Brooklyn ballclub, by whatever nickname it was variously called, played in a junkyard of a field called Washington Park. Described as "ramshackled Washington Park," it consisted "of an old wooden grandstand, rickety bleachers, and a flimsy wooden fence that encircled a cow pasture-type outfield." But this was hardly unique, and apparently, quite major league. Top-level baseball in the early 1900s was played everywhere amidst such appalling confines. So it was indeed momentous when the Brooklyn owner had this wild dream of a shiny new stadium that would hold as many as 35,000 screaming fans.

Ebbets walked the borough searching for an appropriate site. He found it in a smelly garbage pit in Flatbush, fittingly called Pigtown, smack in the middle of Brooklyn. This fetid four-and-a-half acre slum, surrounded by shanties and feeding pigs, would be perfect. It was centrally located, crossed by more than a dozen transit lines and would surely be dirt cheap. Garbage-dirt cheap at that.

But Ebbets discovered that there were 40 different owners of parcels that comprised the property. It would take him three and a half years of tracing the proper holders of deeds and discreetly purchasing the pieces through a dummy corporation to put it together at last in 1911. The last owner had to be traced across the world from California to Berlin to Paris and finally to the nearby city of Montclair, New Jersey. There, with the real motive for buying the man's property kept secret, the owner was approached.

"Why would anyone be interested in land in Pigtown?" the owner wondered aloud to the inquiring agent. Then he added, "Would $500 be all right?"

The $500 was better than all right. Ebbets, now deep in debt but high in hopes, somehow talked his bank into advancing him new funds for beginning construction of his stadium. On March 4, 1912, a black bowler atop his head, the mustached Brooklyn owner pushed a spade into the leveled ground to begin excavation.

A reporter at the scene asked Ebbets what the name of the ballpark would be. "Washington Park, the same as the old park, I suppose," replied the Brooklyn owner matter-of-factly.

"Why don't you call it Ebbets Field?" asked the newspaperman. "It was your idea and nobody else's, and you've put yourself in hock to build it. It's going to be your monument, whether you like to think about it that way or not."

Ebbets thought about it for no more than a moment. "All right," he said, "that's what we'll call it. Ebbets Field."

It took a year and a little more than a month to complete the construction of the park, and its cost of $750,000 also cost Ebbets part of the ownership of the team. To complete construction, he had to include as partners the McKeever Brothers, the contractors themselves. So finally on April 5, 1913, the new ballpark known as Ebbets Field opened before 25,000 happy fans. It was immediately deemed "the most modern and most beautiful baseball stadium in the country." But as modern and beautiful as it was, and though blessed with an opening-day victory in an exhibition game with the New York Highlanders, Brooklyn still finished fifth that year.

At the end of the season, in an attempt to change his team's fortunes, Ebbets made a fortuitous move. He hired as manager of the team the old Baltimore Orioles catcher Wilbert Robinson, a man with roly-poly proportions, a warm sense of humor and obviously some baseball savvy. Within three years, Uncle Robbie, as he was lovingly called, built a potent pitching staff. He acquired three wily veterans, Larry Cheney, Jack Coombs and Rube Marquard, and developed two young prospects, Jeff Pfeffer and Sherry Smith, to bring Brooklyn in 1916 its first pennant in 16 years.

The team duplicated that feat in 1920, this time by a healthy seven games over its nearest opponent, its archrival, John McGraw's New York Giants. But this victory would have to hold the team through the drought of the next 20 years.

Each pennant win, by the way, was followed by a defeat in the ensuing World Series. Thus began a dismal tradition for Brooklyn that would hold until 1955, when that year's version of the Brooklyn Dodgers beat the Yankees in the World Series, four games to three. But back in 1916, they lost in five games to the Boston Red Sox, one game of which was lost to Boston's star left-handed pitcher, Babe Ruth. Baseball's future home-run king had won 23 games in the regular season for the Sox, having led the American League both in earned run average and shutouts.

Ebbets Field, home of the Brooklyn Dodgers since 1913, when Charles Hercules Ebbets took it upon himself to build "the most modern and most beautiful stadium in the country" (National Baseball Hall of Fame Library, Cooperstown, N.Y.).

In 1920, Brooklyn lost in seven games to the Cleveland Indians, this time five games to two, after having taken both the second and third games played in Brooklyn. This World Series was noted for two historic firsts, both at Brooklyn's expense and both occurring in the fifth game of the series, which Cleveland won, 8–1. In the first inning of that game, Indian outfielder Elmer Smith hit the first grand-slam homer in World Series history against Brooklyn pitcher Burleigh Grimes.

But even more dramatic was the unassisted triple play made by Cleveland second baseman Bill Wambsganss in the fifth inning With two men on base, Wambsganss caught pitcher Clarence Mitchell's line drive, stepped on second before Brooklyn second baseman Pete Kilduff could return to the bag, then tagged catcher Otto Miller, who had run from first on the pitch. Never had one man done so much damage in a single play, and never would it happen again in a World Series.

The team made a last-gasp effort for owner Ebbets in 1924 when it finished a slim one and a half games behind the pennant-winning New York Giants. Brooklyn's 37-year-old outfield star, Zack Wheat, had one of his best seasons with 97 runs batted in and a lusty .375 average, not unusual during those days of skyscraper batting percentages. Still, this was topped by St. Louis Cardinal Rogers Hornsby, who hit an incredible .424, the best average ever attained by a major league batter.

Dazzy Vance, the team's ace pitcher, had his best season, too. Vance won 15 games in a row and finished with a total of 28 wins, the best in baseball. He established the National League's single-game strikeout record that season with 15, was considered the League's Most Valuable Player, and led both major leagues in strikeouts with 262 and earned run average with 2.16. The team's first baseman, the much traveled Jack Fournier, led the league in home runs with 27 and was second in RBIs, with 116.

But all this was still not enough to overtake the rival Giants, who had a team loaded with future Hall of Famers. With the likes of George Kelly, Frankie Frisch, Travis Jackson, Fred Lindstrom, Bill Terry, Hack Wilson, and Heinie Groh, they could field a lineup of baseball's best of that day.

When Charles Ebbets died in 1925, Brooklyn fortunes seemed to die with him. For five straight seasons, the inept Brooklyn team, now called the Robins after Wilbert Robinson, its manager and president from 1926 to 1929, finished in sixth place. The Robins were terrible, but also terribly colorful.

Known as the Daffiness Boys and led by Floyd "Babe" Herman, a hell of a hitter and a hell of an incompetent in every other way, they were a band of misfits committing errors by the moment. Herman was a lifetime .324 hitter with astronomical seasons of .381 and .393, but he also had a darker side. His misfortunes on and off the field gave him something close to a monopoly on the list of baseball's ten worst bloopers. Herman's most memorable misplay was doubling into a double play, when he and two other runners ended up sliding into the same third base.

That feat hardly stood alone. Twice in one season, while Herman was on base, another batter's home run was negated by the slow-moving Babe strolling around the bases at such a crawl that the batter passed him. On another occasion, Herman almost caught a ball with his head. He also carried lit cigars in his uniform pocket and read newspapers in the dugout during games.

But the man didn't goof alone. This Babe had lots of company. Players on the road stayed out all night carousing in the visiting city. Players took naps in the dugout during games, probably suffering from the night before. Players carried guns. Players carried on. Most important, players committed errors physically and mentally like few had committed them before.

In an effort to counteract this nonsense, Manager Robinson created a Bonehead Club. Players who made any sort of a mistake would have to contribute ten dollars to the club's fund. The very same day this was announced, Robinson delivered an erroneous batting order to the umpires that cost Brooklyn the game.

New York Sun reporter Eddie Murphy wrote, "The manager of the Dodgers formed a Bonehead Club before yesterday's game and promptly elected himself a charter member."

At yet another time, Robinson proved he was one of the boys. Filling out a lineup card, he realized he had forgotten how to spell a player's name. His solution was simple. Instead of playing Oscar Roettger, he would play Dickie Cox.

While this kind of behavior may have brought laughs from the crowds and even endearment in some quarters, it didn't win many games and certainly not a single pennant. Robinson finally was forced out in 1931 by Steve McKeever, the last of the Ebbets family's partners. But the change of managers in 1932 to Max Carey and in 1934 to Casey Stengel didn't make a dent in the frightful quality of play. Now instead of Babe Herman and his band of misfits, there was a new group of oddballs.

This band had a player named Clyde "Pea Ridge" Day, who sounded hog calls from the mound with every strikeout and rang up a meager sum of two victories. This group had Walter "Boom Boom" Beck, who gained his "Boom Boom" nickname from the sound of baseball bats hitting his ball, immediately followed by the sound of the ball hitting the outfield fence.

There was also Luke "Hot Potato" Hamlin, who couldn't let a ball sit still in his glove, nor many runners stand still on a base. Hamlin was one of Brooklyn's two winningest pitchers in 1937, with 11 wins, as the team finished in sixth place, barely six games shy of the basement.

The most notable achievement for the Brooklyn baseball team during these years was the permanent attachment of the Dodgers nickname in 1933. Finally in that year "Dodgers" was stitched across the front of Brooklyn jerseys, and the use of names like the Grays, the Robins, the Superbas, the Bridegrooms, or simply the Brooklyns were relegated to baseball history. These were finally and forever the Dodgers, after years of only intermittently being called that name.

And where did the name Dodgers come from? It stemmed from Brooklyn residents being called Trolley Dodgers as they ran from the many electric trolley cars that had crisscrossed the borough since 1890. Local historians say that these electric trolleys, "driven by unskilled former horse and buggy drivers, were killing an average of one pedestrian a week by 1895."

Out of this supposed mayhem came the quirky name of Brooklyn Dodgers. And by 1937, the most this team had dodged, except for some notable exceptions that all had happened long years before, was the title of a credible ballclub. They were heavily in debt, they were habitual losers, and they were desperately wanting of decent players.

It was time for someone or something to bring about a dramatic, if not traumatic, change. And, as if by magic, it was about to happen.

2

Larry and Leo

The Dodgers were in hock in 1937, up to the letters of their uniforms and above. The ballclub owed the Brooklyn Trust Company more than half a million dollars, and this was at a time when half a million dollars was half a real money. With telephone lines cut off, with revenues at laughable numbers, with no player on the team worth peddling for necessary cash, the ballclub stood on the brink of disaster.

The heirs of the longtime owners, Charlie Ebbets and Steve McKeever, who had fought tooth-and-nail during the recent years of turmoil, went begging, not for more money but for something even more important. The president of the Brooklyn Trust Company, George McLaughlin, had issued the club a warning. If it could not come up with a new and vigorous leader, it would be in deep trouble. The bank was ready to throw out the pair of them and sell their ballfield for scrap. So they tiptoed into the office of the president of the National League, Ford Frick, for his advice. What can we do to save our ballclub, they asked.

Frick had an answer. Or at least a kind of an answer. He told them they'd need a strong, first-rate general manager who knew his baseball and could stand up to the best and worst of the other teams' management. Frick then conferred with Branch Rickey, the general manager of the always potent St. Louis Cardinals and purportedly the smartest man in baseball, whom he hoped to induce to take the job. Rickey said he was sorry, but he wanted no part of it. But he did have a name to offer.

It was that of Leland Stanford MacPhail, known to friends and enemies alike as Larry. MacPhail was a big, square-jawed redhead with an athlete's mug and a drinker's pallor. He was a former law school classmate

13

of Rickey's at the University of Michigan whom the St. Louis general manager had handpicked in 1930 to take over the Cardinals' struggling Columbus franchise. In a short time, the man had transformed the team into the crown jewel of this multijeweled farm system.

From there, again on a Rickey recommendation, MacPhail went to Cincinnati in 1933 on a mission to revitalize its dying ballclub. Another home run. With more than a touch of show biz and a hell of a lot of expenditure, he brought excitement to the city, profits to the owners and a farm system that worked so well it would produce two consecutive pennants for the team.

Along the way, he also introduced night baseball to the major leagues, the first radio broadcasts of games (described by the melodious Southern voice of Walter Lanier "Red" Barber), as well as the initial use of commercial airlines for travel.

Now Rickey knew that MacPhail was in need of a change of venue. Indeed, "in need" was the fitting phrase. In a recent drunken stupor, MacPhail had kayoed the team's owner, Powell Crosley, and that was over the line for even a very successful general manager.

This kind of behavior evidently was not unusual for Larry MacPhail. Peter Golenbock, in *Bums*, described him in these terms: "MacPhail had his own way of doing things: He was a heavy drinker and had great difficulty keeping his temper when under the influence. He was a loudmouth. He was a boor. But he had a genius for running a baseball team."

Leo Durocher, who soon would begin to play a huge part in this story, seemed to concur. "There is no question in my mind but that Larry was a genius," he wrote in his book *Nice Guys Finish Last*. "There is that thin line between genius and insanity, and in Larry's case it was sometimes so thin that you could see him drifting back and forth. They always said this about MacPhail: Cold sober he was brilliant. One drink and he was even more brilliant. Two drinks—that's another story."

The son of devout Methodists, Branch Rickey had the puritanical air and ways of a Sunday school teacher. This seemed to belie his caring for and recommending the rich and scandalous MacPhail, whose family's fortunes stemmed from Shylock profits invested in new banks. But care for and tout him Rickey did, as if sinfully attracted to his own alter ego.

When interviewed by the Ebbets and McKeever families, MacPhail first played coy. "I'll take the job," he said, "if you lay the kind of money I want on the line for me, give me a free hand and fix it up with the bank so when I want some real money for operating purposes, I can walk in there and get it."

When the men heard his numbers, for himself and for his operating

Larry MacPhail and Branch Rickey, close friends, bitter rivals, and each of them general manager of the Brooklyn Dodgers at different times. It was Rickey who suggested the Dodgers hire MacPhail in 1937 (National Baseball Hall of Fame Library, Cooperstown, N.Y.).

purposes, they gulped and misplaced their tongues. MacPhail reputedly looked at his watch and said, "If I can't do business here, I know where I can."

There was little else the men could do. Not ready to give up their ballclub, they saw this bizarre madman as their only hope. Before MacPhail could find the door, the men found the painful words that gave him all he had demanded.

As a final salvo, MacPhail pointed at the meager office space surrounding him and asked, "Is this all there is?" When he was told that it was, he exclaimed, "When I'm in charge here, we'll have to have more space." Heading for the door, he began telling the bewildered owners which walls would have to be torn down.

MacPhail was worth every costly dollar. He had inherited a team that had finished in the second division 13 times in the last 17 years and, as he had promised, turned it into one of the premier franchises in baseball. Over the next several years, he spent and he spent and he spent. But, of course, that's also what he had promised.

He modernized Ebbets Field (cost: $200,000). He put in lights for night games ($72,000). He bought first baseman Dolph Camilli from Philadelphia ($50,000). He bought minor league shortstop sensation Pee Wee Reese from Louisville ($75,000). He bought outfielder Joe Medwick and pitcher Curt Davis from St. Louis (estimated $250,000). He bought pitcher Kirby Higbe from the Phillies ($100,000). He bought catcher Mickey Owen from the Cardinals ($60,000). He bought Billy Herman from the Cubs ($65,000).

He brought in Red Barber and his melodious drawl from Cincinnati to broadcast the Dodger games, which were the first games ever broadcast from New York City. He hired 15 scouts, bought six minor league teams and signed working agreements with six others to begin a farm system that would rival Branch Rickey's Cardinals, famous as the best in the major leagues.

One of his two most auspicious acquisitions was the perennial juvenile delinquent Leo Durocher. A good-looking hustler with a face that resembled the actor George Raft, with whom he would later bum around, Durocher was a scrapper, a cheat, and an even louder mouth that MacPhail. Known as Leo the Lip or Lippy because of that mouth, he was also a pretty fair ballplayer. He never was much of a hitter in his stints with the Yankees, the Reds and the Cardinals, but by 1937 he was considered the best defensive shortstop in the National League.

Durocher had alienated almost every ballplayer whose life he had touched. From the very greatest to the struggling journeyman, most had enough of him after a single season.

He had grown up in the slums of West Springfield, Massachusetts, hustling at the local pool hall and spending his time with wise guys, card sharks and low-life gamblers. He never got that out of his system, except that in later years the mobsters he befriended had more money and flashier clothes.

Tossed out of high school in the ninth grade for his wild behavior, he was given a job at the local electric company where he played baseball for the company team. In 1925, his terrific play attracted the notice of the Hartford minor league team, which placed the 20-year-old bad boy on its roster. While playing there, he was caught red-handed stealing money out of the other players' wallets. Though his teammates wanted him suspended and banned from baseball, manager Paddy O'Connor, striving for a pennant, begged his players to let him finish the season at shortstop.

"We have a chance to win," O'Connor told his team. "If you let him stay, I'll get rid of him at the end of the season."

Hartford won the pennant with Durocher, then sold him at the end of its year to the New York Yankees, where he remained until 1929. While with the Yankees, Durocher stole from and alienated the very best. He called Babe Ruth "that baboon" and for years was accused of stealing the great slugger's watch. He screamed out at Ty Cobb, "You're an old man, the game has passed you by," then threatened to shove a baseball down the great ballplayer's throat.

He passed rubber checks to New York storekeepers, got drunk and gambled with notorious racketeers. And, incidentally, he played a sensational game at shortstop. His godfather on the Yankees was the team's manager, Miller Huggins, a short and gnome-like figure who admired the way Durocher muscled his way through the bigger players around him. Until Huggins died, Durocher was safe. The old manager respected him as the best fielding shortstop in the league and applauded the gritty way Durocher played.

"He loved me like a father," Durocher wrote in *Nice Guys Finish Last*, "and I loved him like a son. I couldn't hit worth a damn—Babe Ruth nicknamed me 'the All American Out'—but Mr. Huggins kept telling me I'd stick around for a long time if I kept my cockiness and my scrappiness and the fierce desire to do anything to win. 'Little guys like us can win games,' he would say. 'We can beat 'em,' he would say, tapping his head just like Rabbit Maranville, 'up here.'"

But Huggins, sick for a long time, died at the end of the 1929 season. To make matters worse for Durocher, during his contract negotiations with general manager Ed Barrow, he lived up to his nickname of The Lip by a mouth and a half. He told Barrow "to go fuck himself." By this time, no one remained in his corner. The new Yankee manager, Bob Shawkey, put him on waivers, and not a single American League team was interested in this troublemaker. The best shortstop in the league was waived out of the circuit and onto the roster of the Cincinnati Reds.

Though Durocher never changed his wayward ways in Cincinnati, the Reds management put up with him for three long seasons.

"Sidney Weil, the owner of the club," Durocher wrote, "turned out to be the nicest, kindest man I have ever known. He started by giving me a raise in salary to $7,500, and then arranged to pay off all my debts and take a specified amount out of my salary every month. In every way he was a second father to me."

Durocher added, "Not that it did any good."

The Reds at this time were a bad ballclub loaded with over-the-hill veterans and journeyman players. The best they finished in the three years Durocher played for them was seventh in 1930. In 1931 and 1932, they ended up in eighth place, the cellar. But one of the few bright spots on the team was Durocher's sterling play at shortstop.

This caught the eye of the St. Louis Cardinals, whose own shortstop, Charlie Gelbert, had shot himself in the foot in a hunting accident and would never again play up to his potential. They needed a shortstop desperately, and they knew Cincinnati had the best defensive one in the league.

The Cardinals and their general manager, Branch Rickey, had to pay a lot for the man. Perhaps even a lot and an acre. They had to give the Reds their star pitcher, Paul Derringer, who for long years later, including four 20-game winning seasons, would be the foremost pitcher on Cincinnati's staff.

But Durocher fit in perfectly in St. Louis. This was a rough-and-tumble bunch of players as scrappy as the new guy at short. Just like Durocher, they would bend the rules of baseball to take advantage of every situation.

As Durocher has written, ""We typified what big-league baseball was in those days. It was a rough-and-tumble no-holds-barred game played primarily by farm boys. Generally unschooled, generally unspoiled, generally unsophisticated."

Every member of the Gashouse Gang would have agreed with that. This was the team of Frankie Frisch, Pepper Martin, Joe Medwick, Rip Collins and a couple of pitchers named Dean, Dizzy and his brother Paul. These guys wouldn't hold back from slicing you with their spikes, crashing into you as they ran a base, or creasing your skull with a pitched ball. Durocher was born for this environment. They would soon be known as the Gashouse Gang, a name, in fact, given to them by Durocher.

"I don't know whether we can win in this league," Dizzy Dean had once said to him, "but if we were in the other league we sure would win."

Durocher answered, "They wouldn't let us in the other league. They would say we are a lot of gashouse ballplayers."

But they did win in that league in 1934 and finished close to the top in the three other years Durocher remained with the Cardinals. If anything, this experience only fed the worst in the Durocher personality. Like him, his teammates were rabble-rousers on and off the field. They fought like kids in the dugout and in the clubhouse, they were thrown out of hotels while on the road (three in Philadelphia alone), they drank to unconsciousness and pranked till exhaustion.

General Manager Rickey, almost with Bible in hand, had taken on this prodigal ballplayer as his own personal reclamation project. At first, Rickey had hope.

"When he came to St. Louis," he said, "Leo was in trouble. No fewer than thirty-two creditors were breathing down his neck, suing or threatening to sue. I proposed that I go to his creditors and arrange for weekly payments on his debts. This meant a modest allowance of spending money for Leo himself. But Leo agreed."

Rickey also got Durocher his first baseball coaching job. This was as head coach for the U.S. Naval Academy, a position that Durocher could maintain during his off-season, and a role the shortstop thoroughly enjoyed. The general manager took a further step in an attempt to rein in the runaround. He promoted marriage for Durocher, even with a woman of Rickey's own acquaintance, Grace Dozier, a prominent dress designer.

But nothing really worked. Durocher still ran around. Durocher still passed bad checks. Durocher still managed to antagonize teammates. Worse than that, he undermined the team's manager and second baseman, Frankie Frisch. During the 1937 season, he began to taunt the manager, telling him and anyone else in earshot that he could manage the team better than Frisch. Finally, Frisch had enough. He told Rickey one or the other player must go. There was no team big enough to hold the two.

"I think," Rickey said, "that he's afraid you're after his job."

"To me," Durocher wrote, "that kind of thinking is silly. Nobody can take a manager's job while he's winning and nobody can save it if he's not."

Nonetheless, Rickey obliged Frisch and traded Durocher to the Brooklyn Dodgers and to his old friend Larry MacPhail for four players that never amounted to much for the Cardinals. MacPhail and Durocher. A drunk and a bum. Now this was a pairing that seemed made in hell. Except that, for the most part, it turned out to be a pairing made in the other place.

Burleigh Grimes was the manager of the Dodgers in 1938, the year Durocher came to the team. Grimes had been a standout pitcher for Brooklyn. One of the last of the great spitball pitchers, he had hurled nine long years for the team, including the pennant-winning year of 1920, and would later win entry into the Hall of Fame. But as for being a manager, he had been a great spitball pitcher.

In 1937, his first year as manager, he had lost five games more that his predecessor, Casey Stengel, had lost the year before, and had done little to improve the team's mediocre pitching staff. By 1938, MacPhail was already looking elsewhere. He had hired Babe Ruth as a coach with every intention of making him his next manager.

The old Bambino, a compatriot if not a friend of Durocher's from their Yankee days, told Durocher as much early that season. "Stick with me, Leo," Ruth said to him, "I'm going to be taking this club over."

"Dammit, Babe," Durocher shot back. "You've got a lot of gall plotting to undermine this man (Grimes) after he's been good enough to bring you in and give you a job. You are insulting me by even thinking I might be willing to help you."

Durocher wasn't willing to help him again later that season. Hardly. A reporter covering one of the Dodger games wrote that Ruth had given the batter the sign for a hit-and-run that then turned out to be a game-winning play. Hearing about this in the clubhouse, Durocher roared out, "How could that baboon have flashed the hit-and-run when he didn't even know what it was?"

Sitting nearby on a stool was Ruth, who had heard every word of Durocher's taunt. As he began to get up, fire in his eyes, Durocher shoved the old slugger down, slamming him against his own locker. Other players immediately interceded and calmed the two men down. Grimes then drew Durocher aside and told him, "Next time you do that, I'll fine you. He belongs to me."

There have been several versions written of that scene, though it must have taken place essentially that way. But there was no doubt that Grimes, who had done little to improve the Dodger fortunes, would be ousted after that season, and that MacPhail's first choice for a new manager had been Ruth.

Durocher, who had been made captain of the team by Grimes, was not going to sit idly by. He certainly believed that Babe Ruth, for whom he had little love, was inadequate for the job and, given the chance, Durocher would be. As it turned out, several people connected with the organization agreed.

Grimes claimed that he suggested Durocher to MacPhail once he was informed that his own contract would not be renewed. "He asked me if I had any suggestions as to who might replace me," said Grimes. "Yes, I said, I do. You've got a guy on the club who's smart, got guts and ought to make a damn good manager. Durocher."

The traveling secretary of the Dodgers, John McDonald, said much the same. "MacPhail wanted Billy Herman, the Cub second baseman to replace Grimes," said McDonald. "Another candidate was Frankie Frisch. I had suggested Durocher, but MacPhail was vehement. 'Never,' he said. 'The guy can't even manage himself. Look at all the bouncing checks, the unpaid alimony.'"

Yet a short time later, McDonald maintained that MacPhail turned to him while the two were driving in a cab, and said, "Hey John, I just got a great idea. A manager who can also play star ball for us will save us a big salary."

"Who do you have in mind?" McDonald asked.

"Durocher," MacPhail replied.

"That's a great idea," said McDonald. "How'd you happen to think of Leo?"

Thus the first of MacPhail's two most auspicious acquisitions was duly anointed with his ascension to manager, to playing manager, in fact, of the team. Though from all accounts, MacPhail and Durocher were at each other's throats from the very beginning. Durocher placed their first skirmish at a time before spring training in 1939, when he took the team's pitchers and catchers to Hot Springs, Arkansas, for preseason conditioning.

On their very first working day there, Durocher and several of his cohorts went to dinner at the exclusive Belvedere Country Club. The moment dinner was over, Bingo cards were brought out and the new manager purchased several for two dollars each. According to Durocher, he won the jackpot of $660, which he then proceeded to give back by buying champagne for the house.

Early the next morning, MacPhail woke up Durocher with a call. "You're fired!" he roared at him.

"For what?" Durocher innocently asked.

"You're a gambler," answered MacPhail. "I just read it in the morning paper. You won the big Bingo prize."

Durocher then tried to explain that Bingo was "a game old women play at church socials," and that it should hardly be considered gambling.

But MacPhail persisted. "Turn the club over to High," he commanded.

Durocher then spent the next 15 minutes trying to convince the general manager to turn the reins over to Coach Charlie Dressen rather than Coach Andy High. When MacPhail was unmoved by the suggestion, Durocher resorted to three of his favorite words. "Go fuck yourself," he screamed, and slammed down the phone.

Durocher went right back to managing the team the next day, as if nothing had happened, and MacPhail never again mentioned the Bingo incident. But that was a harbinger of what was to happen again and again and still again over the next four years the two men were together. By one count, MacPhail fired Durocher 60 times during their tenure and either "forgot" about it or rehired the man at their very next meeting.

One of the angriest firings occurred just weeks after this incident, and it happened over the playing of a new ballplayer, a quite extraordinary new ballplayer. It concerned the man who was Larry MacPhail's most auspicious acquisition.

The incredible Pete Reiser.

3

A Pistol Is Fired

"He was the best I ever had, with the possible exception of Willie Mays. At that, he was even faster than Willie Mays."
—Leo Drocher

He was born in St. Louis on March 17, 1919. St. Patrick's Day, if you will, to a devout Catholic family. Christened Harold Patrick Reiser—the Patrick in honor of the saint—he wouldn't be called Harold for long. As a kid playing in the St. Louis streets, he loved to mosey around with a pair of toy pistols holstered in his belt and shoot them at make-believe hombres threatening his cowboy heart. Thus, that early on, he was called Pistol Pete, after a cowboy movie hero of the time, and Pistol Pete Reiser he would always be.

During his playing days, he was a sleek, solidly built ram of a man standing an inch short of six feet and weighing 185 pounds. He possessed the speed of a gazelle, the wrist strength of a whip and the full, handsome, drop-dead face of a young movie star. He was born to play baseball, and he played the game perhaps like no one had done before or has done since. There was no pitcher that could not be hit, no base that could not be stolen, no ground ball that could not be beaten out, no fly ball that could not be caught, no fence that could not be ... well, that'll come later.

As if to explain this relentless and reckless way he played baseball, Reiser admitted to his own orneryness as a kid. "I had a bad temper," he conceded to writer Donald Honig. He'd get mad once in a while and chase his sisters around the house with his grandfather's old cavalry sword. "Just to scare 'em," he said, that childlike deviltry still in his eyes.

He had been an exceptional athlete since the first time he could fit his little hand around a ball, but baseball hadn't been his first love; football had been. "My ambition," he told Honig, "was to be the greatest football player Notre Dame ever had."

"I was a hell of a soccer player, too," he added. "In fact, I was declared a professional soccer player when I was fourteen years old."

He had been playing for Holy Ghost Parochial School in St. Louis when he was offered 50 dollars to play in a Sunday soccer game. "That was a lot of money," Reiser pointed out. "Hell, my Dad was making 25 dollars a week and supporting 12 children."

This was a working-class family living in a working-class neighborhood during the heartless days of the Great Depression of the 1930s. Lonnie Frey, the Cincinnati Reds star second baseman of the 1930s and 1940s, grew up in this same neighborhood, just three or four blocks away from the Reisers. Though he never met Pete Reiser or any of his family till long years later he knew they lived thorough conditions similar to the ones he had.

"We were poor," he said, "but we never felt it. We made our due with what we had. If necessary, we made our own baseballs by winding string tightly around a cork and taping over it. And any repairs we needed, in our gloves and such, we'd simply sew up at night."

"Pete (Reiser) grew up in the St. Louis tradition," said an article in a September 1942 issue of the Saturday Evening Post, "fighting the usual battles with gangs from the neighborhoods, like the Sherman Street Creeps or the Marcus Street Rats, playing ball after school, catching the latest installment of a Western thriller on a Saturday afternoon, wearing a special suit on Sundays and rooting for the Cardinals and the Browns. While attending Holy Ghost Parochial School, and later in his two years at Beaumont High, Reiser could hit a long way."

That, it would seem, was part of the Reiser family tradition. Although Reiser's father, George, worked for a printing plant in St. Louis, he had been a baseball player himself, often competing as a pitcher for various semi-pro teams in the area.

"My Dad pitched several no-hitters," Reiser's sister, Julia, reported proudly to me in a telephone interview. "We were a baseball-playing family. All of us kids played ball, but Pete had it in his blood. That's all he wanted to do."

"None of us played hard like him," she said. "Who did? Maybe Pete Rose, and that's all I can think of. Even as a kid, Pete played hard. Maybe too hard."

Pete's dad helped develop the young kid by first playing catch with him in their back yard and later taking him to the fairgrounds where the

Pete Reiser in one of his earliest photos as a professional ballplayer. This was taken in 1938, when he was playing shortstop for the Superior Blues of the Northern League (courtesy of Shirley Reiser Tuber).

ex-pitcher tossed them in at full speed to his own son. The kid was very soon playing with boys much his senior.

"When I was twelve years old," he told Donald Honig, "I was playing ball with guys five years older. My brother Mike used to bring me around to play on his team. The other guys would say, 'What's this kid doing here?'"

Reiser's brother simply smiled and told them, "He'll show you."

And each time, the kid they called Pete showed them. "Maybe it started there," he later said. "Having to try hard, hard, and harder, to prove to them, to live up to the expectations of somebody you admired the hell out of, and to keep on proving it."

"I always felt I could do better than I was doing," he went on, "that there was no limit. I couldn't wait from one day to the next to get out there and prove it."

Reiser tried to prove his abilities in a major test when he was only 15. Lying about his age, he went to a Cardinals tryout camp for kids 16 years old and over. "I wanted to see how good the competition was," he explained.

"I'm fifteen years old and I go to a two day Cardinal training camp," he told his son-in-law, Rick Tuber, long years later. "Eight hundred ninety people show up," he said emphatically. "What kind of chance do you think you'll get?"

All they were allowed to do was run a 60-yard dash, throw to home plate from center field and take three swings at bat. "I had a great arm," said Reiser. "So you made two throws and I thought I threw great. Everyone's going to run sixty yards and no one's going to beat me. Two things I knew I could do was throw and run. And I beat everybody in camp."

Despite what Reiser believed was an outstanding, if foreshortened, performance, the disappointed kid was cut on the very first day.

"Well, Dad, I guess I'm not as good as I thought I was," he said to his father.

"Don't worry about it," his father answered. "You're only fifteen years old."

Several days later, a huge Buick pulled up in front of the Reiser home and Charley Barrett, the head Cardinal scout, stepped out and walked up to the door. "I want to talk to you about your son," he told Reiser's father.

"Well, I want to talk to you, too," snapped his father. "Why'd you cut him?"

"We didn't want anybody else to see him," answered Barrett. "That's why we didn't ask him to come back. We know who he is."

"You know who he is?" asked the stunned father.

Barrett then confessed that Cardinal scouts had been watching Reiser play since grade school and had marveled at what they saw. They didn't want to indicate any interest in him until he could be signed.

"You see," explained Reiser, "in those days if the Cardinals showed any interest in a kid, the other clubs would rush in and try to sign him. That's the kind of reputation the Cardinals had."

But Reiser was still too young to be signed as a ballplayer, so then and there the youngster was signed as a chauffeur for $50 a month. He traveled around with Barrett through much of the South and Southeast that season, where various Cardinal farm teams were located and were playing. At each stop, Reiser would don a uniform and work out with the team, playing the infield and taking batting practice.

When they were ready to leave, the farm team's manager would invariably ask Barrett to leave the kid behind. "Can't," Barrett would say. "He's only fifteen."

"So what," the manager would reply. "We'll change his name."

"Not this one," Barrett would answer, and off he and the kid would go.

To point out just how green he was in those times, Reiser told a story about how Barrett took him to a restaurant early in their trip from St. Louis. Twenty-five miles later, Reiser said, "I was feeling pretty proud of myself because I thought I'd done Charley a favor."

"You know what you did, Mr. Barrett?" he said to him. "You left some money on the table back at the restaurant. But I picked it up for you."

"You did what?" the scout yelled. "By God, boy, that was a tip."

"Hell," said Reiser as he told this story, how could he know what a tip was. "I'd never eaten in a restaurant in my life. How was I supposed to know any different."

The green kid from St. Louis finally did end up being signed to play baseball for the Cardinals. By the time he was 18, he was playing for them in the lower minors and catching the eye of many in the system. Especially that of general manager Branch Rickey, the man they called "The Mahatma" because of his supposed Gandhi-like wisdom.

Rickey, who was considered by many to be baseball's most astute man, had masterminded the development of the sport's farm system and had the best and most famous one in St. Louis. Some of his methods, however, were considered duplicitous, and some of the contracts he had signed with youthful kids willing to give up everything to get into the game were downright illegal.

Or so believed Judge Kenesaw Mountain Landis, baseball's first commissioner, who then ruled the game with an iron fist. Landis had been granted near-absolute power to clean up and rescue baseball after it had been almost destroyed by the infamous "Black Sox" gambling scandal of 1919. In this monumental event, detailed in Eliot Asinof's fine book and its subsequent film, Eight Men Out, the Chicago White Sox conspired to throw the World Series to the underdog Cincinnati Reds. Thus granted his great power, Judge Landis, for better or worse, enjoyed using it.

The judge took a look at what Rickey was doing and reached for a pen. The tall, slender judge, with a white mane and a face as deeply carved as those peering out from the front of a totem pole, decided to issue a new emancipation proclamation. In the spring of 1938, he set free almost a hundred young Cardinal ball players who he believed had been unfairly signed and kept in their farm system.

One of these was Pete Reiser. And Reiser was the only one Rickey cared about.

In answer to this punishment for his baseball illegality, Rickey responded with an even more flagrant breach of law. He made a secret deal with his old pal, Larry MacPhail, to purchase Reiser's contract. Some time later, at a time deemed acceptable by Landis's edict, the young man would be traded back to the Cardinals. After all, Rickey had helped MacPhail into several important positions, including his present one as general manager of the Dodgers. This was the least MacPhail could do for his good friend and benefactor.

MacPhail was recruited to sign Reiser to a Dodger contract and bury him in the Dodger farm system for three years. This was the minimum period of time, dictated by Landis's decree, that the Cardinals were forbidden to own Reiser. By the secret agreement of the two general managers, MacPhail was to hold on to the young man for that length of time and then return him to the coveting arms of Branch Rickey. This young ballplayer was the greatest raw talent Rickey had ever seen, and he wanted him back.

It probably would have worked except for Dodger manager Leo Durocher. No one completely trusted Durocher, and certainly not in having this kind of knowledge. So the manager was never apprised of this illegal arrangement. Unfortunately for the Cardinals, this later would backfire in Rickey's face.

The Dodgers, as promised, signed Reiser. MacPhail made the deal for a measly bonus of 100 dollars, pitiful for even that time, and sent him to the lowly farm team in Superior, Wisconsin, of the Northern League.

"I was a shortstop at the time," said Reiser, "and a strictly right-handed hitter." But the young man learned quickly the disadvantage of hitting from the right side of the plate. Despite the gift of his enormous speed, he was too often narrowly beaten trying to run out grounders. Hitting as a left-hander would give him that extra step. So the eager kid, who had never before hit as a left-handed batter, spent the following season mastering it.

And master it he did. For someone who had never hit from that side of the plate, he accomplished it quite amazingly. Reiser hit a handsome .302, smashed 18 home runs, 27 doubles and ten triples, while displaying stellar abilities at his shortstop position. It was apparent even then that there would be no boundary to hold him.

There is a handwritten "autobiography" by Reiser, penned at about this time, that is in the possession of his daughter, Shirley Tuber, which chronicles the events of his early baseball career. The handwriting is clean, clear, perfectly legible and carefully done as if preserving the story for posterity. Pasted into an old scrapbook containing his early clippings, it offers a remarkable insight into the young man's heart and mind.

"During the spring of the 1938 baseball season," it begins, "I was one of 75 players declared free agent by Judge Landis, High Commissioner of baseball, in a shakeup of the Cardinal farm system teams."

The document then goes on to tell of his beginning days as a player for the Cardinals earlier that year. "I left St. Louis February 14," it continues, "for Winter Haven, Florida, with scout Charles Barrett of the St. Louis Cardinals. I did the driving all the way to Florida, and up to this time, it was the most wonderful thing that ever happened to me. We arrived in Winter Haven on February 17 late in the evening."

He then describes Branch Rickey's Baseball School in Florida, which began the very next day and continued until March 19. Included in this were the names of every teacher there, some of them being Rickey himself; Frankie Frisch, then manager of the Cards; Doc Weaver, the team's trainer; Ray Blades, manager of the team's minor league club in Rochester; and Burt Shotton, of the Columbus team. There are 20 other names he specifies, and one is sure his list is complete.

"We left Winter Haven for Albany, Georgia," he continues, "where the Cardinals had another school. It was while in Albany that I was declared a free agent by Judge Landis. I signed with the Brooklyn organization. Ted McGrew, head scout for Brooklyn, did the signing."

On Shirley Tuber's wall, hang the two documents in a single, simple frame. On the left is a short note signed by Landis that declares Reiser a free agent. And on the right is Reiser's first Dodger contract, granting him a sum of a hundred dollars for joining the team.

Reiser goes on to describe his short stops at Dayton and Winston-

Salem, where he never played a game, and a one-day trip to Ebbets Field in "Brooklyn, New York," from which he was sent to Superior, Wisconsin, of the Northern League. There is where he finally played.

"Superior had a fine, hustling and well balanced team," he writes. "I batted .302, 18 home runs, 30 doubles, 11 triples and scored over 100 runs. I also stole 23 bases. Superior won the Northern League championship by 7½ games. Duluth was runner-up. Superior lost to Crookston four games out of six in the first round of the playoffs. Duluth won from Crookston in the seven game series. Due to a leg injury to my left knee received in an exhibition game, I was kept out of action for the last week and a half of the season and during the playoffs."

Mind you, not even to himself, did he add that this injury might have been the reason his team lost in the playoffs.

There then begins a short Chapter II in the document. "The news of going to Elmira in the Eastern League," he starts, "was a real thrill and a pleasure to me." Reiser goes on to list the other players who were to join him in this step up to the Elmira ballclub, and then concludes with a delightful wrap up of what baseball has so far done for him.

"After the close of the 1938 season," he writes, "I had been in 31 different states through baseball during my two years in professional baseball. The states are as follows...." And what follows is a carefully numbered list of 31 states, set in three carefully constructed parallel columns, and presented in the exact order he visited them, from his home state of Missouri to, finally, Texas!

Though Reiser was now purportedly a member of a rival team, his friend Charley Barrett didn't desert him. That winter, Reiser turned to his old friend for some added help. "If I could just get down to spring training in Florida early," he told him, "I could get a jump on some of these guys."

Barrett, who had been a good friend of Durocher's since his Cardinal days, spoke to the Dodger manager on Reiser's behalf. As a favor to the Cardinal scout, the manager agreed to bring the kid down to Clearwater, Florida, the following spring, where the Brooklyn team trained.

"So I went to Clearwater in the spring of '39," said Reiser, "just to shag and run and get the feel of a big league camp."

"Like any young kid," he went on, "I was eager. Every time somebody was slow getting into the batting cage, I jumped in, which I wasn't supposed to do. Made some of the regulars pretty sore."

Indeed he did, but he made Durocher smile. This kid had nerve by the barrelful, not unlike Durocher himself, and this was something the manager always admired. He also was taken with the kid's speed of foot.

Summary of Pete Reiser
Ball Season during 1938 season.

During the Spring of 1938 Baseball season. I was one of 75 players declared free agent by Judge Landis, high Commissioner of Baseball in a shake up of Cardinal farm systems teams. I left St. Louis Feb 14th for Winter Haven, Florida with scout Charles Barrett of St. Louis Cardinals. I did the driving all the way to Florida. up to this time it was the most wonderful thing that ever happen to me. We arrived in Winter Haven Florida on Feb 17th. late in the evening. the trip to Florida was really wonderful. Rickey's Baseball school opened on Feb 18th and lasted until Mar 19th. besides Rickey himself, other officials of the school were as follows. Frank Frisch. manager of St. Louis Cardinals. Doc Weaver. trainer for St. Louis Cardinals. Whenmayer Clay Blades of Rochester. Manager Burt Shotton of Columbus. Ira Smith of Houston. Tony Kauffman of Decatur. Harold Anderson of Asheville. Benny Borgmann of Portsmouth. Jimmy Sanders of Daytona Beach. Tommy West of Easton. Harrison Wickel of New Iberia. Paul Hanna. coach of Columbus. Ollie Vanek of Greenville. Joe Davis of Cambridge. Dutch Dorman of Duluth. Johnie Anderson of Martinsville. Pete Mordino of Paducah. Carl Mann. director of Sports for United States Olympicar Association. who was principle speaker. Scouts Charles F Barrett by olympicar Association. who was principle speaker. Scouts Charles F Barrett Joe Sulgeon. Pop Kelchner. Jack Ryan. Bob Finch. Branch Rickey Jr. assistant also attended school. We left Winter Haven for Albany Georgia. where the Cardinals had another school. it was while in Albany that I was declared a free agent by Judge Landis. I signed with the Brooklyn organization. Ted McGrew head scout for Brooklyn. did the signing. I reported to Dayton of Middle Atlantic League. at Greensboro N. Carolina. I was therefore 2 3 weeks for spring training. I was sent to Winston Salem of Piedmont League but never played a single game there. after being with Winston Salem for a week. I was called to Brooklyn N.Y. by Larry McPhail. General Manager of Brooklyn. I worked out one day with Brooklyn at Ebbetsfield. left N.Y. following day along with Bill Randall. Ralph Graves and scout Ted McGrew for Superior Wisconsin of Northern League. were I started regular playing season and finished up there. Superior had a fine hustling and well balanced team. I batted 302. hitting. I hove was 30 doubles 11 triples and scored over 100 runs. I also stole 23 bases. Superior won Northern League Championship by 7½ games. Duluth was runnerup. Superior lost to Crookston. 4 games out of 6 in first round of play offs. Duluth won from Crookston in 7 game series. Due to a leg injury being left knee received in exhibition game at Saint Paul Minn. I was left out of action for last 1½ of season. and during play offs.

Opposite and Above: Reiser's handwritten early biography that describes his emancipation from the Cardinals by Judge Landis and his signing with the Dodgers. (Courtesy of Shirley Reiser Tuber)

II

The news of going to Elmira in Eastern League was a real thrill and a pleasure to me. Also going to Elmira from the Champion Superior Blues were Red Randell, Center fielder. Lyn Rumpfield right fielder. Dick Scott, pitcher and Barney DeFray pitcher. After the close of 1938 season. I had been in 31 different states through ball during my two years in professional base ball. The states are as follows.

1 — Missouri
2 — Arkansas
3 — Oklahoma
4 — Kansas
5 — Nebraska
6 — Louisana
7 — Mississippi
8 — Alabama
9 — Tennessee
10 — Florida
11 — Georgia
12 — S. Carolina
13 — N. Carolina
14 — Illinois
15 — Iowa
16 — Indiana
17 — Kentucky
18 — Wisconsin
19 — Minnesota
20 — Virginia
21 — W. Virginia
22 — Ohio
23 — Pennsylvania
24 — Maryland
25 — N. Jersey
26 — Delaware
27 — New York
28 — N. Dakota
29 — S. Dakota
30 — Michigan
31 — Texas

"They had a guy down there," said Reiser, "I think his name was Cesar. He was supposed to be the fastest guy in the Dodger organization. One day, Leo says to MacPhail, 'I got a kid that'll beat Cesar by ten yards.'"

MacPhail spat out, "Bullshit," and the two placed a hundred-dollar bet on a race between the two men.

"I did beat the guy," said Reiser proudly. "Yeah, by ten yards."

That really grabbed the attention of the manager. "But there was one play," said Reiser, "that I think really cemented it with him."

The Dodgers were playing an exhibition game with Detroit, and Reiser, who had been playing second base, was a runner on first. On a ground ball hit by the batter, Reiser took off for second intent on breaking up the double play. Billy Rogell, Detroit's veteran shortstop, took the throw as Reiser came barreling into him. He knocked Rogell on his prat and broke up the double play.

"The throw had me beat," explained Reiser, "so there was nothing else I could do."

"You bush son of a bitch," Rogell screamed. "We don't play like that in spring training."

"Well, I do," answered the brash kid. "I may not be here after that."

"When I get on base, I'm going to cut you from ear to ear," Rogell responded.

"You've got to get on base first," Reiser shot back.

Sure enough, next time up, Rogell got on base. Everyone knew he'd

The flag-winning Superior Blues of 1938. The young Reiser is second from the right, front row (courtesy of Shirley Reiser Tuber).

be gunning for Reiser at second. Durocher, who had been playing alongside Reiser at short, told the kid, "I'll handle the throw."

But Reiser insisted, "I want the throw."

"No," said Durocher.

"I'm taking it," said Reiser again, talking to his manager as if he were the kid next door. "So you stay clear."

On the very first pitch, Rogell took off in an attempt to steal second. Reiser jumped to the base to take the catcher's throw as Rogell came in with his spikes dangerously high. Reiser tagged the man out, eluded the threatening spikes and stepped aside, avoiding any contact with the runner.

"He threw up a ton of dirt," said Reiser, "but never touched me."

From then on, Reiser concluded, "I think I became Leo's pet."

For that and much more. Durocher had witnessed the kid's spunk, he had bet and won on his speed, he had watched him hit line drives like a pistol shooting bullets, he had noted that he could hit from both sides of the plate, and as young as Reiser was, he wanted him in a Dodger uniform.

One day during spring training, on St. Patrick's Day to be exact, which also happened to be the day of Reiser's 20th birthday, Durocher woke up with a severe migraine headache. He turned to the young ballplayer and asked, "How'd you like to play short today?"

Reiser smiled and replied, "Hell, yes."

"Listen, kid," said Durocher. "They've got some mighty good right-handed pitchers. Do you think you can do any good against them?"

"Mr. Durocher," the young man replied, "I can hit any right-handed pitcher who throws a baseball."

And hit he did, and play he did as if someone had written a fairy tale and cast him in the hero's role. In his first time at bat, with two men on base in the game's first inning, Reiser cracked a home run off Cardinal southpaw Ken Raffensberger's first pitch, which turned out to be the winning margin in the Dodgers's 6–4 win over the Cards. In his other at bats that day, he had a base on balls and two singles, the hits this time off right-handed pitchers.

In his second game, this time against the powerful Cincinnati Reds, he hit two singles and two more home runs, the second one slammed over the center field fence 450 feet away, to lead the Dodgers in a 9–1 laugher. Then in his third game, this one against the Detroit Tigers, who were to win the American League pennant that year, he singled in a run in the first inning, helping the Dodgers to a 3–0 lead.

All in all, he got on base his first 12 times at bat, including three home runs, five singles and four walks, while knocking in eight Dodger runs.

By this time, players had begun to kid their manager, asking him, "What kind of bench manager will you make, Leo?" and "Are you going to wave a score card like Connie Mack?"

Pete Reiser had arrived like a locomotive doing a hundred miles an hour, and Durocher gawked at what he saw. He began bragging that this kid was the greatest prospect he had ever seen and would lead the Dodgers into the World Series. "What have I got here? What have I stumbled upon?" he asked. "This is a dream. I never saw anything like this."

But Reiser himself wasn't surprised at what he had done. "I'd been doing it all my life in my mind," he said, "and I'd convinced myself I was going to do it for real when the time came. So I wasn't surprised, I expected it."

And he didn't stop. No one could have expected what followed. In his first time at bat against the Detroit Tigers pitching ace, Tommy Bridges, he hit a home run. In his first game against the Yankees, he hit one off Hall of Famer Lefty Gomez. All in all, Reiser played shortstop in the remaining 33 games of the exhibition season, hitting an inconceivable .485 and turning the heads of everyone who had seen him.

They traveled through Florida with the New York Yankees that season, riding the same train and staying at the same hotels. "One day," said Reiser, "Joe McCarthy (the Yankee manager) walks up to me and says, 'You're going to be my third baseman this year.'"

Reiser asked how he expected that would happen. "I'm with the Dodgers," he told McCarthy.

"We'll get you," McCarthy explained. "I'll tell Ed Barrow (Yankee general manager), and you'll be a Yankee."

A few days later, the Yankee manager repeated the promise. "It won't be long now," he told Reiser, "before you're a Yankee. The deal is almost made."

The deal the Yankees offered the player-hungry Dodgers was unheard of for its time. They were to pay them $100,000 and send them five top minor league prospects for Reiser! Durocher hit the ceiling when he heard about it. "No way," he screamed, and threatened to quit if MacPhail took the offer. But, of course, MacPhail couldn't make the trade. He only had Reiser "on loan" from the Cardinals and was sworn to return him to St. Louis at the appropriate time.

Durocher had his own plans for the kid. He planned to make him his opening-day shortstop with expectations that he would tear up the league. This was the ticket to the pennant if ever there was one.

Meanwhile, Branch Rickey had been reading these incredible accounts of Reiser's heroics and of Durocher's expectations for the kid. All major newspapers of the day carried stories about this new sensation. This was one hell of a way to hide a prospect, he thought. Let the whole damn world in on the secret.

A fuming Rickey called MacPhail and reminded him of all the Cardinal general manager had done for him. What kind of payback was this? The two had made an agreement for Reiser to be returned to St. Louis when the time was safe. Expose the kid like this and the Cardinals would have to hand the Dodgers their entire team to get him back!

MacPhail called Reiser immediately, reaching him in the Dodger clubhouse, to give him the news. He would be sent down to the Elmira team of Brooklyn's farm system for further seasoning. Reiser reiterated what Durocher had promised and had publicly stated. Reiser was to be his opening-day shortstop.

"I don't give a damn what Durocher says," replied MacPhail. "You're going to go to Elmira."

Once MacPhail had hung up, Reiser sat there stunned. Jesus, he thought. He can't do that to me. Not with the spring I had. Go to Elmira?

When Reiser told his manager what had happened, Durocher went berserk. "Like hell you are!" he screamed.

This situation apparently precipitated several vicious and angry confrontations between Durocher and MacPhail. A fistfight took place during which the manager flattened the general manager, a host of firings of Durocher occurred that were soon followed by torrents of tears and immediate rehirings, and, finally, though Durocher had no idea why MacPhail insisted on sending Reiser to Elmira, he accepted the decision and abided by it.

Long years later, baseball writers wrote of how Reiser was returned to the minors that year because of one or another supposed problem. He needed further seasoning, he had hurt this or the other limb, he had to learn to hit a curve ball or swing better against left-handed pitching. Whatever the excuse, either no one knew or no one cared to write about the real reason—MacPhail's disgraceful arrangement with Branch Rickey.

Even in his book *Nice Guys Finish Last*, published in 1975, Durocher wrote: "I never did find out why he didn't want me to play Reiser."

In any event, major league baseball would still have to wait for Pete Reiser.

4

Hidden Away

"I didn't see the old-timers, but Pete Reiser was the best ballplayer I ever saw."
— Bob Cooke, former sports editor
of the *New York Herald Tribune*

The name on a player's uniform designates the name of the team he plays for and belongs to. At least, usually. Whether Pete Reiser in those days was wearing a uniform that read "Elmira" or one that read "Brooklyn," in the eyes and hearts of Larry MacPhail and Branch Rickey, he belonged lock, stock and barrel to the St. Louis Cardinals.

The two general managers had fashioned an agreement that they felt obligated to honor. All they would have to figure out was how to hide Reiser from public scrutiny and how to return him at the proper time to the Cardinals. Do it, that is, without baseball's commissioner catching the stink of the felonious deal.

Except that hiding Pete Reiser in the minors was like hiding an elephant in a classroom. Anyone with eyes was going to see him.

At least, Reiser's 1939 season at Elmira worked to the two general managers' advantage. Beset by several injuries, including a broken elbow and a brain concussion, and certainly demoralized by what had happened in spring training, the young shortstop had a patched-together and incomplete season that curtailed his progress.

"But I did all right anyway," Reiser later said to writer Donald Honig, in his book *Baseball When the Grass Was Real*. "Hit .300."

That and word of his previous exploits proved enough to catch the eye of Clyde Sukerforth, manager of the Montreal Royals, the premiere team in the Dodger farm system. Brought to spring training with the Royals in 1940, Reiser was informed by Sukeforth, "You're my center fielder."

"But I don't want to play the outfield," Reiser complained, portentous perhaps of what was to come. "I want to play the infield."

"Regardless where you play," replied the Montreal manager, "you're going to play on my ballclub."

In spring training, Reiser did. Sukeforth had him play at several positions, both in the infield and the outfield, and was ready to start him as the season opened. But then things changed. Again.

Once the major league season started, the Dodgers released a group of their veterans, shipped them down to Montreal and ordered the manager to play them. This sent Reiser to the team's bench. By this time, boiling mad, Reiser was called to Sukeforth's room.

"I know you're not going to like this," the manager told him. "I've got some real bad news. MacPhail said to send you to Elmira."

Reiser hit the ceiling. "Bullshit," he screamed out. "No way you're going to send me to Elmira."

"My hands are tied," Sukeforth told him. "MacPhail promised the people in Montreal a winner, that he would not take one player away from the Montreal ballclub. He's afraid that you're going to do so well that he'd have to break his promise and take you up to Brooklyn. He does not want to offend the people who are supporting a valuable franchise."

Still dumb to what was really going on, Reiser had little option. But before going back to Elmira, he boarded a train back home to St. Louis. There he spoke to his father and told him he was ready to quit baseball.

"I'm better than anyone in Montreal," he complained. "I should be up in the big leagues by now."

His father calmly patted Reiser's shoulder. "When you're old and wise enough to be a general manager," he told him, "you'll tell yourself what to do. Now if I were you, I'd listen to Mr. MacPhail."

That and a call from Bill Killefer, both manager and general manager of the Elmira ballclub, helped soothe his ego and ease his wounds.

Killefer was an old-time catcher whose career started way back in 1909 for the St. Louis Browns. He was famous for many years as the battery mate of pitching immortal Grover Cleveland Alexander in his days with the Philadelphia Phillies, and was part of their pennant-winning team in 1915.

He had also been a manager for the Chicago Cubs and the Browns, as well as for several minor league teams. Reindeer Bill, as he was called, had been around, and around, and he understood the plight of ballplayers during these days of unrestricted servitude.

"You come to Elmira," he said to Reiser, "and I'll make you a promise. If you're going good before July 1, and the Dodgers don't bring you up, I'll sell you to the highest bidder."

When Reiser asked Killefer how he'd accomplish that, he was told that he was being optioned outright to the Elmira club. "I'm the general manager," said Killefer, "and I can do what I want. I don't have more than a year or two left in this game anyway, so the hell with them. You should have been on the Dodgers in 1939."

"But you'll get fired," Reiser said.

"To hell with them," said Killefer. "I'm ready to retire anyway."

The young ballplayer wanted to believe what he was told. "All right," he agreed, "but, boy, if I'm not up there—"

Killefer cut him off. "You'll be there, kid," he said. "Don't worry."

And it was Killefer who ultimately forced MacPhail's hand.

By mid–June, Reiser had been tearing up the Eastern League, where Elmira played. He was hitting .378, creating havoc on the base paths with his base-stealing prowess, and fielding—wherever they played him—with a golden glove, a rifle arm and a reckless go-get-'em style.

Killefer then lived up to the promise he had made Reiser. He did have the power to trade the young man, and he told MacPhail he would do so if he didn't bring up the player to the Dodgers.

By this time, MacPhail and Rickey had devised the way Reiser would be sent to the Cardinals. The two clubs were in the process of a major trade that would send Brooklyn the Cardinals' great slugger and future Hall of Famer, Joe Medwick, as well as veteran right hand pitcher Curt Davis, who had won 22 games for St. Louis the year before. In return, the Cardinals would be sent Pete Reiser and a trio of inessential players, including outfielder Ernie Koy. Certainly, it was Reiser who was the crux of the deal.

MacPhail was stymied. With all sorts of newspaper accounts glorifying the potential of Reiser and now, with this barefaced threat by Killefer, his hands were tied. Just as this dirty bit of larceny was about to take place, it couldn't be done. Reindeer Bill had ridden to the rescue.

MacPhail called Rickey immediately and told him the news. There was no way he could get Reiser to the Cardinals. "They'd lynch me here if I traded Reiser away even up for Medwick right now," said MacPhail. "Durocher has talked too much and the reporters have written every word. The fans are so excited about the kid that there would be a scandal. I just can't give him back to you."

Of course Rickey had to back off. If their little scheme had been publicized, the two men would be facing more trouble than either had ever known. Judge Kenesaw Mountain Landis had always lived up to the "Mountain" of his name.

In the final trade for Medwick and Davis, the Dodgers had to send the Cardinals the then staggering sum of $250,000 to take the place of the young Pete Reiser. This was something that could not be adequately explained to the inquiring press nor to Brooklyn's board of directors.

As the end of June grew near, Reiser went to see Killefer. "It's getting pretty damned close to July 1," he reminded him.

Killefer grinned. "You're going to Brooklyn tonight," he told him. "You've been called up."

Killefer then revealed to Reiser the intrigue between MacPhail and Rickey and how sadly it had held back the young man's progress. "Do you know why you didn't stay there (in Brooklyn) in '39?" he asked. "Because you were the property of the Cardinals."

Many years later, in Donald Honig's book *Baseball When the Grass Was Real*, Reiser recounted much of what had developed for him at that time

"There were two things that could have happened to me in those years," Reiser said. "They could've sold me to the Yankees and I probably would have been the Yankee third baseman for a long time. And if I played for the Cardinals, I probably still would have been an infielder, probably at third base, because they had guys like Slaughter and Terry Moore in their outfield. Plus the fact if I would have been declared a free agent in '39, there's no telling how much money I could have got to sign. So you see how your whole life changes."

This was a startling admission. Yes, indeed, if any of these options had taken place, Pete Reiser would probably have spent his entire baseball life as an infielder, and an outstanding one at that. And furthermore, far from the demons that were awaiting him. He recognized this and understood completely all its implications.

But that was not to be the case. Reiser's life was about to change, and no one could have believed how much, as he left to join the Brooklyn Dodgers on June 22, 1940.

5

Dem (Not Such) Bums

"They'd lynch me here if I traded Reiser away even up for Medwick right now. Durocher has talked too much, and the reporters have written every word."
— Larry MacPhail to Branch Rickey

It was a sportswriter named Sid Mercer who was responsible for hanging the name "Bums," later Brooklynized to "Dem Bums," on the Dodgers. This occurred during the grief-ridden days of the 1930's when the team held something close to a lease on the National League basement. Quoting a disgruntled fan who constantly shouted, "Ya bum, ya!" from his seat behind home plate in Ebbets Field, Mercer called him "The Spirit of Brooklyn" and mentioned him often in his writings.

Several newspapers picked up the name and used "Bums" in their headlines as a synonym for Dodgers. When, years later, the incomparable sports cartoonist Willard Mullin drew a lovable tramp in rag clothes and made him his insignia for the team, this became a nationally known icon. As Ellen M. Snyder-Grenier, in her book *Brooklyn! An Illustrated History*, points out, "not only of the Dodgers but of Brooklyn as well."

But by 1940, that image had begun to change.

The combination of general manager Larry MacPhail and field manager Leo Durocher had accomplished a good deal since back in 1937, when they put their minds together—and their wills in clash. By 1939, they had been able to lift the once woeful club to a third-place finish, which, in Durocher's words, was "the highest Brooklyn had finished in the memory of man." Ending the season six games ahead of their traditional rivals, the New York Giants, was an added plum.

By the following year, the world outside the daily sports pages was becoming a far different place. A world war had settled in, both in Europe and in Asia, though we were still reluctant to give it that name. Hitler had marched through and taken much of Western Europe, while France, one of the supposed stalwarts of Western Democracy, teetered on the edge of collapse.

America still debated its role in this conflict and just how much aid it could chance to give its European friends. So as best it could, this nation shut its eyes to the daily headlines, fenced itself in with its national priorities, and enjoyed such things as the World's Fair that flourished in New York City, and, of course, baseball, the national pastime.

In retrospect, it seems strange that this blindness was a national affliction. Though perhaps it always is and we don't realize it till we take a look back at our past through a rearview mirror. Anyhow, what was going on in the world at this time deserves being noted, if only to point out its insignificant effect on baseball.

Thus all that was on Leo Durocher's mind in 1940 was his hope to better his achievement of the year before. Period. But by the time spring training rolled around, most of his hopes had turned sour. In *The Dodgers and Me*, Durocher's early autobiography, the former Brooklyn manager wrote:

"We had an outfielder who wore a pink corset because he had a bad back, and a relief pitcher who whizzed through our training camp base at Clearwater on a motor bike, giving vent to wild cowboy yells…. We paid $10,000 for a pitcher who stayed out late and then was on the verge of breaking me in half and $25,000 for an outfielder who ate salads only and was so weak he couldn't wave his bat."

The Dodger players "changed as frequently as the bill in small-time vaudeville," Durocher complained. "Players came and went as though we were working behind swinging doors."

Joe Vosmik, the man with the pink corset; Roy Cullenbine, the outfielder who ate salads; Steve Rachunok, a 200-pound pitcher who couldn't throw a fast ball but liked late-hour living; Chris Hartje, a much-publicized catcher who had come with MacPhail's blessing and couldn't stay off the booze. And so on.

Added trouble came by way of one of the team's few genuine big-time ball players, first baseman Dolf Camilli. A strong home run hitter, he was, according to many, the best fielding first baseman in baseball. Camilli, who had hit close to .300 and knocked in more than a hundred runs during the season before, was expected to match these numbers in 1940.

However, at spring training, Camilli refused to sign a new contract until he was given a $1,000 raise to $15,000 a year, as well as traveling expenses for his wife and kids. MacPhail being MacPhail refused. He wasn't "running a kindergarten," he told the first baseman. He did not intend to pay the expenses of Camilli's eight kids.

This simply added insult, shameful insult, to injury. There were four Camilli kids, and though the general manager was constantly corrected, he persisted on keeping his own count.

Durocher described the scene that had taken place in an office of the hotel lobby in Clearwater, where the quite powerful Camilli had literally picked MacPhail right off the floor by his jowls.

"I didn't know what to do," Durocher wrote. "Dolf was strong as Strangler Lewis (a prominent wrestler of the time). I thought Larry was a goner."

For weeks, Camilli threatened to return to his home in California for the season, and Durocher, contemplating the year without his most important hitter, saw any possible pennant hopes flutter away.

MacPhail finally gave in. "Tell Camilli he is going to get that extra thousand bucks he is crying about," he said to Durocher. "But don't let him know that it is coming from me. This is one argument I want to win."

The manager had to tell his star that he, Durocher, would be guaranteeing the money. "I'll see that you get it," he said to Camilli. "It may not be today, or next week, but you'll get it."

That finally put the matter to rest, and the manager went on to his other problems, which he had by the bushel. Despite the successes of the previous season, the Dodgers were a team with gigantic gaps. Still without benefit of a thriving farm system, they were forced to enter the major league market to buy players. With all the money MacPhail had been granted—and by this time, he had spent the owners into near hysteria—Durocher still had ended up with too many players long in the tooth or chomping on their baby ones. Thus the revolving door Durocher spoke of. Out went Vosmik, in came Jimmy Wasdell. Out went Wasdell, in came Joe Gallagher.

The acquisition of Dolf Camilli from the money-starved Phillies in 1938 was a rare good move. So was the deal that had made the young rookie shortstop, Pee Wee Reese, a Dodger. The youngster, who would eventually end up in Cooperstown, had been purchased from Louisville of the Boston Red Sox farm system for $75,000, and was expected to steal the shortstop position from his manager. Reese, of course, did more than that. He soon became one of the best fielding shortstops in baseball and, in later years, one of the game's premier clutch hitters.

The first time Durocher saw Reese, in spring training that year, he told himself, "Leo, you can rest your aching tootsies."

But MacPhail would have none of it. He had contracted Durocher as a manager and as a shortstop, and he expected both from him.

In his book *Nice Guys Finish Last* Durocher wrote, "He knew I was the premier fielding shortstop in the business, see, because everybody told him I was."

When Durocher pointed out that he might have been that six years before, but that he was now an aging 34-year-old, MacPhail simply replied, "You can play another two or three years."

Durocher tried to explain that Reese could easily handle balls that Durocher couldn't get close to. "What we got here," he told MacPhail, "is a diamond that you found in Africa. What we got to do is polish the diamond up, and he is going to be

Dodger Manager Leo Durocher, couldn't believe the abilities of the young Reiser when he saw him in the spring of 1939. "This is a dream," said Durocher. "I never saw anything like this" (**National Baseball Hall of Fame Library, Cooperstown, N.Y.**).

as good a shortstop as they ever heard of in the major leagues."

"I'm paying you five thousand dollars to play shortstop," MacPhail shot back.

"Reese is going to be the shortstop," insisted Durocher.

"If you're not out at shortstop tomorrow," MacPhail said, "you're fired!"

By this time, already inure to these supposed firings, Durocher paid no attention to this latest salvo. "The only time I ever played shortstop," Durocher wrote, "was when Reese was hurt, which kept me very busy in his first year and practically retired me thereafter."

The rest of the Dodger starting infield, second baseman Pete Coscarat, third baseman Harry Lavagetto and utility infielder Johnny Hudson, were hardly the bricks with which to build a pennant contender, though Lavagetto certainly was the premier player of the lot.

The Dodger pitching staff was headed by Whitlow Wyatt, a fireballing castoff from the American League, whose best years were to come in his Brooklyn uniform, and by Fred Fitzsimmons, who had been a standout knuckleballer for the New York Giants and was entering his third and best year for the Dodgers. Except for Hugh Casey, who would become one of the game's finest relief pitching stars, the rest of the staff was on the belly side of mediocrity.

The team's first-string catcher, Babe Phelps, was a lifetime .310 hitter nearing the end of his career, and his fielding capabilities made you awfully glad he could hit. But there always had to be a good fielding backup for Phelps, who couldn't play his position much more than a hundred games a season, and you were somewhat glad he couldn't. During this season, backing him up was Gus Mancuso, long past his prime, but still first rate with his glove.

Phelps also wouldn't go near an airplane. When the team traveled home after their first Western trip that season, a most successful beginning for the Dodgers, two airplanes were chartered as a special reward for their accomplishment. The catcher refused to get aboard.

Durocher argued, "If you're number is up, you're going to go, whether you're in a train, walking on the sidewalk, or in a plane."

Phelps had an answer. "Suppose you're up in a plane," he told Durocher, "and the pilot's number comes up. Where does that leave you?"

Such was Phelps, and the manager gave no answer.

But the team's biggest problems were in the outfield. They could not put together three players who could safely defend the outfield walls and at the same time hit more than a lick. One was too weak to swing, another would swing at everything. One fielder couldn't go to his right, one to his left, and the other anywhere at all.

Yet, to everyone's surprise, they started the season like a shot out of a cannon. With Camilli hitting well at first, with Reese sparkling at short, with eight different pitchers winning at least one game, with outfielder Dixie Walker, another American League castoff, suddenly finding his hitting stroke, and with the rest of the outfield somewhere and somehow finding cohesion, they jumped into first place with nine consecutive victories. By the end of the first month, they still maintained that position, if ever so slightly, over the Cincinnati Reds.

Of course, very few believed this team had any chance of staying there. By the beginning of June, they were in second place, three games behind the Reds, and their fortunes severely threatened. In a game on June 1 with the Cubs, Chicago pitcher Jake Mooty struck Reese on the head with a stinging fast ball that landed just behind his left ear. The 20-year-old shortstop sensation had to be carried off the field on a stretcher and immediately taken to nearby Illinois Masonic Hospital.

Luckily, no fracture was found, though doctors warned that Reese "must remain quiet" and be kept at the hospital for at least a week. The rookie did suffer dizzy spells for a while and could not return to the Brooklyn lineup for two weeks more.

It is interesting to note that as Reese's dizzy spells continued, the club went looking for a replacement. There were several newspaper accounts during this time about a 19-year-old shortstop named Emil Rey, who was brought in to work out with the team. Rey, who never appeared in a major league lineup, was forgotten as soon as Reese began to improve. But one does wonder whether the name of Pete Reiser, a quite accomplished shortstop, had ever been mentioned.

In any case, it was time for some magical changes, and Larry MacPhail believed he was going to pull a rabbit out of his hat. Better yet, a duck. He had fashioned his deal with Branch Rickey to bring to the Dodgers Joe Ducky Medwick, the powerful hitting Cardinal outfielder, who may have walked like a duck but swung a bat like an angry gorilla. This transaction, too, had been originally formulated as a means of finally sending Pete Reiser back to the Cardinals.

But this idea, as it has been previously explained, had been squashed by Elmira general manager Bill Killefer, and the entire transaction had to be reconstructed. Fortunately, in every way for the Dodgers. Not only would they now get Medwick, they would also be able to keep Reiser.

Medwick had been one of the National League's great sluggers, and one who would ultimately end up in the Hall of Fame. He had hit well over .300 since his beginnings in baseball in 1932 and had once led the league with an astronomical .374 batting average. Durocher believed that the abilities of this muscular and handsome slugger were made for the modest confines of Ebbets Field, and his presence in the Dodgers lineup would give them a terrific chance at the pennant.

Along with Medwick, the Dodgers got the very fine veteran pitcher Curt Davis, a sidearm right-hander who had won 22 games for the Cardinals the previous season and would have several good years for Brooklyn. In exchange, the Cardinals got four expendable Brooklyn players and a ton of money that, because of Reiser's exclusion in the deal, was said to amount to $250,000.

Years later, in looking back at the trade for Medwick, Durocher wrote, "When Rickey is willing to let a contending team have that kind of a player, you have a right to suspect that he has spotted a certain decline setting in."

Medwick's numbers for the Cardinals that season had indeed slipped. In addition, the manager had gotten disturbing feedback from some old pals on the Cardinals. The big outfielder had had some major run-in with St. Louis manager Ray Blades, and many on the team believed Medwick was playing strictly for himself and not for the benefit of the team. In fact, Medwick, once the darling of the fans, was now being loudly booed.

Still, if there was any trouble with the outfielder's hitting, Durocher, a longtime friend, felt sure he could straighten it out. "I know Joe will be a better ball player for me than he has been," Durocher was quoted in *The New York Times* as saying. "He'll hustle his head off ."

"He's coming with a good bunch of fellows that he likes and who like him," he told reporter Roscoe McGowen. "It's going to make all the difference in the world."

It was suggested that there might be an upward adjustment in Medwick's contract, which purportedly had called for $18,000 a year. Medwick, in fact, had reluctantly signed the pact only after a major squabble with the St. Louis management.

"I wouldn't be at all surprised," said Durocher. "Medwick's return for this year may be at least $25,000, assuming Joe hits and plays in the manner he has shown himself capable in the past."

As for Medwick? "I'm the happiest guy in the world," he said. "Nothing ever happened to me that tickled me so much."

The fans as well as the press in New York greeted the news excitedly. It had been long years since the team had a player of this magnitude. There was a rush in ticket sales and enthusiastic hype in all the newspapers. "Flatbush in fever over new players," read a typical headline. In the next few days, the headlines grew even more energized as the revitalized team began a mild winning streak that gave them the league lead once again. If only for a moment...

On June 18, the Cardinals came to town for a series and immediately knocked the Dodgers out of first place, beating them, 3–1 and holding Medwick hitless in four tries. The Cardinals were staying at the Hotel New Yorker, where both Medwick and Durocher were also staying.

On the following morning, Durocher and Medwick rode down in the elevator with Bob Bowman, the Cardinal pitcher slated to pitch against them that afternoon. Durocher later said that on the ride down he had given Bowman "one of my lovable remarks about his chances for survival, which gave him a perfect opening."

Bowman answered it quickly. "I'll not have any trouble getting you out anyway," he said.

Medwick immediately had a response. "I doubt if you'll ever get to pitch to Leo," he said. "We'll belt you out of there before you get down the lineup that far."

The now irate Bowman would have the last word. "I'll take care of both you guys," he said. "Wait and see."

That conversation played out dramatically and sadly in the game later that day. The first three Dodgers at bat tore into Bowman's pitches for line-drive base hits that scored a run and left two men on base. Next up was cleanup hitter Joe Medwick.

On Bowman's first pitch to Medwick, the ball was thrown high and inside and straight at the batter's skull. It came in too quickly for Medwick to get out of its way, and the ball smashed him ferociously in his temple. As Durocher has described it, "He dropped like the trunk of a tree."

Medwick fell hard on his back, unconscious before he hit the ground. The ballpark erupted in mayhem.

There were fights all over the place that day, on the field between players and in the stands between enraged fans. MacPhail, who had just spent a small fortune to get the man who was being carried off the field on a stretcher, was probably angriest of all. He raced down from his box to a position in front of the Cardinal dugout, challenging one and all to come out and finish the battle Bowman had begun.

MacPhail didn't let it rest. Based on what Bowman had said in the Hotel New Yorker elevator, he pleaded with District Attorney William O'Dwyer to investigate the beaning of Medwick, the earlier one of Pee Wee Reese, and his contention that National League teams were out to destroy his team's pennant chances by taking out their key players.

O'Dwyer, who had recently played a key role in bringing to justice gangland's infamous assassination squad, known as Murder, Inc., was now being asked to deal with what MacPhail had cleverly termed, "Beanball, Inc." And the D.A. did!

Though there were 32 pages of testimony and much time spent in questioning players and managers, nothing really came of this. The National League office also took up the case and came to much the same conclusion. "After careful investigation," National League President Ford Frick decided, "the National League office finds no proof of the charge brought by the Brooklyn club that pitcher Bob Bowman of St. Louis deliberately and with premeditation beaned Joe Medwick in the game played at Ebbets Field June 18. The charges therefore are dismissed."

The most important occurrence that did take place from this incident was the introduction of plastic batting helmets. Before the next season had begun, MacPhail had them made and ordered for the team.

"Guaranteed to withstand baseballs propelled at a hundred miles an hour," he announced proudly. "Now let them throw at us all they want. They can't hurt us."

Pee Wee Reese later returned to the lineup apparently recovered from what had happened to him. But Joe Ducky Medwick, whether from the ravages of the years or specifically from this beaning by Bowman, was never the same. His abilities slowly diminished, and many players would swear that the incident had made him plate shy.

Leo Durocher, in his biography *The Dodgers and Me*, indicates the moment when he realized that Medwick would never be the same. "Joe was up in the last of the ninth," he wrote, "against the Pirates, the score tied, the bases loaded, three on, one out. The game was crying to be won, but Joe pulled away from the pitch and dribbled into a double play.'

From that time on, Durocher placed the cleanup hitter lower in the batting order. "He did not belt the ball when it counted," he wrote, "or for distance."

But by the All-Star break, the Dodgers were still nip and tuck in their battle with Cincinnati for first place. And wonder of wonders, despite the variety of fears Durocher had in spring training for the Dodgers, they somehow placed six men on the National League All-Star team, more than any other club in the league. Joe Medwick, Babe Phelps, Cookie Lavagetto, Pete Coscarat, Whitlow Wyatt and manager Durocher himself were named to the team, with all but Durocher getting into the 4–0 winning effort over the American League.

Just about this time, Pete Reiser, with that heroic assist from Bill Killefer, was finally called up to the Dodgers.

6

Finally

"In my estimation, Pete Reiser was the greatest natural talent who ever lived."

—Donald Honig, author of
Baseball When the Grass Was Real

The house that Charlie Ebbets had built in Brooklyn had neither the class nor the glamour of the House that Babe Ruth had built in The Bronx. Yankee Stadium, the so-called Ruth's House, which in terms of baseball's comparative engineering was much more a mansion, had all the size and appropriate magnificence to fit the plethora of World Championship flags that adorned the place. Built for two and a half million dollars, it was an all-concrete stadium that could seat well over 70,000 with more than ample breathing room.

It had its opening on April 18, 1923, with all the fanfare of a Fourth of July celebration . The military band playing there that day was, in fact, led by John Philip Sousa, America's own king of the patriotic marching band. Upwards of 74,000 people turned out for the event, up to then the largest crowd ever to witness a game. The first ball would be thrown out by the state's governor, Alfred E. Smith, soon to be his party's nominee for president.

More than a hundred writers from all over the nation were there as reporters. One of them, Fred Lieb of the *World*, in the next day's paper christened the place "the House that Ruth Built," and forever that name would stick.

As if from a script, in the third inning of the game Babe Ruth hit the Yankee Stadium's first home run. Ironically, it was hit off pitcher Howard

Ehmke of the Boston Red Sox, a member of the team that had sold him to the fortunate Yankees.

As for the Polo Grounds, the longtime home of the New York Giants, right across the Harlem River from the stadium, it had tradition, if not class or glamour. Once it was the home field for both the Giants and the Yankees, until Babe Ruth's presence in a Yankee uniform hastened the building of his team's own ballpark. The Polo Grounds had been the playing field for many baseball immortals over the years. Great players like Christy Mathewson, Joe McGinnity, Bill Terry, Mel Ott, Frankie Frisch, Carl Hubbell and Babe Ruth himself all performed there.

The original Polo Grounds, which had been just north of Central Park, opened in 1883 as a field in which to play polo, much as the name indicates. When baseball was played there, the area was so huge that two games could be played at once. This present one, the fourth to bear the name, seemed as preposterously laid out for baseball as the original. In this ballpark, a batter could hit a 249-foot home run in right field but not get close to the wall with a 475-foot smash to center. Still, the Polo Grounds boasted size, a seating capacity of 55,000 and an accumulation of baseball history.

The runt of the litter, certainly in playing area and seating capacity, was Ebbets Field in Brooklyn. Originally built by Charlie Ebbets in 1913, in its time it was considered a great advancement in construction and engineering. But, of course, back then, so was the Ford Model T. This ballpark barely reached 400 feet at its deepest part in center field, and its stands could hold a minuscule 34,000 spectators.

At its front, the structure sat like a three-story building with a wide, canopied, open entranceway. The name, Ebbets Field, was riveted in huge block letters onto an opening at the top, much like the marquee of a movie theater. Views of the exposed grandstands were clearly visible above the first floor of office space about a third of the way down the street to both the left and right. Its address was 55 Sullivan Place in the Crown Heights section of Brooklyn, and what it lacked in grandeur, it more than made up, if you will, with fan-deur.

The fans of the Brooklyn Dodgers, you see, were probably the most distinctive and die-hard the sport had ever seen. Through thin and thick— which there was hardly much of—they came out to root like hell for their home team, and win or lose, they enjoyed every damn moment of it.

As Peter Golenbock in his book *Bums* pointed out, "There was an informal, non-professional quality to Ebbets Field and the Dodgers. It was very personal. The fans loved the players. The players loved the fans. All a player had to do was walk out onto the field, and the fans would begin waving at him and hollering to be waved back at, and they would throw down little vials of holy water and religious medals, and when a ballplayer had a birthday, there would always be one or two homemade cakes in the clubhouse for him."

When Larry MacPhail had Ebbets Field renovated in 1937 and 1938 with improvements that included new paint, improved bathrooms and artificial lights, annual attendance went from 400,000 to more than double that the following year. Now that the Dodgers had a team that was apparently going places, their attendance figures would soar.

Some of these fans also became quite famous. To the players, to the press, to other fans who took up their chants and their nonsense. Perhaps most famous was a woman named Hilda Chester, who sat in the center field bleachers and rarely missed a game. Hilda had a growly foghorn voice that she used to successfully rouse the crowd as well as the guys on the field. After a debilitating heart attack caused a doctor to prohibit her from any further yelling, the Dodgers presented her with a huge cowbell that she clanged out there in her seat till the cows came home. Which, fortunately, they never did.

Five rabid musical fans put together a group called the Dodger Sym-Phoney, which paraded atop the dugout and through the stands playing their ragtag versions of ragtime music. The group greeted the umpires with their rendition of "Three Blind Mice," opposing pitchers who were being relieved with "The Worms Crawl In," and a rival batter who had just struck out and was about to take his seat in the dugout with an embarrassing crash of cymbals.

All this spontaneously took place without a ballclub hireling like the San Diego Chicken or the annoying Philly Phanatic to artificially drum up support.

This was the warm, welcoming environment Pete Reiser walked into when he finally arrived in Brooklyn on June 22, 1940. "I felt great," he would later write about his trip down from Elmira. "I rode the bus all night into New York. Couldn't sleep a wink, I was so excited."

He then related a story about being at his first game there and his meeting with one of those Dodger fans. As Reiser left the park, he was tapped on the shoulder, as he put it, by "the meanest-looking son of a bitch you ever saw."

"You don't know me, do you?" the man asked.

"I don't think so," said Reiser.

The man told him he knew him from Elmira.

"Oh, you from Elmira?" said Reiser.

"No," the man replied. "I'm from Brooklyn. But you and the Elmira

Pioneers came up there last year and played an exhibition game at the prison. I just got out," he continued. "And I want to tell you I appreciate things like that from you athletes. Listen, anybody gives you any trouble in this town, I want you to know I'm gonna be out there every ball game. You just whistle up to me. Anybody gives you any trouble, they're dead."

"Welcome to Brooklyn!" joked Reiser, concluding his story.

Early on he also had a funny encounter with cowbell-clanging Hilda Chester. It was in the seventh inning of a game, and Reiser was taking his position in center field. "Hey, Reiser!" someone called from the stands, and he realized it was Hilda.

"There could be 30,000 people yelling there at once," he told writer Donald Honig, "but Hilda was the one you'd hear. I look up and she's dropping something onto the grass."

It was a note that she instructed Reiser to give to Durocher. "So I pick it up and put it in my pocket," Reiser recalled. "At the end of the inning I started heading in.

"Now MacPhail used to sit in a box right next to the dugout, and for some reason he waved to me as I came in," he went on. Reiser returned his boss's hello with a wave and then continued into the dugout. Before he sat down he handed Hilda Chester's note to Durocher.

"Next thing I know," said Reiser, "he's getting somebody hot in the bullpen. I think it was Casey. Meanwhile, Wyatt's pitching a hell of a ball-game for us. In the next inning, the first guy hits the ball pretty good and goes out. The next guy gets a base hit. Here comes Leo. He takes Wyatt out and brings in Casey. Casey got rocked a few times, and we just did win the game, just did win it."

Once the game was over, an angry Durocher went into his clubhouse office and slammed the door behind him. The players waited silently for their manager to show up. They had always been instructed to keep their uniforms on till he gave them word to remove them. Finally Durocher walks in and points a finger at Reiser.

"Don't you ever give me another note from MacPhail as long as you play for me," Durocher ordered.

"I didn't give you any note from MacPhail," answered Reiser.

"Don't tell me!" he screamed at Reiser. "You handed me a note in the seventh inning."

"That was from Hilda," said Reiser.

"From Hilda?" screamed a disbelieving Durocher. "You mean to say that wasn't from MacPhail?"

"I'd never even looked at the note," said Reiser, recalling the incident. "Just handed it to him. Leo had heard me say something to MacPhail when I came in and figured the note was from Larry. It seems what the note said was: 'Get Casey hot, Wyatt's losing it.'

"So what you had," said Reiser, finishing his story, "was somebody named Hilda Chester sitting in the center field bleachers changing pitchers for you. You talk about oddball things happening in Ebbets Field, you're not exaggerating."

But for Reiser, having finally arrived in Ebbets Field and with the Dodgers, the most oddball thing that happened to him was spending his first weeks glued to the Brooklyn bench. For all that had taken place to get him here—the Landis ruling, the Rickey shenanigans, MacPhail's thoroughly illegal burial plot and Bill Killefer's upstanding bravery, the young man could have been back in Elmira. There, at least, he still would be playing ball.

But on the bench is where Reiser sat for more than a month as the Dodgers continued to lose ground in their effort to keep up with the front-running Reds. On July 23, having just lost three out of four games to the Cardinals and now behind Cincinnati by five full games, Brooklyn began a crucial three-game series with the Reds at Ebbets Field.

It began with a midweek doubleheader and, finally, it was time for the youngster to get up off the bench. This, at long last, would be Pete Reiser's first day playing as a Dodger.

July 23, 1940, was the date of this historic moment in Reiser's life. And what kind of a day was it? One look at the front page of the next day's *New York Times* would seem to suggest that nothing changes much but the calendar. The Republican candidate for President, Wendell Willkie, was promising cuts in big government. An important public official was being criticized for unethical behavior. The United States was lashing out at the Soviet Union.

And a young ballplayer of unlimited promise was beginning his major league career.

A short item in the *Times* took note of this, announcing that "Reiser, boy wonder of the spring training trip two years ago, started in right field for Brooklyn." The "boy wonder" meekly made out in his first at bat, but he walked up to the plate in the fifth inning at a crucial moment, with a chance to break open the game for his team.

The game had been a 2–2 tie when Joe Medwick had opened the inning with a double off the left field wall. Cleanup hitter Babe Phelps then followed with a hard single to right, bringing Medwick home and giving the Dodgers a 3–2 lead. First baseman Dolf Camilli walked, moving Phelps to second and bringing up Reiser. No one out, two men on base, and Reiser in his first game ready to show what all the shouting had been about. In the words of Sam Spade in *The Maltese Falcon*, it was "the kind of stuff that dreams are made of."

Reiser was quickly flashed the signal to bunt and move the players along. On the first pitch, as the runners took off, he dropped his hands down on the bat and pushed it softly at the incoming ball.

And missed.

Reds' catcher Ernie Lombardi caught the ball cleanly and in one motion threw down to second base, catching the lumbering Phelps as he tried unsuccessfully to get back to the base. Okay, one out and Reiser still up. Still a chance to make this first day a memorable one.

Not this day. Without time to even catch his breath, one pitch later he swung and weakly grounded into an inning ending double play. The dreams would have to wait.

As it turned out, the Dodgers lost both games to the Reds that day, 4–3 and 9–2, slipping further behind the streaking leaders. Reiser was hitless in all three at bats in the first game, and in the second, failed as a pinch

The Dodgers finally saw Pete Reiser swing his powerful bat in midseason of 1940, and they soon couldn't stop watching (National Baseball Hall of Fame Library, Cooperstown, N.Y.).

hitter in the ninth inning for pitcher Newel Kimball. A quite inauspicious start for the 21-year-old player, probably overwhelmed in his first moments in the major league sun. But at least his name was in a National League box score, and there was no place to go but up.

The Brooklyn team continued its losing ways, including a streak of 13 losses in 19 games, and fell further behind the Reds. Reiser's only other appearances in July were several fruitless pinch-hitting efforts. One of these was portrayed in *The New York Times* as follows: "Pete Reiser essayed to pinch hit for the second time and ran his strikeouts to two." (Well, at least, he was being noticed!)

Things changed dramatically for him, however, during the following month. The Dodgers remained in the pennant race, if only by their finger-tips, and Reiser got a chance to really play. A note in the August 3 issue of the *Times* stated, "Reiser may be the Dodger third baseman soon. Durocher worked him out at third yesterday and would have put him in the lineup had Hartnett (Cubs manager) started a right hander. Leo wants to give Lavagetto a few days rest."

A day later, Reiser did play. "Manager Durocher made what seemed an extraordinary but justifiable move in the nightcap," read the *Times*. "He benched Medwick, Cookie Lavagetto and Coscarat. Pete Reiser, rookie outfielder, played his first game at third base and handled three simple chances without trouble."

Batting fifth in the order, he also got his first major league hit, a single off Chicago pitcher Claude Passeau. He went one for four, scored two runs, was credited with a successful sacrifice hit, and all in a 7–6 winning effort for the Dodgers.

Two days later, still batting fifth, he got another single in three tries, this time against the third-place Giants. On August 9, in an extra-inning game with the Giants, he successfully pinch hit for pitcher Curt Davis, with a single in the seventh inning that led to the Dodgers tying the game. He finished the game in right field, getting a second hit and a walk in a 12-inning Dodger win. Slowly, it appeared, the young man was being moved into the lineup.

As he received more and more playing time, he was shifted from position to position. Several games he played at third, several in right field, and later that month, he was moved to shortstop. After Reese had broken a heel bone and had been retired for the season and Durocher, his replacement, had injured his throwing arm, Reiser was selected to fill the position. He was certainly revealing himself as a player of enormous versatility.

One of his efforts at short was described by the *Times* this way: "Reiser made two nice plays, both on balls hit by (Billy) Herman and his judgment was good after fielding (Stan) Hack's hit to deep short in the sixth. Todd tried to go all the way home, but Pete fired to Mancuso and got Al Todd easily at the plate."

Reiser hit his first triple in a game against the Phillies and his first home run on August 21 against Bill McGee of the Cardinals. This time he was batting as the right fielder, and the hit was described as "a clout atop the pavillion roof" that tied the game for the moment.

In this continuous dance around the positions of the playing field, the place Reiser was most comfortable at was third base. When regular third baseman Cookie Lavagetto suffered a burst appendix during a road trip in Cincinnati, Reiser was moved from short to third and remained there for the rest of the season.

Reds manager Bill McKechnie, Reiser reported, "came up to me one day and said, 'You're the best third baseman in this league. I think you've found your position.'"

It is interesting to note that back in 1939, when Yankee manager Joe McCarthy promised Reiser that his team would be trading a pot load of money and several players for him, he expected him to be his third baseman. That, Reiser would remember, was when then Yankee third baseman Red Rolfe was considered one of the premier players in baseball.

Reiser made his preference known rather simply. "I loved third base," he later said.

At least during the last weeks of the 1940 season, Reiser did play at third and played the position superbly. Brooklyn didn't win the pennant that year, finishing 12 games behind the winning Reds and only four ahead of the reinvigorated Cardinals, who became more competitive without Medwick than with him. As the season progressed, it became obvious that the Cardinals would be the team for the Dodgers to beat—or get beaten by—in their next quest for the pennant.

Durocher blamed the team's ultimate failure on the series of Dodger injuries. "I still think we would have won the pennant that year," he said in *The Dodgers and Me*, "except for the mishaps we suffered. Reese had been beaned, so had Medwick, and then Wyatt had still been bothered by his bad knee. Just as we pulled ourselves together for one final lunge at the pennant Lavagetto went out with appendicitis, and we had to play Reiser at third. Then Reese went out again with two broken bones in his ankle, and old man Durocher had to go in to play short."

A slight mix-up in the chronology, but you get the idea. This was a better ballclub than the final standings suggested, and Durocher certainly had a point. Still finishing second was no mean trick for the Dodgers. This was the best a Brooklyn team had done since 1924, when one of Wilbert

Robinson's better clubs finished a game and a half behind the pennant winning Giants.

As for Reiser, finding a home at third base, if only temporarily, gave him stability and greater confidence at the plate. And he delivered. Playing in 58 games, several as a pinch hitter, he batted just short of .300 at .293. This was the fourth highest average of all Dodger batters, slightly behind the three leaders, Walker, Medwick and Phelps.

He had begun to hit with power, too, compiling a .418 slugging percentage. This included 11 doubles and four triples in what was essentially one-third of a season. The youngster also scored 34 runs, an impressive total for the number of games he played. As for his fielding, it seemed outstanding wherever they played him, and so far they had played him almost everywhere.

In finally reaching the major leagues, Pete Reiser had begun to make his mark. No one was quite certain at what position he would play the following spring, but everyone knew he would certainly play. His spectacular spring training performance of 1939, as well as his .378 average, his daredevil base stealing and his intrepid play in the field for Elmira earlier that year were not flukes. Those people, like Branch Rickey and Leo Durocher, who suggested that this was the greatest natural baseball player they had ever seen weren't talking through their baseball caps.

In the words of the old Dodger war cry: "Wait till next year!!"

7

A New Shopping Spree

The Dodger management didn't wait till next year to start strengthening the team. The pair at the helm, Larry MacPhail and Leo Durocher, decided to go on a shopping spree that winter. Despite Durocher's claim that the club's failures in 1940 were due to their lengthy injury list, the two men realized there were gaping holes at several positions.

With the Brooklyn farm system still very much in its infancy, the Dodgers were filled with players purchased from other clubs. For them, going to market was nothing new. Except for second baseman Pete Coscarat, who was a product of their minor league system, Reiser was the closest to being a second. And that serpentine story has already been told.

They knew they needed at least one more front-line pitcher and, if they could get one, a sure-gloved catcher to back up (or perhaps even front up) the good-hit, very-bad-field Babe Phelps. This 225-pound veteran backstop, whose substantial size had him nicknamed "the Blimp," had also soured management by his refusal to fly. He would do that again the following spring.

The pitcher they went after was a 25-year-old wild man named Kirby Higbe. A fireballing right-handed pitcher, he had won 12 and 14 games in consecutive seasons for the Philadelphia Phillies, perennial dwellers in the National League basement. The 14 games he had won in 1940 were almost a third of the team's entire total, indeed an impressive accomplishment. Considered one of baseball's better pitchers, woefully stuck on a less than mediocre team, Higbe had been last year's strikeout leader while compiling a respectable 3.72 earned run average.

The catcher they decided to pursue was Mickey Owen, the Cardinals' first-string catcher for the last three years. A tough young competitor, still in his mid-twenties, Owen was one of the league's best backstops, if only a mediocre hitter. St. Louis general manager Rickey had his eye on a young catching prospect in the Cardinal farm system named Walker Cooper, who he rightly believed would soon become one of baseball's best. Owen, he felt, was therefore superfluous.

MacPhail knew he'd have a job getting both players, especially if Rickey learned of his acquiring Higbe. The Cardinals feared the Dodgers most in the coming race for the pennant in 1941 and would never give up Owen if Brooklyn had purchased a pitcher of Higbe's caliber. There was only one thing to do: Keep the Higbe deal secret.

In November, MacPhail made his secret deal with Philadelphia owner Gerry Nugent, giving the Phillies three players and $100,000 for the pitcher. Nugent, always in need of cash for this faltering ballclub, pocketed the money and kept his mouth tightly shut.

As Durocher noted in his book *Nice Guys Finish Last*, it's not easy to deal in secret, considering the amount of paperwork and the number of eyes under which that paperwork must pass. The commissioner saw all contracts, and bulletins from League headquarters reported all trades. How, then, do you get the commissioner to help keep such a thing confidential?

Durocher believed he had figured it out. He felt that Landis's complicity was induced by Rickey's illegal arrangement with those Cardinal farmhands, including Reiser, back in 1938 — because perhaps Landis "hated Rickey so much for playing fast and loose with the spirit of the rules that he would be willing to play fast and loose with the spirit of the rules this one time."

Durocher then explained that the rules said only that the trade and the exchange of contracts had to be filed, not made public. The teams were the vehicles for making the announcements. "The information in the League bulletins was a service," he concluded, "not a legal mandate."

Whether Durocher was correct in his assumption or not, the commissioner's office did remain silent. Word never was released about the Dodgers' acquisition of Higbe until the deal had been completed for Mickey Owen. The Dodgers completed that trade for Owen in early December, giving the Cardinals and Rickey $65,000 and two players, Dodger backup catcher Gus Mancuso and a minor league pitcher.

"This was in no small part due to Nugent," Durocher wrote in *The Dodgers and Me*, "who hush-hushed the Higbe deal so well that the Giants thought they had a fine chance to buy Owen after he had already become our property!"

The Giants actually believed they had a chance of getting Higbe too. Durocher claimed that Giant general manager Horace Stoneham was boasting to pals in Toots Shor's popular Manhattan restaurant in November that New York was sure to get Higbe.

So it was with great joy that MacPhail finally called a press conference and made his auspicious announcement. "The New York Giants," he began, "despite what they have to say, have no chance to land pitcher Kirby Higbe from Philadelphia. Higbe is owned by Brooklyn!"

Sadly, however, the Dodgers lost Phelps. Judging by his actions, the big catcher's feelings were irreparably hurt by the acquisition of Mickey Owen. Still afraid to fly, he informed Durocher that he would not take the plane down from his Maryland home to the team's training camp in Havana. The manager suggested that instead he take the train to Miami and, from there, a ship across to Cuba.

Phelps reached Miami, and as Durocher has written, "He must have taken one look at the dock and the water and decided he was no more of a sailor than he was a flyer."

Phelps quickly retreated to his home in Odenton, Maryland, to cure a so-called cold but more, it would appear, to sulk. He had been the Dodgers' first-line catcher since 1936 and, despite his shortcomings as a fielder, his big bat had kept him in the lineup, and often batting cleanup, since that time. The threat of Mickey Owen—and it wasn't certain that he would completely take over Phelps' job—was more than the big catcher could handle.

During the season, his emotions, as well as his conduct with the team, did not stay on an even keel. He would drift home constantly and no one could reason with him. Finally, Babe Phelps retired from the Dodgers after playing only 16 games that season. He gave up his $10,000 contract, as Durocher put it, "to smash baggage at Odenton for fifty bucks a week."

This was a blow to the team. A bigger problem that soon arose, however, was the weakness at second base. Pete Coscarat, despite his selection as an All-Star the previous year, was not the player Durocher envisioned in that position.

"I hollered for Billy Herman," said Durocher, which according to the manager, "was like asking for the moon."

Herman was a Chicago Cub fixture at second base since 1932 and was perhaps the premier player in the league at this position. An excellent fielder and a brilliant baseball mind, he was also a potent hitter who constantly had a better than .300 average. Once he had led the league in doubles and once in triples, and was, of course, a perennial All-Star.

"Get me Billy Herman," Durocher promised MacPhail, "and we'll win the pennant."

One morning several weeks later, the general manager woke Durocher at 5 A.M. The manager was a breath from apoplexy when MacPhail said simply, "Say hello to your new second baseman."

Durocher said he "almost fell out of bed" when he realized it was Billy Herman on the phone. And there was Herman telling him that he would be reporting to the Dodgers that afternoon.

This was another wily stroke of negotiation by the irrepressible MacPhail. It was later revealed that he had spent a long night with the Cubs general manager, Jimmy Gallagher, and field manager, Jimmy Wilson, drinking and dealing for Herman. The two Chicago representatives, probably proud to show their drinking skills, downed one whiskey after another without letup. MacPhail, on the other hand, instead of drinking his usual lineup of spirits, was secretly pouring them down the sink.

"No mean sacrifice," commented Durocher, "for a man like MacPhail."

At 4:30 A.M., while MacPhail was as sober as he'd ever be, Wilson and Gallagher were too bleary to know whom they were giving away or what they were receiving in return. The deal that had been consummated had the Dodgers giving up $65,000 and a pair of journeymen players, Johnny Hudson and Charlie Gilbert, for a future Hall of Famer. Not bad for a long evening's work.

The Dodgers had gone to market and had come home with the goods. They were in a tremendous position for the coming pennant race.

8

Coming Into His Own

"Out in Los Angeles, they think Duke Snider is the best center fielder they ever had. They forget Pete Reiser. The Yankees think Mickey Mantle is something new. They forget Reiser, too."
—Garry Schumacher,
New York baseball writer

It takes more than one player to turn a team around or to turn an also-ran into a pennant winner. Even Babe Ruth couldn't do that. In Ruth's first year with the Yankees in 1920, the team finished in third, the same position they had finished in the year before when a man named Sammy Vick had batted a paltry .248 as their right fielder. Of course, they did win the pennant in three of the next five years, though managing to fall to seventh place in 1925. The point is that it takes a team to win a championship.

Ted Williams in his 19 years with the Red Sox played in only one World Series. Ty Cobb, in 24 years, played in but three, and none in his last 19 years. As for Hank Aaron and all his home runs, his Braves, whether in Milwaukee or in Atlanta, appeared in two World Series.

But in 1941, for all that the additions of Kirby Higbe, Mickey Owen and Billy Herman did for the Dodger cause, it was the addition of Pete Reiser in his first full season in the major leagues that meant the most. Still, when Reiser reported to spring training that season, there remained the question of exactly what position he would be playing.

"I figured I could beat out Lavagetto," he later told writer Donald Honig. "I went to spring training in '41 figuring I was the Dodger third baseman."

But MacPhail and Durocher called him in to discuss an entirely different idea. "You want to play for the Dodgers?" MacPhail asked him.

"Damn right I do," replied the eager Reiser.

"Well, then you learn to play center field," said MacPhail.

"Hell, I thought anybody can play center field," Reiser said to Honig. "All you had to do was run a ball down. Nothing else to worry about. So with help from Charley Dressen and Freddy Fitzsimmons, I spent that spring becoming a big league center fielder. When the season opened in '41, I felt I'd never played anywhere else."

Actually, he made another major change that spring. Reiser stopped batting as a switch-hitter and became a strictly left-handed batter. It is ironic to recall that he began his baseball days swinging only from the right side of the plate. Now he had chosen to make a 180-degree turn.

"The Dodgers almost blew their stacks," he remembered. "But I got hard-nosed about it."

Paul Waner was the one who suggested this switch to Reiser. One of baseball's greatest batsmen, Waner had led the league three times during his long tenure with the Pirates and would ultimately end up in the Hall of Fame, boasting a sensational .333 lifetime batting average. Now 38 years old, he had come to the Dodgers presumably to become the team's right fielder. But after only 19 games in a Brooklyn uniform, he was traded to the Braves. Before he went, however, he had turned the Dodger rookie into a strictly southpaw swinger. The veteran had been watching Reiser bat one day during spring training and pulled him aside.

"Why in the hell do you switch-hit?" he asked the kid.

"Because I'm a natural right-hand hitter," Reiser answered.

"But your stroke left-handed is perfect," said Waner. "I know you've got more power right-handed, but you're an entirely different hitter. You uppercut right-handed, left-handed you don't. With your speed, you stay left-handed, kid."

When a player of Waner's stature makes a suggestion about hitting, you listen. For the likes of the eager young Reiser, you give it a try. "So, once in a while during an exhibition game," he said, "when there was a left-hander out there, I tried it. No problem. Left-handers didn't make a bit of difference. But I still had to convince Leo."

Reiser tried to convince Durocher in a game with the Yankees, in which they were pitching their star southpaw, Lefty Gomez. "I hit him pretty good right-handed," he told his manager, "but I'll hit him better left-handed."

Reiser, who owned up to being a much too cocky kid for making this promise, did exactly as he had pledged. "I made Leo a believer," said Reiser.

But that was only the half of it. MacPhail had to be convinced, too. And, according to Reiser, "MacPhail was going to fire him (Durocher) for letting me hit left-handed."

The young rookie stubbornly stood his ground. Feeling sure that he had found the best side of the plate for himself, he wasn't going to move. He had started, remember, as a right-handed batter, and one who had gained the most incredible plaudits for his hitting. To gain the extra step down the first base line, he had taught himself to bat left-handed. Then, as a switch-hitter, he had become the astounding prospect that tempted other clubs to offer half their teams for him.

Now he had the audacity to throw this all away. He wanted to reintroduce himself as a left-handed batter, with only three years experience as a part-time southpaw swinger. And he wouldn't budge an inch. "I didn't care how much dust MacPhail kicked up," said Reiser. "MacPhail got so goddamned mad that he came within an ace of trading me to the Cubs in the Billy Herman deal."

But Reiser stuck to his guns, and MacPhail, later seeing how those guns could shoot, would finally change his mind.

Spring training in 1941 was held both in Clearwater and in Havana. Reiser was impressive in both places. Though promised the center field position, he still bounced around from short to third to right field to center. Durocher also had him hitting at several different places in the batting order. Reiser led off, he batted second, he batted fifth and he batted third, the place that would ultimately be his.

Early in March, an article by Roscoe McGowen in the *New York Times* pointed out, "Young Peter Reiser, definitely in the spot as the regular center fielder, is not unhappy about the matter. 'I feel pretty good out there,' he said. 'Of course when you've played another position, everything's different, but I like it there and I think I can make it.'"

"If Reiser's batting in the Giant-Dodger series(in Havana) is a sample of what may be expected," McGowen went on, " it may be easily understood why Lippy Leo Durocher wants to play him there regularly. Pete topped all Dodgers with an average of .545 and came to bat more times than any other except Pee Wee Reese. Reiser's hits included one of the two Brooklyn homers off of Giant pitching. Carl Hubbell was Pete's victim."

At about that time, MacPhail made a rather presumptuous statement. Fulfilling the promise he had made when both Reese and Medwick were beaned the previous season, he announced the use of a batting helmet, or as he termed it, a "protector" for batters.

"The biggest thing that has happened to the game since night baseball," he trumpeted. "Every player in the Brooklyn organization will wear the protector, and I want to make a prediction that within a year every player in the major leagues will be wearing it."

Despite the man's braggadocio, compounded by coupling this innovation with the beginning of night baseball, another of his accomplishments, this was an extremely important occurrence. Just the first step toward what would become a baseball way of life, at the very least, it had addressed a serious and dangerous problem. This device created a pocket on each side of the cap that could be zippered open and the guard placed inside. Depending on which side of the plate the batter hit from, the guard was placed facing out toward the pitcher and his incoming throw.

"They designed it with the idea of making it as light and as inconspicuous as possible," MacPhail said, "and it would cover the vital parts of the head where serious injuries have resulted from a player being hit by a pitched ball."

"The plastic has the strength to withstand the weight of a baseball traveling a hundred miles per hour," he continued. "It won't completely eliminate the possibility of a player receiving a slight concussion, but it should entirely eliminate fractures."

Made from a plastic developed in a Delaware laboratory, it was created jointly by Dr. Walter Dandy and Dr. George Bennett, a pair of physicians from Johns Hopkins. The Brooklyn general manager said it was "stronger than metal and weighs practically nothing."

"You'll never notice you had it on," said Medwick, who acknowledged that both he and Reese had worn the device the previous day. "There's not enough difference in the weight or the feeling to bother anyone."

"My players are solid for this device," said MacPhail, "and they're all going to use it."

Though, sadly, it was far from the panacea MacPhail had predicted, the device would soon play an important role in a debilitating injury to Reiser. But MacPhail's interest in and promotion of its manufacture was one of those important examples of progress he so often brought to baseball. For all his warts—and his character had a nation full of them—one had to respect the man.

By mid–March, Reiser was winning headlines and, perhaps more important, getting hits by the bunch. A huge number of times that spring, he had multihit games. Several times, he got three hits in a game, one time he had four, and many, many times he ended up with a pair.

One story in *The New York Times* pointed out, "Reiser has hit at a .423 clip in all the games played since the Dodgers arrived in Florida from Havana. His blows include a homer."

Another said, "Pete Reiser, who made his daily hit a rousing double to right in the first inning, contributed the best catch of the day when he took Bill Baker's liner at his shoetops in the fifth."

Early in April, still another story said, "He (Medwick) was overshadowed by Master Pete Reiser, the juvenile who rediscovered his batting eye to rifle two doubles and two singles and drive in four runs."

Even without a hit, he made news. "Three times," read one account, "Pete Reiser, who went hitless, grounded into what might have been double plays for most players, but the youngster's speed merely made them force outs."

Another story paid homage to his fielding. "Only one ball was hit dangerously," read the report, "and a great running catch by Peter Reiser in right center nullified that threat. York hit the ball, and in this spacious park it looked like a triple, but Reiser pulled it down with his gloved hand."

The young man was being noticed and praised by contingents of sports writers, a group usually reluctant to go out on a limb for a rookie player. (Yes, by even those who erroneously called him "Peter," as if that had been his given name. And by those, too, who had written of Pee Wee Reese celebrating his 22nd birthday on March 17, when it was Reiser whom they had meant.) They took note of the completeness of his abilities—his hitting, his fielding, his speed, his energies, his gutsy and fearless way of playing, and realized the rarity of the combination.

The center field job was his and, apparently, so was the third slot in the batting order. Durocher was already talking about a new "Murderer's Row" for the Dodgers, that name given to several Yankee batting orders of famous power hitters of the past and present. This one of Durocher's consisted of Pete Reiser, Joe Medwick, Cookie Lavagetto and Dolf Camilli.

In an interview on April 1 with Tommy Holmes, leading baseball writer for the *Brooklyn Eagle*, the team's home paper, Durocher went even further than that. "I wouldn't trade him (Reiser) even up for any player in the National League," he told the reporter.

Holmes didn't let Durocher stand alone. "Some of you back home may think Durocher's opinion of Pete Reiser exaggerated," he wrote, "but ninety percent of those who have played with or followed the Dodgers this spring will concur."

He continued this paean to Pete by pointing out that Reiser hadn't made an error in the 22 games he's thus far played nor "missed any fly ball that you'd think any center fielder might have caught." Holmes continued to praise the young rookie, noting his tremendous speed, his judgment of fly balls, his amazing throwing ability and, perhaps most of all, his spectacular hitting.

"Batting third in the Dodger lineup," the reporter wrote, "he has been shut out of the hit column only three times in the 22 games. He has 35 hits in 94 times at bat for an average of .372. He has extra base power to all fields and may be the fastest man in baseball beating out an infield hit. Two hops to shortstop and Reiser is usually safe at first."

"And so when Durocher says he wouldn't trade Reiser for any player in the league," he concluded. "don't think he's kidding."

A poll of National League managers taken during spring training picked the Cincinnati Reds to win their third consecutive pennant that year. Six of the eight managers voted for the Reds, and one, Frankie Frisch of the Pirates, picked the Dodgers. Durocher was the lone holdout. The manager refused to participate in the balloting, saying he did not want to place himself in the spot.

As the season was about to open on April 15 someone, at least, gave the Dodgers a chance to win it all. And everyone connected with the Brooklyn ballclub hoped their new center fielder would come through in a way so many had predicted.

They had no idea.

9

Rookie of the Year

"Any manager in the National League would give up his best man to obtain Pete Reiser. On every bench they're talking about him. Rival players watch him take his cuts during batting practice, announce when he's going to make a throw to the plate or third base during outfield drill. They just whistle their amazement when he scoots down the first base line on an infield dribbler or a well-placed bunt."
—Arthur Patterson, *New York Herald Tribune*

The first time there was a Rookie of the Year award with actual balloting by sports reporters was not until 1947, when Jackie Robinson was chosen as the winner. But back in 1941, if balloting had taken place, it would not even have been close. Pete Reiser in his first full season as a major leaguer was hands down the major leagues' Rookie of the Year and certainly a great deal more. And that would have been a foregone conclusion before much of the season had even been played. The young man was startling to watch, to play against or to play alongside of. There were so many facets to his ability, and each was a rare jewel in itself.

He could dominate a game like no one playing then. His awe-inspiring strengths lay in every phase of the game. His hitting, of course, which players, managers and reporters all believed was the best in the league. His incomparable fielding skills, including one of the most powerful arms in baseball. His speed, which could be approached by no one. And his daring and indomitable way of accomplishing it all. If ever there was a perfect baseball player, it was Pistol Pete Reiser.

Baseball pundits gawked at what they saw, and writers gushed like kids at their first movie in trying to describe it. Was he the most incredible sight in a uniform since Joe DiMaggio or Joe Cronin or Ty Cobb himself? Or, perhaps, as someone would later put it, was he the coming of the first Pete Reiser? This man's baseball immortality appeared a near certainty.

A bigger question that year was who would eventually win the National League pennant. For most of the season, the Dodgers and Cardinals fought tooth and nail in a classic seesaw battle that wouldn't be resolved till the last days of the season. This was supposed to be what baseball was all about, and neither of these teams disappointed.

One thing about Pete Reiser, however, became apparent. An ominous chink showed up in the young rookie's armor very early in this campaign. Then, even as his athleticism and his abilities expanded, it grew still more threatening. But that's getting ahead of things.

As the Dodgers marched into the pennant wars that year, they were led by a lineup of veterans, mostly in their thirties, and by two strong young hopefuls, Pete Reiser and the sterling shortstop from Louisville, Pee Wee Reese. The team had coupled the kids as roommates the season before in the Hotel Granada in Brooklyn when they were home and in the various hotels on the road.

Ironically, the two were named Harold at birth, had very similar surnames and were known by quite similar nicknames. The two were often mixed up. In fact, reporters during spring training had written about Pee Wee's birthday celebration on St. Patrick's Day when it really was Pete's birthday. Furthermore, both had come to the major leagues as shortstops, Reiser having been transformed into a third baseman and later a center fielder because of Reese's spectacular performance at short.

The two had become good friends very quickly, often went on dates together, enjoyed similar sporty—if not, garish—clothes, and purportedly exchanged them with each other. The two were also very close in age, Reiser having been born on March 17, 1919, Reese on July 23 of the year before.

They were similar in build, incredibly similar in name, and often mistaken for each other, and the Dodgers' great future, it was supposed, was to be built on both their backs.

As the season opened, however, the Dodgers' immediate present didn't begin with the expected bang. With Reiser, their new center fielder, out of the lineup because of a sprained muscle in his side, the team dropped the opening two games to their archrivals, the New York Giants. Reiser finally returned for the third game of the series, but his four fruitless at bats did nothing to prevent a third straight loss to the gleeful Giants. A woeful beginning for a club so filled with hope.

Then Reiser and the Dodgers woke up. Brooklyn won six of the next

Peewee Reese, the Hall of Fame shortstop who had been Reiser's close friend and roommate. He and Reiser were adoringly known as the Gold Dust Twins (National Baseball Hall of Fame Library, Cooperstown, N.Y.).

seven games as the rookie went on a batting rampage. There were three days when he had a pair of hits, one in which he had four, and, in that short run, he had raised his batting average to an impressive .355. Reiser's hits included three doubles, a triple and a home run—a dazzling display of his power—as he scored eight runs and knocked in four. He had reached base, in fact, 22 times in his 37 trips to the plate. The boy wonder looked like he was everything he had been cracked up to be.

Perhaps, too, the Dodgers were everything they had hoped to be. By April 23, they had lifted their record to 6–4 and had raised themselves to second place right behind the Giants. With the Phillies, the league's worst team, now coming to town, Brooklyn was ready to run roughshod over them. But, sadly, there suddenly appeared a disquieting bump in the road.

As Hy Turkin, the *Daily News* correspondent, wrote in the following day's paper, "The Dodgers kayoed their pet stooges, the Phils, 4–0, at Ebbets Field yesterday, but in turn lost a decision to their perennial nemesis, the beanball."

Last year, it was Joe Medwick, Pee Wee Reese and Hugh Casey. This time the errant pitch struck the head of the young rookie, Pete Reiser.

It happened in the third inning when Reiser batted for the second time in the game. He had singled home the Dodgers' first run in the opening inning and now faced the Phillies' fireballing right-hander, Ike Pearson. Pearson's first pitch, a sidearm fast ball, came in too high and too far inside for the batter. The young rookie saw the ball and attempted to jump back, hoping to elude the pitch. But he couldn't draw back fast enough. The ball seemed to sail, according to *News* reporter Hy Turkin, and right at Reiser's head.

There was a sound like a rifle shot as the ball hit the rookie squarely on the right cheekbone, just under the temple and too low for the complete protection of MacPhail's headgear. Reiser was knocked cold, landing on his shoulder blades, his knees rigid in the air.

Not till he was carried off the field on a stretcher and brought to the clubhouse had he begun to regain consciousness. He was still badly dazed when they rushed him by ambulance to Brooklyn's Caledonia Hospital.

"You could plainly see the imprint of three stitches where the baseball hit him," said the attending physician. After examining wet X-ray plates, a second physician, Dr. D. A. McAteer Jr., concluded, "Reiser has a mild concussion and a localized blood clot. He's a very lucky man because he certainly would have had a fractured skull if it weren't for the helmet which absorbed part of the shock."

"He'll remain under observation for three or four more days," the doctor continued, and then he would probably have a "very sore face." McAteer, who was the son of the Dodgers' regular physician, suggested that Reiser would not be able to play for a week or two.

Of course, General Manager MacPhail chimed in with a triumphant huzzah. "Ike Pearson's wild pitch actually struck Reiser's helmet," he declared boldly, "don't let anyone tell you different. The helmet saved him from a fractured skull." (This, however, seemed to contradict the imprint of three baseball stitches that the initial physician had found on the side of his face.)

In an interview with writer W. C. Heinz that appeared in *True* magazine in 1958, Reiser said that he woke up at 11:30 that night in the hospital. "I was lying in bed with my uniform," he told Heinz, "and I couldn't figure it out. The room was dark, with just a little night light, and then I saw a mirror and I walked over to it and lit the light and I had a black eye and a black streak down the side of my nose. I said to myself: 'What happened to me?' Then I remembered."

At this time, word had been received that this was not the first time Reiser had been beaned. During Reiser's first year in pro ball, back in 1937, he had been hit in the temple by a pitched ball in a game played for Newport of the Cardinal chain. He was knocked unconscious by the throw and was carried off the field.

Learning this, the Dodger management was reluctant to rush the rookie back into the game. Unless he was rested for a proper period of time, they feared, this second occurrence might have an adverse effect on the young man.

"A reliable source," read an item in the *Daily News*, "said both Durocher and President Larry MacPhail are strongly in favor of giving Reiser a good rest."

What the phrase "a good rest" may mean is open to debate, but Reiser returned as a regular in the Dodgers lineup on May 2, just nine days after his severe injury. By this time, the team had compiled a 14–5 record, and was just a game behind the league-leading Cardinals. The National League race now had all the appearance of a fiercely fought two-team affair. The preseason choice of six of the league's managers, last year's winner, the Cincinnati Reds, seemed out of it by this juncture.

When Reiser finally returned, he faced up to his own fears about being hit again. "I was a little worried at the time," he told writer Donald H. Drees some time later. "Such an accident makes batters gun-shy and a sucker for an inside curve at the head. I knew that as I stepped up to the plate against the Cubs."

"Bill Lee was the pitcher," he recalled, "and he cleared up my doubts in a hurry. His first pitch was a high curve at my head. When I didn't shudder or jump out of the way, I knew I had it licked."

The young rookie was soon thriving again and once more winning accolades for all his multitalents. "Young Pete Reiser," read one report, "brought the fans to their feet and hope back to their hearts in the ninth when he dynamited one of Ken Heintzelman's fast ones far into Bedford Avenue after Pee Wee Reese had walked with two out."

Another wrote of his tremendous speed: "Reiser turned a possible put-out into a hit in the third by his great speed." Still another of the accuracy of his arm: "Reiser made a magnificent throw on the fly to Owen to cut off Cooper at the plate in the fifth." And yet another of an amazing catch he had somehow made.

Reiser was back in action, and the Dodgers were about to take over first place from the Cardinals. More good news came on May 7. The deal to get premier second baseman Billy Herman from the Chicago Cubs had been finally consummated by Larry MacPhail. Get Herman, and this team wins the pennant, Durocher had promised his boss, never believing MacPhail could accomplish it.

Actually, the deal seemed so impossible that the members of the press couldn't believe it either. "MacPhail, trying to release the news to the papers," reported *The New York Times*, "spent a trying early-morning half-hour on the telephone. The most trying part of the job was convincing listeners that he was Larry MacPhail and that Herman had been bought.

"Some felt they were being ribbed, and MacPhail beseeched them to 'Call me back. I'm in Jimmy Gallagher's (Cubs' General Manager) room at the Commodore where we just signed the papers.'"

"Eventually," the story concluded, "the skeptics were fully convinced; half of them, anyway."

Herman immediately went to work for the Dodgers that day, going four for four in his very first game and helping them to a 7–3 victory over the Pirates. As Roscoe McGowen of the *Times*, put it, "He even knew enough to duck out of the way of a screaming drive by Pete Reiser in the third. If he hadn't, the Dodgers would be seeking another new second baseman."

The first-place Cardinals moved into town the next day, and two days later, after two consecutive Dodger wins, the Brooklyn team moved into first place. But the second game also had a dangerous and costly occurrence.

"An injury to Pete Reiser, brilliant young centerfielder, cast the only gloom on a happy day for the Brooklynites," reported *The New York Times* on May 9. "Pete crashed into the metal gate in the second inning in making a gloved-hand catch of Slaughter's drive and had to leave the game. He was temporarily dazed but ran off under his own power."

The injury was worse than the *Times* described. The moment Enos Slaughter hit the ball, Reiser saw it heading for dead center. The young centerfielder turned and raced back for it, his eyes only on the ball. He caught it at full speed 400 feet away at the center field wall and against the giant iron exit gate that had been built into it.

Reiser crashed both his head and the base of his spine against the gate and still managed to hold on to the ball. He was a bloody mess when he returned to the bench. There was a gash in his head and blood was pouring through the seat of his pants. In the clubhouse, the Dodger physician managed to stem the blood with a metal clamp at his spine.

"Just don't slide," he advised Reiser. "You can get it sewed up after the game."

After this injury, the first against an outfield wall for this converted infielder, he would not return to action for nine days. This was, after all, the second time in little more than two weeks that the prize rookie had suffered a head injury and a subsequent concussion. But the Dodgers were in a tough pennant race, and on May 19, Reiser returned to the Brooklyn lineup.

Auspiciously, one would add. In a three-game series at Chicago against the Cubs, Reiser got five hits, including a pair of bunt singles and a long double. But the Dodgers lost all three games as their pitching momentarily turned sour. Despite Reiser's continued hot hitting, their losing ways continued. They lost a pair of games in St. Louis to the now front-running Cardinals, making it six losses in a row for the disheartened team.

Licking their wounds, they now looked forward to their usual safe haven, back home in Ebbets Field facing the lowly Phillies. As the doctor might say, take a couple of Phillies games and call me in the morning.

It worked.

They broke their losing streak the very next day as Reiser's potent hitting continued, propelling his batting average for his first 20 games of the season to a resounding .357.

Things got even better. There was a dramatic face-off during the next game that would show the essence of baseball and, more important, the mettle of this young player. It happened on May 25 in the Dodgers' second game of their series with Philadelphia, just about a month to the day after Reiser's frightening beaning. The best description of this encounter appeared in the following day's *New York Times*, written by reporter Louis Effrat.

"A month ago," wrote Effrat, "Pete Reiser was skulled by a pitch thrown by Ike Pearson of the Phillies and wound up in the hospital, his career in jeopardy, his life in danger. Fortunately, Pete came out of it apparently none the worse for his experience. At Ebbets Field yesterday, Reiser faced Pearson for the first time since the accident on April 23, faced him in a situation that couldn't have been more dramatic if it were part of a Hollywood scenario. The big test had arrived.

"The Dodgers and Phillies were tied at 4-all, the bases were filled and two were out when Reiser strode to the plate to bat against the man who had brought disaster to the young outfielder the last time they came together. Was he frightened? Did he flinch? The result, more than anything else, answers these questions, for Reiser blasted a 3-and-1 pitch against the screen in centerfield for a mighty home run inside the park.

"So it was that Reiser passed his test and the Dodgers routed the Phillies, 8–4, before a crowd of 12,941 and Brooklyn now is sporting a two game winning streak."

A further description of the hit called it "a tremendous drive on top of the exit gate, 399 feet away. By the time (Joe) Marty got his hands on the ball, Reiser was on third base and he continued all the way scoring standing up for his third circuit clout of the campaign."

Mind you, Ebbets Field was one of the smaller parks in baseball. It did not have the outfield acreage of Yankee Stadium or the Polo Grounds, where inside-the-park homers were hardly rarities. In the Brooklyn ballpark, it was an event, and one that could only take place with a greyhound of a ballplayer.

There is a conflicting story about Reiser's beaning that tells a very different tale. In this report, Reiser left the hospital a day after the beaning by Pearson with strict orders not to play for a week. He then went immediately to the ballpark, where the Dodgers were once again playing the Phillies, and took a seat behind the dugout. Durocher spotted him and asked Reiser how he felt.

"Not bad," replied the young rookie.

"Get your uniform on," Durocher ordered.

"I'm not supposed to play," Reiser replied.

Supposedly, Durocher simply wanted him to sit on the bench because it would make his teammates feel better about his injury. Reiser suited up and did exactly as his manager had requested. But by the eighth inning, the score was tied, 7–7, and Ike Pearson, the same man who had beaned Reiser, was coming in to pitch for Philadelphia.

"Pistol," Durocher was quoted as saying, "get the bat."

Reiser did so and promptly hit Pearson's first pitch into the center field stands for a base-clearing home run and an 11–7 victory for the Dodgers. As Reiser, who could barely walk, slowly circled the bases, writers in the press box marveled at how steadfastly he stood up against the man who had beaned him just two days ago.

Nope, it never happened. It actually happened as described earlier in this text. Neither Leo Durocher nor an acquiescing Larry MacPhail acted in such a negilgent and thoughtless manner. At least, not that time.

It is apparent that this story came from Reiser himself and from his faulty memory of what had occurred. What is significant is that Reiser would remember it that way. After all, he would always remain a staunch defender of Durocher, and a staunch defender against those who would lambast the manager for sacrificing this player's well-being for the sake of a pennant. Yet, here is Reiser describing a fictional Durocher doing much the same in prodding him to go beyond his physical capabilities. This should not be forgotten considering what would happen later.

In any case, Reiser's true heroic blast against Pearson, as well as the subsequent victory, seemed to propel the Dodgers into further heroics. With the rookie getting three hits in one game, a pair in the second, and three hits more in a third, they beat the Phillies three more times and inched closer to first place. That third game had been a 5–5 tie until the 12th inning, when Reiser slammed a long double that scored Billy Herman with the winning run.

By this time, the rookie's hitting barrage had raised his batting average to .387 and to his place as the league's leading hitter.

Reiser's hitting continued to power the Dodgers to their eighth and ninth consecutive wins, over the Giants and the Cards, and to a flat-footed tie with St. Louis for first place. During this time, Reiser had a 12-game hitting streak in which he had batted .423, knocked in 14 runs and hit six doubles, a triple and that grand-slam homer.

More and more, it seemed, as goes Reiser, so go the Dodgers. Of course, this was a potent team with many important ingredients. The first baseman, Dolf Camilli, was a superb fielder and a potent home run hitter. Though Billy Herman was not the Herman of past years, he was still one of the standout second basemen in the league. Reiser's roommate and friend, Pee Wee Reese, though not enjoying his best year at bat, was a startlingly good shortstop with incredibly flashy moments. Cookie Lavagetto, at third, was a timely hitter with occasional streaks and a fine fielder at his position.

Joe Medwick, in left, was surely not the Medwick of his great years, but he was still a substantial batter and a quite decent fielder. Dixie Walker, in right field and often a backup for Reiser in center, seemed to improve with age. He had been the Dodgers' leading batter the previous year and would outdo his numbers in this present one. Catcher Mickey Owen was not the batter they had expected him to be, but he crouched with the best at his position.

The Dodgers pitching staff was excellent. They were led by John Whitlow Wyatt, a nonachiever in the American League during his twenties, who enjoyed several superb years for the Dodgers while passing through his thirties. Wyatt had tremendous speed and fine control and for many years participated in heralded pitching duels with the Cardinals' ace pitcher, Mort Cooper. Years later, Reiser said, "In the early 40s, he was the best right-handed pitcher I ever saw."

Right behind Wyatt, if not alongside, was the former Phillies' fireballer Kirby Higbe, who after a slow start measured Wyatt win for win down the stretch. Curt Davis, the drag-along in the Medwick deal, proved a happy surprise and was still a wily, curve ball pitcher. And Hugh Casey, later to become a formidable reliever, was more than an adequate fourth starter.

In almost every way this team was the equal of their St. Louis rivals, with one distinct advantage. That, of course, was in center field. In fact, the Cardinal center fielder, Terry Moore, many baseball minds had considered the best fielding outfielder in the game. Now experts wondered if this new sensation, who certainly seemed the best batter in the league, was also its best defensive outfielder.

In any case, the battle for first place continued to seesaw and Reiser continued to sparkle. His batting average continued to stay in the .360s and, on occasions, would rise higher, while he maintained his lead in the batting race.

In mid–June, the Dodgers finally said good-bye to their forlorn former catcher, Babe Phelps. The Babe had gone into a grump at the time of the Mickey Owen acquisition, and no words of encouragement could rescue him from it. When he finally insisted he was ill and had to go home, though doctors found nothing wrong with him, the fiery and never tongue-tied Durocher blew up.

"I don't want him on my ballclub," cried the manager. "He's off. I've got a bunch of players trying to win a pennant and Phelps apparently doesn't want to play, even when doctors tell him that there's absolutely nothing wrong with him."

Without Phelps, but with three hits by their Pistol, including a home run, three runs scored and two knocked in, the Dodgers beat the Cards, 12–5, in St. Louis and moved closer to the top. During that Sunday game, Reiser was feted in this his hometown by "A Friends of Pete Reiser" committee. Amongst an array of gifts, the young outfielder was presented with a set of golf clubs.

"The committee," remarked Dodger Secretary John MacDonald, "included all the pitchers in the National League," who he suggested had hoped he'd give up baseball and take up the game of golf.

But Reiser's assault on the league's pitching arms continued. In one game, the young rookie had three hits, in another a pair, and in still another four. Reiser was hitting .371, and the Dodgers were still nipping at the tail of the Cardinals.

Whitlow Wyatt was the Dodgers' pitching ace for many years, a 22-game winner in the 1941 pennant drive, and Reiser's favorite pitcher (National Baseball Hall of Fame Library, Cooperstown, N.Y.).

The Dodgers stayed close to their St. Louis rivals during the next few weeks, and Reiser showed the width and the depth of his talents. As sensational a hitter as he was—and perhaps even then, he was the best hitter in the league—that was just the start of things. He could win for you everywhere.

Item: "Without sufficient time to warm up, Casey almost blew Wyatt's ball game and only an amazing relay from center field—Pete Reiser to Pee Wee Reese to Lew Riggs—which caught Lonnie Frey trying to stretch a long blow into a triple, kept Brooklyn on even terms with Derringer."

Item: "Reiser led off with his first hit in seven tries. Riggs dropped a sacrifice bunt and was safe at first while Reiser ran to third on Frank McCormick's bad throw.

"Then after Dolf Camilli fanned, Dixie Walker's sacrifice bunt put over the decisive tally. McCormick tried to nip Reiser at the plate, but that was like trying to catch lightning in a bottle. Pete was almost to the dugout when Lombardi's big hand swung around in a mock tag."

Item: "Werber singled in the opener's 15th and was nailed trying to take an extra base by Reiser's expert throw to Reese."

Item: "Pete Reiser's speed set up a two run sortie in the fifth. After he forced Herman, Reiser scampered to second on Medwick's single, stole third and drew a balk when he started to break for home.

"The Pirates found Reiser too fast again in the seventh. Although they moved in for his bunt, Pete beat the throw to first with plenty to spare. Lavagetto singled and he and Reiser put on a double steal, Bill Baker throwing to second too late when he saw there wasn't a chance to catch the fleet Reiser. Medwick's single scored both, created the final score and sent Wilkie to the clubhouse."

Item: "First Reese beat out a hit to deep short. After Herman flied to right, Chuck Dressen put on the hit-and-run sign and Pete Reiser's 'squib'—a sliced roller into the hole vacated by Arky Vaughan as he went to cover second—dribbled just beyond the infield. Reiser, running with Cobbian daring, made two bases as Reese went into third. Lavagetto's single to right scored both."

Item: "Reiser exhibited one of the finer points of baseball when he slid home safely in the first. Lavagetto grounded to (second baseman) Harry Marnie, who threw to the plate, but Reiser slid past Warren, touching home with his hand as he went by."

Item: "Pete Reiser, the spirit of the 1941 Dodgers, gave his teammates a lift in the first when he tripled after Billy Herman had slammed a single to center. Cookie Lavagetto's infield grounder send Pete Reiser dashing home a moment later. Reiser sounded off again in the third when he dropped his seventh homer onto the cobblestones of Bedford Avenue"

Simply put, Reiser could beat you with his speed, he could beat you with his arm, he could beat you with his daring, and just in case you had forgotten, he could beat you badly with his bat.

In an interview given at this time, Leo Durocher crowed, "If there ever will be another Ty Cobb, his name will be Reiser."

The Dodger manager boasted of the kid's speed, declaring, "I'll take

Reiser for speed against anyone in baseball today." As for his hitting? "He has no weakness that I've ever seen or that any pitcher has yet found," said Durocher. "When he learns a little more through experience he may easily move into the .400 class."

"He came to us as a shortstop," he continued. "I had Reese at short and we needed a good center fielder who could cover ground. I asked Pete if he could play the outfield. He told me without any touch of bragging, 'I can catch if you need me there.'

"I found out he could. He has already shown how well he could play third and short. He can play any position on the club and look good at them all. This is remarkable for a young man of twenty-two."

Durocher went on to crow about the young man himself. "What sort of fellow is he?" he asked rhetorically. "A great kid. As good as he is, Pete is always anxious to learn. He and Pee Wee Reese, who are about the same age, are two pals. They room together and each thinks the other is the best there is. Pete still has a few things to learn—say about base running—but he is learning fast. And I don't think I ever saw anybody who loved baseball more."

As the Dodgers went into the All-Star break in early July, Reiser had an 18-game hitting streak still going, his third long streak of the season, and Brooklyn stood in first place, three games ahead of the Cardinals. In their last game before the break, the Dodgers had beaten the Braves, 5–2, with Reiser collecting three hits, including a home run, and knocking in two of his team's runs.

Six Dodgers had been picked for the National League All-Stars, more than any of the other clubs' selections. They were Whitlow Wyatt, Billy Herman, Cookie Lavagetto, Joe Medwick, Mickey Owen and, indeed, Pistol Pete Reiser, the youngest ever to be chosen as an All-Star. Three of these men were named for the starting lineup: the battery of Wyatt and Owen, and Reiser, who would be batting third and playing centerfield.

The All-Star Game of 1941 was not a happy affair for the National League team. Leading the American League, 5–3, going into the bottom of the ninth, the senior league let it all get away. In one of his historic moments, Ted Williams stunned the crowd and the National Leaguers by hitting a long home run with two out and two men on base to win the game, 7–5.

On the other hand, young Reiser had a washout. In four trips to the plate, he struck out twice, grounded into what was for him a rare double play, and finally reached base by aid of a two-base error. But, after all, this was only a 22-year-old rookie who everyone expected would be a perennial All-Star for long years ahead.

Several months later, in part of a statement given to reporters, Durocher spoke of Reiser's nervousness in the All-Star game being the reason he performed so poorly. But nervous or not, that cooling off of his continued as the season picked up again. In the first game after the break, Reiser's 18-game hitting streak was ended by Cincinnati pitching, and over the next few weeks, his batting average dropped into the .330's. He also lost the lead in the batting race, at one time to Nick Etten of the Phillies and at another to Johnny Hopp of the Cardinals.

The Dodgers likewise suffered. They were, after all, facing a brilliant Cardinal team in this pennant race. St. Louis had two powerful batters in first baseman Johnny Mize and right fielder Enos Slaughter, who would both end up in the Hall of Fame. They had three strong bats in the hands of third baseman Jimmy Brown, left fielder Johnny Hopp and their great defensive center fielder Terry Moore. Marty Marion was a brilliant short stop and Frankie Crespi a fine second baseman. The Cards had a superb rookie catcher in Walker Cooper, Mort's younger brother, and a stronger bench than Brooklyn's. Lon Warneke, Ernie White, Mort Cooper, Max Lanier and Harry Gumbert gave them a much deeper pitching staff.

Many experts predicted that this contingent would overtake the Dodgers and, in the end, would win the pennant. During July, it appeared that they would. Brooklyn's lead of three and a half games over the Cards on July 11 became a flat-footed tie by July 23 and a three-game lead by the Cardinals on the last day of July.

Sometime during this period, the Dodgers "mismanaged" to lose nine out of 12 games, and their pitching too often seemed porous. To worsen matters, in early August Reiser suffered still another injury. After getting three consecutive hits in a winning effort against Chicago, on August 3, he left the game in the seventh inning suffering from a severe sciatica condition in his right side. A day later, he was confined to New York Hospital and remained there for four days. Not till August 10 did he return to the Brooklyn lineup.

With this sudden reversal of fortunes for the Dodgers, General Manager MacPhail went to market once again. This time he returned with pitcher Johnny Allen, a 36-year-old veteran from Cleveland, and a pair of minor leaguers from Nashville, pitcher Tom Drake and outfielder Tom Tatum. The two Tom's would mean little, but Allen, who had won 20 games for the Indians back in 1936 and had an incomparable 15–1 record the following year, would help the Dodgers the rest of the way.

These purchases prompted a funny and telling piece by sports columnist and Information Please panelist John Kieran in the *New York Times*. It in essence explained the difference between the Dodgers and the Cards that year. The Cardinal players were younger and were primarily products of their farm system, the Rickey machine that produced standout players like a faucet pours forth water. Except for Reiser and roommate Reese, the Dodgers were veterans bought on the trading block, often for outrageous prices.

"Wonderful gent, that Larry the Red MacPhail," wrote Kieran. "He's a purchasing agent extraordinary. Whenever the pennant prospects of the Dodgers sag even a trifle, the gallant MacPhail gallops off in all directions and comes back with fresh hirelings to add strength to the Flatbush Flock."

He went on to point out that the purchases of Muscles Medwick and Curt Davis the past year was the signal that they were in the running for the pennant. "But they didn't run fast enough," wrote Kieran. So the Purchasing Agent went into action again.

In came Higbe, Owen, Herman and now Johnny Allen. Kieran also pointed out MacPhail's apparent weakness for outfielders. "He couldn't resist outfielders," he wrote, "and bought every one that was advertised for sale, good, bad and indifferent. Medwick, Dixie Walker, Joe Gallagher, Joe Vosmik, Jimmy Wasdell, et al., for instance."

"What more the Purchasing Agent Extraordinaire can buy," he went on, "to bring that pennant to Brooklyn this ba°ed bystander doesn't know…. Where the next leakage or seepage will show itself nobody can guess in advance. Maybe there will be no leakage or seepage, and the assembled Dodgers—it's an assembly job—will go ahead to capture the pennant. But if there is any hole, Larry the Red MacPhail will put on his buying suit again and do business to nail a pennant to the Brooklyn flagpole."

During the month of August, the race remained a nip-and-tuck battle between the two clubs. Each team took turns at the top, with no more than two games separating them. This also was not Reiser's best month. His batting average slipped into the .320s, and he often relinquished his lead in the batting race to either Johnny Hopp or Nick Etten.

Still, he had his moments. A headline in the August 19 issue of *The New York Times* read: "Homer By Reiser Wins in Ninth, 6–5." The subhead read: "Pete also triples with two on, then scores for Dodgers in three run third."

The accompanying story described the rookie's ninth-inning home run, a long blast over the 40-foot right field wall in Ebbets Field, that rescued the ballgame from the clutches of the Pirates and moved the Dodgers a game ahead of the Cards.

"As Pete's drive cleared the high right field screen," reported the *Times*, "dozens of fans piled out of the lower stands and rushed onto the field to escort him around the bases."

In another victory four days later, "The game ended with a kiss for Pete Reiser, Brooklyn's young center fielder star," said the *Times*. "As Reiser ran in, a young woman dashed out of the lower stands and kissed Pete. The crowd roared and shrieked its approval of the tribute."

"A few moments before that," the newspaper explained, "Reiser had made the game's most spectacular play, a diving, rolling catch of Charley George's looping fly to short right center."

As the end of August drew near, John Kieran wrote two columns pointing out the differences between the Dodgers and the Cardinals. In one article, he suggested that "the Brooklyn Dodgers have to hurry."

"The Dodgers have some regulars on the sunny side of thirty," he pointed out, "but more on the shady side. Pete Reiser and Pee Wee Reese are mere infants," he granted, but the rest of the team is fighting the calendar. The Cards, on the other hand, are "filled with players under thirty" and should have many chances over the years.

The baseball wit's second column reminded readers of the history of the Brooklyn team. "It used to be," he wrote, "that the Flatbush Flock was cherished throughout the baseball world for the wackiness of the Brooklyn heroes, on and off the diamond."

"This was how," he explained, "the country came to adopt the Dodgers as The People's Choice in baseball. Notre Dame is The People's Choice in football, but not for the same reason. There is no humor in football. It's a very serious game. But there is humor in baseball and, over a long span of years, the Dodgers furnished most of it."

"If it went by a popular vote," he concluded, "the Dodgers would win in a walk. But since it is to be decided by pitching, hitting and fielding, the result is in considerable doubt."

On the last day of August, despite Reiser's four hits in eight times at bat, the Giants beat the Dodgers in a doubleheader. The Cardinals, by dint of a no-hitter pitched by their veteran, Lon Warneke, moved into first place two points over the trailing Dodgers. There was a month of baseball left for the two contending teams and less than 30 games to be played by each of them. But this season was far from over.

10

Down to the Wire

"How many guys does God make like this?"
— Sportswriter Tom Meany, talking about Pete Reiser

The beginning of September 1941 was the second anniversary of what had become World War II. The front pages of American newspapers were filled with ongoing battles and real threats to spread the war to American shores. While the Soviet Union was attempting to stem the Nazi onslaught all along its borders and the British were fighting off the daily pummeling by German planes, the Japanese were warning the United States and Great Britain that they would retaliate for the two countries' freezing Japan's foreign assets. All this while the Japanese premier was supposedly in the midst of peaceful negotiations with the United States.

That was what was on the front pages of newspapers. The back pages were what too many Americans would restrict themselves to reading. Much of that space was devoted to the spectacular pennant race in the National League between the Dodgers and the Cardinals. The American League race was long over. The Yankees, double-digit games ahead, would clinch the pennant by September 4, the earliest ever in league history. This team was a powerhouse, and whoever would face them in the World Series was courting death by baseball massacre.

Thus far, the only prominent ballplayer who had been drafted into military service was 30-year-old Hank Greenberg, the great Detroit Tigers slugger who had led his team to three pennants and, in 1938, had threatened Babe Ruth's record with 58 home runs. He had been called up by his draft board early in the season after he had played in his team's first 19 games. More players would be drafted that winter, and by the end of the 1942 season, few in their twenties or early thirties would still be around playing ball.

But the talk of most towns during this September was the spectacular race for the National League flag. It remained breathlessly close as the month began, the two teams more or less matching wins and losses during the early days. The Dodgers beat the Giants, 13–6, while the Cards beat the Reds, 6–3. Brooklyn beat the Braves, 6–5, while the Cards took a doubleheader from the Pirates, 5–3 and 6–3. The Dodgers won, St. Louis was rained out. And so it went.

Through this period, Reiser regained the batting touch that had escaped him for a while the previous month. He soon had many multihit games, his average soared once again, and he proved pivotal in several key games as the Dodgers moved in front and took a three-game lead.

"Reiser decides nightcap," read one *New York Times* headline. "Laurels will have to be awarded not only to Camilli and Medwick," read the accompanying story, "but to young Pete Reiser, for it was his single that set the stage for Medwick's tying blow and his line single to left that brought Mickey Owen across with the run that ended the game."

By September 10, Reiser had put together another of his hitting streaks, this one for 15 straight games. He had also regained the lead in the batting race, his .336 average now 11 points ahead of Johnny Hopp. It was all coming down to the next several weeks, the final weeks of the season.

An all-important final Western swing began, and began disastrously, as the Dodgers lost twice to the Cubs in Chicago while the Cardinals won twice hosting the Phillies at home. The Dodgers suddenly were left with a slim one-game advantage: and all in the win column. They had played two more games than their rivals and had won them both.

In the first game of that Chicago twin bill, Reiser was beaned once again, this time by a powerful fast ball by Cub pitcher Dick Erickson. Years later, Reiser described the details of that incident to writer Donald Honig. His was an explanation that clearly described the young man's grit as well as his hard-nosed interpretation of the ethics of playing baseball.

"Ike Pearson zonked me in Brooklyn early in the year," he recalled, "and then later on Paul Erickson hit me in Chicago. What provoked the Chicago beaning was something that happened on our previous trip."

He then told of how he had come all around from first on some player's double and crashed into the Chicago catcher, who had been blocking the plate. "I knocked him on his ass and scored," Reiser said.

Jimmy Wilson, the Cubs manager, tore out of the Chicago dugout and told Reiser, "We'll get you for that, bush."

When Reiser got up during that Cubs series, he could hear the taunts from their dugout. "Stick it in his ear," the Cubs called out.

"Erickson winds up," said Reiser, "and the next thing I know Landis is visiting me in the hospital."

Baseball Commissioner Landis, who had been sitting in a box behind the dugout, had heard the same catcalls Reiser had. "Do you think that Paul Erickson threw at you intentionally?" he asked the young man.

"No, sir," Reiser answered.

"You didn't hear, 'Stick it in his ear?'" said the judge.

"I heard something like that," replied Reiser.

"Then why don't you think he threw at you intentionally?" insisted the commissioner.

"He doesn't have that kind of control," Reiser said. "I lost the ball in the shirts in center field."

"Then you won't accuse him of throwing at you?"

"No, sir," said Reiser.

"He was skeptical," Reiser continued to Honig. "He was no dummy, the judge. But he had to accept it. Christ, in those days all you heard was 'Stick it in his ear.' 'Put him in a squat position.' 'Drill him.' If you got hit, you got hit. And nobody ever said excuse me. You wanted to play ball, you played the way it was played."

For the rest of that season, both the Dodgers and the Cardinals played with a never-say-die determination, and no one with greater tenacity or talent than Pete Reiser.

Smack in the middle of their road trip, the Dodgers had an all-important three-game set with the Cardinals at St. Louis' Sportsmans Park. If perchance the Cards could win two of the three games, they would move into first place.

The Dodgers won the first game, 6–4, as Reiser chipped in with a triple and a single. St. Louis then took the second game, 4–3, though the young rookie again had a pair of hits, including a double.

The third and deciding game was a classic, a name given too often to important or well-played games. This one was, indeed, a classic. This was a pitching duel between Whitlow Wyatt and Mort Cooper, two performers who would wage many extraordinary battles during that and the next seasons. Wyatt was going for his 20th. Cooper was striving to get his team into first place.

For seven innings, young Cooper had a no-hitter in a scoreless game. But in the eighth inning, Dixie Walker hit Cooper for a double to right center, and Billy Herman immediately followed with another two-bagger in the same area. As *The New York Times* described it, "Walker, running as if a horde of red demons were on his heels, galloped across with the all-important run."

The all-important winning run, as it turned out. That was the ballgame. The Dodgers beat the Cards, 1–0, increased their lead to two games, and Wyatt, for the first time in his life, had won 20 games in a season.

But the race was hardly over. Brooklyn continued its winning ways the following day in Cincinnati, beating the Reds, 7–5, as Reiser once again had a pair of hits including a double. His batting average by now was .337, well in front of any other batter. The down side of that day, however, was that the Cards won two games from the Giants, reducing the Dodger lead to one and a half games.

The very next day, the Dodgers and Reds played in what again might be called a classic. It also points up the difference of endurance, for whatever reasons, between pitchers then and those of today. For 16 innings, the two teams were locked in a scoreless tie. The Reds' pitcher, Paul Derringer, was still on the mound while the Dodger starter, Johnny Allen, another of MacPhail's fortunate mid-season acquisitions, had toiled for 15 complete innings.

Manager Durocher had a lot to say about this key game in his book *Nice Guys Finish Last.* "At the end of nine innings," wrote Leo, "Johnny had pitched a one-hitter and we had got him exactly no runs. 'Stay in there, Johnny,' I said. 'We'll get 'em for you.'"

Durocher had made this same promise inning after inning since way back in the third. Allen would come off the mound, dripping sweat like a fat man in a Turkish bath, and his manager would try to comfort him with his ill-kept promise. But it was still a scoreless game when Allen batted in the 16th inning and hit an infield grounder that was fumbled by the fielder. Running like hell, the pitcher tripped over the base and spun into the dirt. Allen then had to be carried off the field in a scary state of exhaustion.

"Our leadoff man in the seventeenth inning," wrote Durocher, "was Pete Reiser, and Derringer had been getting him out all day by pitching him tight. Now, for such a great control pitcher, Derringer had a peculiar way of pitching. At the very moment of his delivery he would take his eyes off the plate and focus on a point right in front of him, like a spot bowler. As Pete was picking out his bat, I told him to jump back in the batter's box just as Derringer was bringing his arm forward. Pete jumped back about a foot and hit the ball 450 feet into the right field bleachers."

The Dodgers would eventually score five runs that inning, but the game was not over yet. It was quite late in the day by then and darkness was quickly moving in. In those days, baseball rules dictated that lights could not be turned on once a game had begun. If it was too dark to finish an inning, the score would revert to the previous one.

The Reds were obviously well-versed in the rule. When their third baseman, in an attempt to prolong the inning, let a simple pop-up drop in front of him for a hit, umpire Larry Goetz gave Reds manager Bill McKechnie a stern warning. This game would be played to its finish, he told him, in pitch blackness if necessary. As darkness fell, Dodger relief pitcher Hugh Casey, in his attempt to get the game over, pitched so quickly that he walked the first two men up. Goetz then came out to speak to him. "We'll play this game to a finish," he said, "if we have to put miner's lights on our caps. Don't let that worry you."

"Five more minutes," Durocher wrote, "and we'd have needed them."

The game finally ended after the Reds had loaded the bases with two outs. Then, in the growing darkness, a batted ball appeared to be headed in Durocher's direction. Durocher couldn't see it, but then suddenly he barely spotted Reese bending over, scooping up the ball and tossing it to Herman for the final out.

But it was Reiser, if with Durocher's help, who had turned the tide of the game, and it certainly seemed that as the race grew hotter, so did Pete Reiser.

A couple of days later in Pittsburgh, the young man continued this incredible display, leading his team to a 6–4 victory over the Pirates. "Two-Gun Pete Reiser," read the *Times*, "became the key man in the devastating Dodger rally today by exploding a mighty two run triple to the right center field exit gate, 429 feet distant, to give his mates their first lead."

This was, once again, his second hit in the game, the earlier one being another of his league-leading doubles. But the sad part of that day for Brooklyn was that the Cardinals had won a doubleheader against the Braves. This meant they were still clawing at the Dodger heels only one game away, and all in the win column. The Dodgers had ten games left to play, the Cardinals had 11.

Brooklyn moved further ahead as they took a doubleheader from their favorite cousins, the Philadelphia Phillies, 3–2 and 6–1, while the Cardinals lost their touch momentarily, letting the Cubs come from behind to score six runs in the ninth and beat them, 7–3.

Reiser continued to hit. He doubled in the first game in his only official time at bat and scored two of his team's three runs. After Herman had walked in the sixth inning, Reiser crashed his double against the scoreboard, sending the runner to third. Herman scored on Medwick's fly ball, and Reiser's speed brought him to third on the play. He then raced home with the winning run on Lavagetto's ground-ball out. In the nightcap, he got two more hits and an all-important run batted it. The young man was on fire, and he had chosen the perfect time to become ignited. Down the stretch, with the final result still up in the air, he would not play a game without producing at least one hit. Quite an amazing feat for a 22-year-old rookie in his first pennant race.

The very next day produced a near reversal of what had happened the day before. This time the Dodgers split their doubleheader with the Phils, at Shibe Park, while the Cards took their two games from the Cubs. The Dodger lead was back to a slim one game.

Reiser was the key player once again for Brooklyn. This time, in the Dodgers' 8–3 victory in the first game, he got two hits, including a triple. The hot-hitting rookie knocked in four of the Dodger runs and scored two more. After Reiser's two-run-producing triple, *The New York Herald-Tribune* pointed out, "the outcome of the game was never in doubt." In the losing second game, incidentally, Reiser added two more hits and another run batted in.

The day also produced evidence of the awesome excitement in New York, and especially in Brooklyn, for the Dodger cause. Not since 1920, 21 long years before, had a pennant been won by a Brooklyn team. Dodger fans, perhaps more fanatical than anywhere else in the sports world, had waited patiently, if never silently. Now, though a pennant still remained steps away and at a last moment could be denied, these fans were not to be denied.

"Approximately 18,000 loyal Dodger rooters came by train, plane and automobile," Rud Rennie wrote in *The New York Herald-Tribune* about this invasion of Philadelphia. "Thirty-nine busloads unloaded outside the park. They came in costume, with a band, bells, horns, bottles, banners, placards and boundless enthusiasm. One woman brought a huge frosted cake and gave it to Fred Fitzsimmons.

"The people from Brooklyn took charge. They moved right onto the field for the Dodger batting practice. No police were around then to herd them back into the stands. So Brooklyn had little or no batting practice. The fans stole all the balls."

Rennie went on to describe the frivolity of the crowd, the dancing of drum majorettes, the music of a marching band and the counter-melodies of the traveling Dodger Sym-Phoney. All this, even after the games had been completed.

But the pennant race was still very much in doubt, and all this celebration could yet go for naught. During the next several days, however, the Dodgers did move closer to their goal, if only because the Cardinals were running out of time. Almost trading wins and losses, the two teams went down to the wire, the Dodgers leading by a game and a half and only three days of games left to play.

It all came to a close on Thursday, September 25, and in grand fashion. Behind their ace, Whitlow Wyatt, who had won his 22nd game, the Dodgers trounced the Braves, 6–0, while the Cardinals were beaten by the Pirates, 3–1. The Dodgers had won the pennant for the first time in 21 long years. And they had won finally in what had been, in the words of the *Herald-Tribune*, "the longest and closest two team pennant struggle in the history of baseball."

The conclusive blow was a two-run home run by Pete Reiser in the seventh inning that finally put the game out of Boston's reach. It was Reiser's second hit of the day, still another multihit performance for the rookie who had all but carried his team on his young shoulders through these final weeks.

This had been a close two-team race since the beginning of the season, no team ever more than four games in front of the other. The Dodgers had been in first place eight different times, and so had the Cardinals. But

The Brooklyn Dodgers of 1941, champions of the National League. Reiser is fourth from the left in the front row. He is sitting between Reese, third from left, and coach Jake Pitler (National Baseball Hall of Fame Library, Cooperstown, N.Y.).

now at the end of this 154 game season, it was the Dodgers alone and supreme at the top, and all of Brooklyn ready to go wild.

There was a bit of a scare for the Dodgers in their next-to-last game of the season, a surprising loss to the Phillies, 7–3. During practice before the game, Reiser injured his right arm while making a throw to home plate and was immediately scratched from the starting lineup. He was taken to the clubhouse, and four doctors were called in to examine his arm.

"I had just thrown the ball when I felt something snap," he told them. "It was painful and I was worried whether I had broken anything. But after awhile the pain went away and I feel fine now."

Still, he was taken to the hospital so X-rays could be taken. If Reiser was out, most believed, the Dodger chances against the Yankees would be nil.

Good news came in bunches the following day. Reiser would be fine, and the Dodgers assured the world that he would play and start in the opening World Series game. The team then went out and beat the Phils, 5–1, in the season's finale. This was also their 100th win of the year, the first time any Dodger team had ever managed that.

Reiser was also proclaimed the winner of the batting title, at .343, the youngest and only rookie ever to have accomplished this feat. In addition, he led the league in doubles, triples, runs scored and slugging percentage, an awesome achievement for any player, an incredible one for a rookie of 22.

The only other important hitting categories, home runs and runs batted in, were won by his teammate, first baseman Dolf Camilli, who had hit 34 homers and knocked in 120 runs. Later on, Camilli would also be chosen as the league's Most Valuable Player, with the young rookie, Pete Reiser, trailing him. It was a clean sweep for the guys from Brooklyn.

Now bring on the Yankees!

11

Three Strikes and Yer—

"He could do everything. He had a good arm, he charged ground balls, he could hit, he could hit with power, he could throw, run, he could do it all. He knew how to play the game."
—Ralph Branca, Brooklyn Dodgers
pitcher and teammate

The history of the World Series goes back to 1903, when the Boston Red Sox, representatives of the newly formed American League, beat the Pittsburgh Pirates of the National League five games to three. The first time the Dodgers got into a World Series was in 1916, when they lost to the Red Sox, four games to one. Four years later, they won their pennant again, and with it the right to play the Cleveland Indians for the championship.

That time, they lost five games to two in a Series made memorable by several important firsts. This marked the first time that a pitcher hit a home run, the first time that anyone hit a grand-slam home run, and perhaps most memorably, the first time anyone had made an unassisted triple play. This last accomplishment was by a second baseman with the unlikely name of Bill Wambsganns.

The New York Yankees didn't get the chance to compete in a World Series until the following year, 1921, the second year of the so-called Babe Ruth era. They lost that one to the Giants, five games to three, all of them played in the Polo Grounds that the two teams shared as home field. The following year, they lost once again to their landlords and hometown rivals from New York, this time four games to none. This also was the first of what would now permanently remain a seven-game elimination series.

It seemed to have taken the building and occupying of the new Yankee

Stadium for the Yankees to finally win. In 1923, with their third consecutive pennant, they once again played the Giants—in games at the Polo Grounds and at the Stadium—and this time beat them, four games to two. Since that time, they had participated in seven other Series, winning six and, in fact, winning four straight times from 1936 to 1939.

Now, after a one-year layoff, they were about to enter a World Series boasting the earliest pennant-clinching in American League history, as well as winning the title by the amazing total of 17 games. Most experts gave little chance to the Dodgers, who hadn't won a pennant in 21 long years and hadn't managed this one till the final week of the season.

But tell that to the Brooklyn Faithful, a half million strong, who celebrated Brooklyn Dodger Day chasing their motorcading heroes down the streets of the borough, from Prospect Park to Borough Hall.

"They climbed trees that would not hold their weight," said *The New York Herald-Tribune*. "They fainted and were trampled on. They bowled over several police and walked on them. They dove under the hooves of prancing police horses. They dodged speeding motorcycles."

All this and more for hours on end till they all were finally exhausted and went home. By some strange miracle, no one was injured. Not a single soul, according to police reports, though 15 children were reported lost.

Leo Durocher proclaimed his team of underdogs ready for the Yankees. "We ain't a-scared of them," he told reporters. "My boys think they can win, and so do I."

"We won," he continued, "with another club on our necks all the way. Sure, it was a strain, but I don't think our boys are tired. And my pitchers will have just enough rest before the Series to be ready."

The manager did grant the possibility that two of his star players could be nervous. "Reese is just a kid," he pointed out. "Two years and boom—he's in a World Series. You gotta expect him to be nervous. And Reiser may be a little jittery. I don't know. I say that because he was nervous in the All-Star game. But if he is nervous at the start, I don't think it will last."

Nervous or not, after jubilation and parties and parades, after special editions of several New York newspapers devoted to this unprecedented Subway Series—where a five-cent train ride could take you to any of the ballparks and another nickel back home—the first of October arrived and it was time to play ball.

"The Dodgers, apparently not the least bit awed by the formidable character of the opposition," said the quite proper *New York Times* on Series opener day, "practiced with the same air of jauntiness that had marked their work through their amazing pennant campaign."

"They are confident," the paper went on, "that their redoubtable home run clouter, Dolf Camilli, and their freshman luminary, Pete Reiser, will prove more than a match for DiMaggio and Keller."

The *Times* sports columnist, John Kieran, added, "It's the crowd from the wrong side of the railroad tracks invading the restricted residential area, bent on mischief. It's the uprising of the downtrodden, the poor against the plutocrats."

He went on to point out that this Dodger team of today was quite different from their ancestors of old, "when baseball in Ebbets Field was a sight for psychiatrists, when the athletes were licensed zanies and nobody was interested in the club officials except possibly a few charity workers."

These guys have a chance was what he meant to say.

The rush for hotel rooms was extraordinary. So was the rush for tickets, for which prices went up and up, greedily if not illegally. This was expected to be one of the greatest series in recent memory. Very few would be disappointed.

The first game, taking place in the vast confines of the Yankee Stadium, was a sign of what was to follow. In a brilliant pitching duel between two veterans, Curt Davis of the Dodgers and Red Ruffing of the Yankees, the team from the Bronx narrowly won, 3–2. This was their tenth consecutive victory in World Series competition, an astonishing record that went back to October 9, 1937.

Each team managed only six hits, with most of these coming from unexpected sources. For the Yankees, their two power-hitting outfielders, Charlie Keller and Tommy Henrich, went hitless, and Joe DiMaggio, who had amazed the baseball world that year with his 56-game hitting streak, was held to a single in four tries. The expected Dodger sluggers, Reiser, Camilli, Walker and Herman, were all held hitless, with their league's home run leader, Dolf Camilli, striking out three times.

The Yankees' first runs came in the second inning when second baseman Joe Gordon homered after catcher Bill Dickey had doubled. The Dodgers got back one in the fifth, when after two were out, Reese singled and Mickey Owen hit a triple to score him. In the sixth, the Yankees added their third run as Keller walked and Dickey and Gordon followed with singles.

The Dodgers scored again in the seventh. Lavagetto reached base on an error, Reese singled him to second, and Lew Riggs, pinch-hitting for Owen, brought Lavagetto home.

The score remained that way till the ninth when the Dodgers took up threatening bats again. Medwick started the inning with an infield single, and after Lavagetto fouled out, Reese got his third successive single of the day. But with the tying and possible winning runs on base, Herman Franks, the team's second-string catcher, meekly hit into a game-ending double play.

Though they had lost the game, the Dodgers had shown the crowds and themselves that the Yankees could be beaten. On their second try the following day, the Dodgers proved it.

"Incredible as it may seem, the Yankees can be defeated in a World Series game," began the startling story in the next day's *New York Times*. It then went on to describe Brooklyn's streak-breaking 3–2 victory.

This was another well-pitched game, with the Dodger ace, Whitlow Wyatt, winning while going the entire nine innings, and Yankee pitcher Spud Chandler sharing the losing effort with reliever Johnny Murphy.

The Yankees picked up single runs in the second and third innings and might have had more, if not for some misguided base running. But it seemed that Chandler had things well in hand, giving up only one hit over the first four innings.

Then came the Dodger fifth. A walk to Camilli, a double by Medwick, a throwing error by Gordon and a single by Owen brought in the two tying runs. The Dodgers might have had more, but Wyatt, one of baseball's best hitting pitchers, grounded into a double play with two men still on board to end the inning.

In the sixth, the Dodgers went ahead and stayed there. Walker got on base via a second error by Joe Gordon. A hit-and-run single by Herman brought Lavagetto to third. "In this interesting situation," wrote John Kieran, "it was up to Pete Reiser, the idol of Flatbush and the National League leading hitter of 1941, to do something. And he did. He struck out. The third swipe he took at one of Murphy's curves was as fierce as anything seen on the premises since Babe Ruth went away."

But that was just the first out. Camilli, still looking for his first hit, came up next. This Dodger star delivered a hard hit single to right that brought in Walker with the winning run. So after ten winning games stretched over four World Series, the Yankee streak was broken. And the Dodgers were hungry for more.

Moving back home to the friendly confines and friendlier fans of Ebbets Field, the Dodgers felt sure they could take down the Yankee aristocracy. The Bombers from the Bronx pitched their young lefthander, Marius Russo, himself born and bred in Brooklyn, against a fat and forty righthander for the Dodgers named Freddie Fitzsimmons. In his 17 major league seasons, Fitzsimmons, who hailed from way out Midwest in Indiana, had pitched only for New Yorkers, the uptown Giants and this Brooklyn team.

Besides bringing his sizable girth and his long years to the mound, Fitzsimmons also brought one of baseball's best knucklers. His slow, off-speed deliveries seemed a perfect antidote for anxious Yankee bats, and for six and two-thirds innings, the fat man proved a master. Over that period, Fitzsimmons had pitched a four-hit shutout. But over that same time, Russo had done much the same.

After two Yankees were out in the seventh inning, and the game still a scoreless tie, the Yankees had Gordon sitting on second base and pitcher Russo, a pretty fair hitter, coming to the plate. Russo was up there to hit, and hit he did, a screaming line drive that headed straight for the pitcher's mound. The ball landed with enormous impact and sound right above Fitzsimmons' left kneecap then rose into the air for perhaps 30 feet over the Brooklyn infield. It finally came down into the glove of Peewee Reese, who took it for the third out and the end of the inning.

But the damage was done. So was Fitzsimmons. The pitcher limped off the field, screaming epithets to the heavens, and was immediately taken to the hospital. There he'd sit out, if not lie out, the rest of the Series.

That was the turning point of this game. Hugh Casey replaced the knuckleball pitcher in the eighth, and his throws were less than tantalizing. The first batter up, first baseman Johnny Sturm, hit the ball long and hard toward right center, but Reiser, after a long run, was able to pull it down. It was the last batter Casey got out. Four straight Yankee hits produced a pair of runs and the exit of the Dodger reliever.

Brooklyn finally got a run in the bottom of that inning. Dixie Walker opened the Dodger half with a long double to right, then after two were out, Reese singled him home. This was still one run short and it would stay that way. The Yankees won the game, 2–1, with the help of a shattered kneecap, an occurrence that the *Times* termed "as freakish a mishap as ever has been seen in World Series play."

The Dodgers were down, but hardly out. The team felt that with a little more luck it could have won the first game of the Series, and with a little less impact this third one. Well, they hadn't seen anything yet.

The batters on both sides had come alive in this the fourth game of a pitcher-dominated Series. Kirby Higbe, one of Brooklyn's two stellar 22-game winners, started for the Dodgers and lasted less than four innings. Atley Donald, a lesser light on the Yankee mound staff, lasted one-third of an inning more.

Down 3–2 going into the bottom of the fifth, the Dodgers started the inning with a long double to right by Dixie Walker. Up next was Pete Reiser, who after being shut out over the first two games, had awakened with a double against Russo the day before and a single earlier that day against Donald. Reiser wasted no time. On Donald's first pitch, the young rookie blasted the ball far over the scoreboard in right field for a two-run home run and the lead in the ball game.

Ebbets Field erupted as fans went wild. Like one, they rose to their feet and yelled and whistled and applauded as Reiser strolled the bases to bring in what they hoped was the winning run. Finally the Dodgers were ahead on their own turf and set to tie up the Series. That finished the Yankee pitcher and, it appeared, the Yankees. For the remainder of that inning as well as the next three, the score remained, 4–3. Johnny Allen and Hugh Casey had done their job well pitching for the Dodgers, and Marv Breuer and Johnny Murphy had done much the same for the Yankees.

Going into the ninth, Hugh Casey was still on the mound for Brooklyn. Days short of his 28th birthday, he had won 14 games for the Dodgers that year, pitching both as a starter and as their premier reliever. Now there were only three outs left for Casey's first World Series win.

The first two batters were apple-pie easy. Yankee lead-off hitter Johnny Sturm grounded weakly to second baseman Pete Coscarat. Red Rolfe did even less with his bat. The third baseman bounced the ball right back to Casey, who threw him out by more than ten feet. Tommy Henrich was all that was left. He hadn't had a hit all day nor much in the three previous games.

Dodger fans sat on their hands and took deep breaths, readying themselves for triumphant applause and exultant shouts of joy. They had finally shown these uptown nobles what the hell their team was all about.

Pitching carefully to Henrich, Casey worked the count to three and two. One more strike and this game was over. Casey reared back, and in the words of Leo Durocher, in *Nice Guys Finish Last*, "threw his bread-and-butter pitch, a hard sinker breaking low on the outside corner of the plate. Henrich missed the ball by a foot."

The umpire, Larry Goetz, called out, "Strike three!" and apparently the Dodgers had won the fourth game of the Series, 4–3, tying things up, two games apiece.

But, no.

As *The New York Times* reported it, "Before the first full-throated roar had a chance to acclaim this brilliant achievement there occurred one of those harrowing events that doubtless will live through all the ages of baseball like the Fred Snodgrass muff and the failure of Fred Merkle to touch second."

Mickey Owen, one of baseball's best fielding catchers, had somehow let the ball get away. Before he could get his hands on it again, somewhere near the Dodger dugout, Henrich was across first base safely and the game was still very much alive.

"When Owen did not shift his feet, but gave it a casual reach with his glove," said Durocher, "the roof fell in on our heads."

Obviously shaken by what had occurred and not giving himself time to settle down, Casey hurriedly went back to work. DiMaggio was up, and he smashed a hard single to left, sending Henrich to third.

Up came Keller. A third out would still end things right here and send the Dodgers home with their second win. Casey quickly got two strikes on this powerful apelike batter, who had appropriately earned the nickname of King Kong. Again, one more strike and this game was in the books.

Durocher said he whistled out to his pitcher and made a motion with a hand across his chest. This was the signal to pitch high and inside to Keller and give him nothing good to hit. For some reason, Casey paid no attention. He threw a fast ball right down the middle and Keller greeted it like his worst enemy. He sent the ball flying high and far toward right field, missing a home run by a few feet. It crashed against the 20-foot screen in right for a double, scoring the two Yankee runners and giving the Yankees the lead. Permanently.

Durocher second-guessed himself many years later in his book *Nice Guys Finish Last*. He chastised himself for not offering Casey some calming words after Henrich had gotten on base. He criticized himself for keeping Casey in after DiMaggio had gotten a hit and the left-handed Keller was coming to the plate; in hindsight, he felt he should have replaced Casey with lefty Larry French. Instead, he wrote, "I did nothing. I froze."

The Yankees scored two more runs before they finished work for the inning, with Dodger left-hander Larry French finally coming in to get the last out. Too stunned to make a final stand, Brooklyn went out meekly without a runner reaching base in their half of the frame. The final score was 7–4, and Dodger spirits could never recover from this.

Years later in recalling the game, Reiser said, "When I saw Henrich swing at that third strike, I figured the game was over. Then I saw the ball rolling away and it seemed to gain speed as it rolled."

Still, Reiser wasn't worried. There were two out and, to him, it still looked like an easy game. "But when those extra base hits began to roll off the Yankee bats," he went on. "it was all over and I felt a strange sinking feeling when the game was lost."

Nobody on the club ever mentioned the third strike to Owen, according to Reiser. The players all believed that the pitch was such a sharp-breaking curve that no catcher in baseball could have caught it.

Whitlow Wyatt faced Ernie Bonham in the final game, which the Yankees won in a lifeless struggle, 3–1. Reiser hit a resounding triple in the first inning, and his fly ball scored Wyatt with the Dodgers' only run in the third.

There was the smell of trouble in the Yankee half of the fifth inning when DiMaggio was brushed back by a Wyatt fastball. The Yankee Clipper angrily rushed to the mound as players from both teams immediately joined the congregation.

"DiMaggio mumbled something to me," Wyatt said after the game, "and I mumbled something to him."

When he was asked what those words were, Wyatt answered, "I wouldn't say. Joe is a great guy and I like him."

Many years later, Reiser cleared up the little mystery. "DiMaggio had told him," said Reiser, "that Wyatt's brush-back pitch was trying to keep him from making a living." 'Hell,' answered Wyatt, 'you're trying to keep me from making mine.' The two then smiled at each other and returned to their positions."

But as tough as Wyatt or Reiser or the rest of the team fought, it wasn't enough to overcome the Yankees or the Dodgers' abundant misfortunes that year. Despite Reiser's slow start in the first two games, he rose to the occasion, just as his manager had predicted. The rookie ended up knocking in more runs and getting more extra base hits than any of his teammates. He had batted in three runs, and his four hits, which were as many as any Dodger had amassed, had included a double, a triple and the home run that should have won the fourth game.

As the Series ended, it was time for the old Dodger war cry—Wait till next year!

Yet again.

12

The Gold Dust Twins

"It's my opinion that Pete Reiser is the greatest ball player in the National League. On my ballclub, Reiser is first pick and there isn't one close enough to make a real run for second money."
— Jimmy Cannon, nationally syndicated
sports columnist for the *New York Post*

Sportswriters began calling them the Gold Dust Twins some time during the heat of the 1941 pennant race. After all, the two did stand out, and stand out like gold, from the rest of the Dodger team. Most of the others were veterans and castoffs, a silver-haired brigade, if you will. Reiser had reached his 22nd birthday early in the season, Reese his 23rd, later in August.

Each of them was given at birth the name of Harold, but they would be known better by their nicknames. Pete and Pee Wee were who they were, and these names, strangely, also were quite similar. Harold Reiser's "Pete" had stemmed from his adoration of a cowboy star named Two Gun Pete. Harold Reese's "Pee Wee" had come from his childhood days as a marble shooter when he finished second in the marble-shooting championship of the State of Kentucky. Their surnames were also quite alike, really only three letters apart.

They were roommates and pals who were constantly written about, separately and together. Two bachelors who sometimes went on dates together, went shopping together, exchanged clothes, helped each other work through batting and fielding slumps. They had been brought up to the major leagues and to the Dodgers at just about the same time in 1940.

Each had once been owned by another team, and each had never played for that team. Reese had been owned by the Red Sox, Reiser by the Cards. Reiser was certainly headed for greatness of an awesome kind. Reese was sometimes astounding in his play at shortstop, though still the jewel needing polishing that Durocher had once described. And often, indeed, he was a batter of consequence, hitting successfully at the most urgent moments, as in the past World Series.

Their temperaments were quite different, but so, in fact, are those of many fraternal twins. "In personality," wrote Tom Meany in an article for *Colliers*, "Pete and Pee Wee are as far apart as the Phillies and a Major League baseball club."

"Pete is stolid, silent and retiring," Meany observed. "Pee Wee is lively, jocose and self-assured."

But that was trivial considering the rest. Their names, their ages, their sizes, their star potential were so similar that dubbing them the Gold Dust Twins was a fitting tribute. But never were the two as twinned as they were on March, 29, 1942, when on the very same day, each ducked out of spring training camp to secretly marry the woman of his life.

The two young rookies went their separate ways at the end of the 1941 World Series, Reiser back to St. Louis, Reese on down to Louisville, each to bask in the glory and adoration of their hometown fans and family. And each returned the next spring with so much more. Reiser had met his wife, Patricia, at a friend's party that winter. Reese had first seen his wife, Dorothy Walton, washing her hair in her Louisville back yard. "I didn't know a baseline from a clothesline," she later said. But evidently it didn't matter.

Neither did Patricia Hurst Reiser know the first thing about the game nor have any idea of the sudden fame of her handsome suitor. Seventeen-year-old Patricia actually came from a family with celebrity of its own. Her cousin was the popular novelist and screen writer Fannie Hurst, who had written such best sellers as *Back Street* and *Imitation of Life*, both made several times into successful Hollywood films. She had also created and written several major Hollywood movies herself, as well as having gained prominence as an important philanthropist.

Reiser described his meeting with young Patricia as if it were a moment of magic. "The first day I got back from the World Series," he said, "a friend called me to invite me to a party."

Reiser declined, telling his friend that he didn't have anyone to bring with him. "Don't let that bother you," he was told. "My girl has a friend that she'd like you to meet."

"So I joined them," said Pete. "It was the first time I had ever seen Patricia in my life. I didn't look at another girl after that."

The beautiful Patricia Hurst, whom Reiser met in the autumn of 1941. Once he had seen her, said Reiser, "I didn't look at another girl" (courtesy of Shirley Reiser Tuber).

And he meant that, it would seem, for the rest of his days. The two would always stay close and deeply in love through all the ups and downs that awaited them like a corkscrew road twisted around a mountain.

Back in St. Louis after the season, Reiser used the bulk of his World Series money to build a beautiful, roomy house in the suburbs for his parents and his siblings. His special gift to himself was a den plastered with paraphernalia and clippings from his incredible rookie season. No, they didn't make much money in those days. Not even the batting champ and the Rookie of the Year.

But a drastic change of fortune was laid on all Americans at that time. On December 7, 1941, of course, the United States was finally brought into the raging World War by the Japanese attack on Pearl Harbor. This altered the life course of all Americans and quickly affected the status of baseball. Players and, more important, players of importance and note, were beginning to be drafted into service, while many more were awaiting their induction.

Detroit's Hank Greenberg had gone into the Army early the previous year, his loss having transformed a pennant winner one season into a second-division club this past one. During this winter, the Cleveland Indians pitching great, Bob Feller, had enlisted in the Navy. Cecil Travis and Buddy Lewis, the core of the Washington Senators, both left for service, leaving their team in ruins. The Yankee rookie first baseman, Johnny Sturm, was called up during the winter, leaving the world champions with a huge opening to fill.

As for the Dodgers, Cookie Lavagetto had volunteered for the Navy and was sworn in as an aviation machinist by the start of spring training.

General managers and managers in both leagues were holding their collective breath, wondering who on their teams might be going next.

John Kieran's suggestion, in his *New York Times* column during spring training, spoke it well. His advice to baseball scouts was to "look for good hitters over 44 years of age, married, with six children and no teeth."

Toward the end of March, just as the 1942 season was about to begin, the total number of major league players already inducted into Service was calculated at 64, 42 from the American League and 22 from the National. This would be the equivalent of the rosters of two teams of players, or one-eighth of the then 16 teams.

Still, against the backdrop of this all-threatening war, there was no question that baseball would continue. President Franklin Delano Roosevelt had deemed it good tonic for his countrymen's morale, and the game would be played without interruption throughout the war years. Though quality would be diminished greatly in 1943 and 1944, this coming season would still be one of near prewar quality.

Teams were naturally searching for veterans in their mid- and late thirties or youngsters barely out of their teens, both in categories safer from conscription. But this didn't always work. Draft numbers were randomly selected, and no one was really totally draft-safe. For the Dodgers, the two players they most feared losing were their two young stars, the Gold Dust Twins, Pete Reiser and Peewee Reese.

A rather bizarre article by the Associated Press appeared in newspapers in early April, declaring that baseball parks would be the best possible place to be during an air raid. "If you're watching a major league baseball game when an air raid comes," it read, "don't go away. You probably will be sitting in the best bomb shelter in the neighborhood, and you might miss part of the game."

"Club officials," it continued, "preparing for their first wartime season in about a quarter of a century, agree that fans could find no better protection in the event of an enemy raid than the steel-and-concrete stands. In New York, where all three clubs are making extensive plans to care for spectators in such an emergency, an official has decreed that afternoon games not be interrupted, even by a raid."

The man who made these remarks was Harry M. Prince, chief civilian protection adviser of the Office of Civilian Defense. He also suggested that "the ball players will be the soldiers in that situation." Ostensibly, they would remain on the field and continue to play ball as enemy planes circled above. "The show must go on," he was quoted as saying. "Otherwise it would be like actors rushing off a stage. If they show panic, you can see what might happen."

Apparently, people didn't laugh at this. They probably were too frightened at being drawn into the unknowns of war, with almost half of those living then never having lived through one previously. What this does seem to indicate was the state of near holiness in which baseball was enshrined, how important the game was to the lives of the people, and that, somehow or other, it must and would be played.

For the Dodgers, their loss of Lavagetto and the possibility of losing a benchful of service recruits, sent Larry MacPhail once again to his checkbook and to his trading frame of mind. His foremost acquisition was Floyd Arky Vaughan, the longtime All-Star shortstop for the Pirates, who was destined for a berth in the Hall of Fame. To nail this fine fielder and superb hitter, who had batted over .300 for ten consecutive seasons and was now slated to play third base for the Dodgers in place of Lavagetto, the team had to surrender four players that they would barely miss. Those players traded to Pittsburgh were Pete Coscarat, Luke Hamlin, Jimmy Wasdell and the disgruntled Babe Phelps, all backups and utility players in the Brooklyn scheme of things.

That trade, however, was only the start. The Dodgers also purchased the hard-hitting Don Padgett, who could play the outfield as well as catch, from the Cardinals for $30,000. But before Padgett could have a single at bat for his new team, he was taken into service, and as the government had decreed, the money was returned by the Cards to the Dodgers. For added outfield insurance the Dodgers bought Johnny Rizzo from their Philly cousins for an undisclosed sum of money. Rizzo was a strong home run threat who had hit more than 20 homers two times in his four preceding big league seasons and, it was hoped, he would duplicate that feat for his new team.

Considered a troublemaker with the Reds and the Phillies, his two previous clubs, Rizzo didn't frighten Durocher, more than a bit of a mischief maker himself. "He can storm at me, the rest of the players or opposing players all he wants," said his new manager, "but I'm going to try to cure him of arguing with the fans. I know he's a good ballplayer."

Brooklyn also picked up veteran catcher Billy Sullivan from the Detroit Tigers for a reported fifteen thousand dollars, outfielder and utility infielder Frenchy Bordagaray, who had been released by the Yankees, and 36-year-old shortstop Charlie Gelbert, who had all but retired. Gelbert, it seemed, was close to the prescription John Kieran had given for this year's model player. Strange but evidently quite true, baseball was building for the immediate future on the backs of 30-plus-year-old veterans.

As the Dodgers gathered for their training season, first in Havana and then moving on to Clearwater, Florida, Durocher was nigh delirious in praise. "I've got just the kind of club I've always wanted," he proclaimed. "What I mean is that every one of these boys is a winning type of player. They all love to play and always want to win."

MacPhail added his endorsement. "I'm not picking anybody to win the pennant," he said with some unusual restraint, "but I think we've got a better club right now than we had when the 1941 season ended."

The general manager took a breather for a day, looked at the players he had brought together, and decided to amend his forecast. "If I were picking a club to try to win this race," he said, "I would have to start with the Brooklyn Dodgers. We've got so many good players down here, I think, Brooklyn could put two teams in the league. And I don't think that second team would finish last either."

There was some truth to MacPhail's declarations, though it would take the poetic license of a Shakespeare to cover his remark about fielding a second team. This surely was an improved club over last season's pennant winners. The only player lost to the draft was Lavagetto, and in his place came Vaughan, a prodigious performer and a perennial All-Star.

The outfield had stayed in tact, with Reiser, a season of experience and a year older, a good bet to outdo his initial stunning numbers. They had also gotten Johnny Rizzo, who if kept on Durocher's leash, could be a potent reserve if not an everyday player. The pitching staff—led by Whitlow Wyatt, Kirby Higbe and Curt Davis—would benefit from a full season of both Larry French and Johnny Allen, along with the young rookie Ed Head, who had impressed everyone in his short appearances at the end of the previous season.

In addition, the Cardinals had traded away their strongest hitter, Johnny Mize, and were taking their chances with outfielder Johnny Hopp and the untried rookie Ray Sanders at first base. Mize and Medwick, once the heart of their batting order, were now taking their swats with teams from New York City. Still, as everybody knew, general manager Branch Rickey always had something hidden up the sleeve of his starched white shirt.

Pete Reiser was certainly doing his part that spring. By the end of March, he was hitting .350 and just beginning to hit his stride when a curious piece of news appeared. Reiser, it seemed, was considering a return to switch-hitting.

"There are some left-handers in the league like Lanier (Max of the Cardinals), Melton and Hubbbell (Cliff and Carl of the Giants), and Olsen (Vern of the Cubs), who have given me a great deal of trouble," declared the young man.

"Of course, I'm only experimenting right now," he went on, "and if I don't feel comfortable at the plate swinging right-handed, I'll be back on the other side against all pitching."

Durocher appeared to give the idea little concern. "Why should Reiser be a switch-hitter again?" he quipped. "What's the sense of making it tougher on the pitchers?"

Coach Charlie Dressen, who seemed to have fostered the notion, thought it could add 15 or 20 points to Reiser's batting average. Combing last year's statistics, it was found that from July 1 on of the previous season, Reiser had hit .275 against lefties, or close to 70 points less than his season batting average.

More important to Dodger management, it seemed, was the marital status of Reiser and his roommate, Pee Wee Reese. News of Reese's marriage was the first to be disclosed. In the Thursday, April 2, issue of *The New York Herald-Tribune*, under a Daytona Beach dateline, it was reported that "Reese and Miss Dorothy Walton of Reese's home city, Louisville, were married here Sunday, the Dodgers' star shortstop revealed today. Reiser, center fielder and Reese's roomie, acted as best man and Reiser's fiancée, Miss Patricia Hurst, of St. Louis, was bridesmaid."

That put Reese's wedding at March 29, four days prior to this item.

Three days later, the same *Herald-Tribune* reported, "Pete Reiser, Brooklyn's star center fielder and champion batter of the National League, was fined $200 today by Leo Durocher, the manager. Reiser went AWOL and missed the Dodger trip to Ft. Benning so that he might drive his fiancée, Miss Patricia Hurst, to Atlanta. He was unable to gain Durocher's permission to take the day off so he took it upon himself to 'jump the club.' There being no KP duty among Dodgers, Durocher decided a $200 fine would be sufficient."

Not till the following day was it divulged that Miss Hurst was really Mrs. Reiser. But the $200 fine was not rescinded. Not even in lieu of a wedding gift.

"While announcements were in order," the *Herald-Tribune* wrote this time, "Leo Durocher insisted this morning the $200 fine plastered on Pete Reiser for his failure to take the bus ride to yesterday's game at Ft. Benning would stand despite the news his star center fielder had been married."

"He's been married for several days," said Durocher. "And he was refused permission to go directly to Atlanta. Bridegroom or not, the fine sticks."

The truth was that the Reisers were married on March 29 in Titusville, Florida, the very same day the Reeses had wed in nearby Daytona Beach.

Newlyweds Patricia and Pete Reiser, married on March 29, 1942, the same wedding date as Dorothy and Peewee Reese (courtesy of Shirley Reiser Tuber).

By the time all this news was sorted out and finally revealed, the newlyweds were comparative oldyweds.

The disclosure of these events in such dribs and drabs and days after the fact does suggest the apprehension felt by the two players. Years later, Reese recalled when the two friends had first thought of getting married.

During spring training, the two smitten bachelors had had dinner with Dixie Walker and his wife, and the thought simply jumped out at them.

"The two of us," remembered Reese. "We went back to our room and the two of us decided we'd get married. But when we told MacPhail and Durocher, they almost split a gut. They didn't believe in players getting married in spring training."

That was good reason to do it secretly, though it didn't stem any outburst from MacPhail. The general manager went berserk when he heard the news.

"Well, there goes the pennant," screamed MacPhail.

Somehow, he believed that marriage—like those participated in by most of the players he had traded for and coveted—sucked the athletic skills out of ballplayers. It had never occurred to him that these weddings might indeed be blissful. After all, they might just save his two stars from a 1-A status in the draft and keep them in their Dodger, rather than Army, uniforms for the coming season.

Actually, MacPhail was having a hard time of it ever since losing the Series to the Yankees. Reiser told of a strange story that he had heard in St. Louis during the off-season that suggested how difficult things were going for the general manager. The disheartened MacPhail, it was said, had offered to sell the entire Dodger roster to the Browns for three or four million dollars and all the Brown players.

"I kept hearing rumors," said Reiser, "that the owner of the Browns, Don Barnes, was running around St. Louis trying to raise the three million. The banks wanted to know what he wanted the money for. He told them, 'I'm buying the Dodger ballclub for St. Louis.'"

"I don't know if MacPhail really would have gone through with it," continued Reiser, "but can you imagine what would have happened in Brooklyn if the St. Louis Browns players had all turned up there one day wearing Dodger uniforms?"

It should be pointed out that the St. Louis Browns had finished in a tie for sixth place in the 1941 American League race, just one spot out of the basement. That was as high as they had gone in long years.

In Peter Golenbock's book *Bums*, the author writes further of MacPhail's outlandish behavior. "Having been denied a World Series victory," he concluded, "MacPhail bore down as hard as ever on Durocher. At Cincinnati, MacPhail's unstable nature had led him to the brink of a nervous breakdown. Unable to control his drinking, furious at having lost the 1941 World Series in so improbable a way, MacPhail was back on the edge. His bouts with Durocher were becoming more emotional, less rational."

The two men continued fighting—and often resorted to fists—all through spring training. Whether it was precipitated by one or another player's purported excessive gambling or drinking or staying out too late or, yes, even getting married, the two men—one drunk and disruptive and the other volatile and passionate—fought and made up and fought and made up. And then acted as if nothing had happened.

Durocher was fired and rehired in the same preposterous manner as in years before, the two men finally ending up bawling in each other's arms, forgiving and promising to forget it all. At least till next time.

MacPhail would constantly hire detectives to follow his players around, then, learning of what would usually end up as minor indiscretions, put the blame on his manager. One such incident involved pitcher Johnny Allen and a private detective's report on his supposed doings during the team's stay in Havana that spring. Furious with the report, MacPhail screamed at Allen, fined him, and suspended him as the whole team looked on. "It was awful," wrote Durocher in *Nice Guys*. "From what I heard, he achieved new heights of invective even for MacPhail." Allen, just as angry as MacPhail, "stalked away," declaring he would not return.

Of course, it was Durocher who then had to come into the breach to paste up things between the prodigal outfielder and his dysfunctional general manager. This caused another frenzied firing of Durocher and another bleary-eyed make up between the manager and MacPhail.

Was this any way to run a ballclub? Was this any way for a general manager and his field general to act with each other? Well, it had worked last year. It had, after all, produced a pennant winner and one that had gotten within a finger span of a World Series championship.

In this new season, however, it would cause a disgraceful and calamitous tragedy, and one that would wrest from them and their team the dream they held most dear.

13

A Season to Remember

"Some people can feel a wall close to them. I know I could. I didn't look back, but I could feel like it's there. I'd slow down. Pete was never aware of a wall. He'd go right through the damn thing."
— Gene Hermanski, Dodger outfielder 1943–1951

The old Dodger war cry of "Wait till next year!" seemed about to be fulfilled. For long years, Brooklyn players and fans had repeated that vow like a mantra, and not till the previous year's pennant win was there even partial satisfaction. Now, in the lingo of Pee Wee Reese, who once played for the immies championship of his home state of Kentucky, this would be the year for winning all the marbles. This year, Brooklyn could take the National League pennant and then continue on to defeat whoever showed up for the American League in the 1942 World Series.

Because of the war, this was, of course, a very special year. On opening day, April 14, John Drebinger, sports reporter of *The New York Times*, put it as follows.

"Pledged to carry on in the traditional manner," he wrote, "professional baseball today will launch another Major League campaign—the sixty-seventh without interruption for the National circuit; the forty-second for the American.

"This year baseball, like virtually every other national institution, faces a special mission. The game, it is felt, can contribute to the prosecution of the war—witness President Roosevelt's suggestion that more night games be scheduled to provide amusement for defense workers—and it is to this end that the pennant races are dedicated."

The Dodgers began things as if the pennant races were dedicated to them. In the first game of the season, they beat their rival Giants, 7–5, at the Polo Grounds. Reiser got a hit and scored a run in four tries while his new groommate, Reese, got a double and a home run and knocked in two runs. Both their brides were at the game, cheering them on from seats near the Dodger dugout. A photograph of the two pairs of newlyweds appeared in a collection of New York papers the following day, four bright, smiling faces welcoming in this new, hopefully improved season.

By this time, Reiser and Reese had appropriately given up their roommate living while at home in Brooklyn. The Pee Wee Reeses had found a place for themselves along the water in Bay Ridge. "We weren't very near the ball park," Dottie Reese later confided, "and, of course, we didn't own a car. It took a bus and two trains to get to Ebbets Field, so I didn't get to see many games that year."

The Reisers remained closer to Ebbets Field, living in an apartment house less than 20 minutes away. Several other Dodger couples—the Hugh Caseys, the Joe Medwicks, the Whitlow Wyatts, the Newell Kimballs, the Ed Heads, the Arky Vaughans and the Billy Hermans—all lived in the same complex. Patricia Reiser thus had lots of empathetic company and became close to several of the wives.

Meanwhile, the team's winning ways continued through most of the following two weeks as they took on their rival Eastern teams, the Braves and Phillies, as well as the Giants. In that time, the Dodgers compiled an impressive 11–3 record and a hold on first place. Reiser, however, didn't manage as well.

Going hitless for several games, being benched one time against a left-handed pitcher and, in practice, testing his ability to hit right-handed again, he hit a mere .235 over his first nine games. Only once in that time did he perform like last year's batting champion. In an effort against the Braves that the Dodgers won, 9–5, he singled in his team's first run and later homered with a man on base to score the tying and, ultimately, winning run.

For a brief moment, one wondered whether MacPhail was right. Perhaps marriage had taken away the elusive essence of his hitting.

Forget it!

Reiser slowly came back to life. On Brooklyn's first Western trip, playing against what was considered the cream of the league's crop, he began again to come up with his two- and three-hit games. He did, however, have two consecutive fruitless appearances against a couple of Pirate southpaws. Reiser went without a hit in five tries against left-handed Ken Heintzelman and ended up with nothing in four tries against Aldon Wilkie.

But left-hander Howie Pollet of the Cards didn't faze him. Reiser got two hits in three tries against Pollet and three hits including a double and a homer against a parade of St. Louis pitchers.

By the first week in May, Reiser was back on target, and the Dodgers were sitting in first place, a game and a half in the lead. Fourth in the batting race by this time, Reiser had upped his average to a solid .325.

Things got even better for both Reiser and his team. Against the Giant great Carl Hubbell, who was still a formidable pitcher and one who threw from the left side of the mound, Reiser hit a homer and a double and knocked in two of the Dodger winning runs. He followed that with a couple of hits against southpaw Johnny Vander Meer, a consistent winner for the Reds for many years who had attained immortal fame by winning two consecutive no-hitters. One day later, Reiser's hit knocked out the same Lefty Aldon Wilkie, who had horse-collared him a week before, to lead a Brooklyn win over the Pirates.

His purported troubles against left-handed pitchers appeared more and more a fiction, and the Dodger chances for a second straight pennant more and more a reality.

Leading a strong Dodger offensive against the Pirates, Reiser got three doubles in four at bats while knocking in two runs and scoring another, as Brooklyn beat Pittsburgh, 8–3. The victory gave the Dodgers a solid four-game lead in the pennant race and brought Reiser's batting average up to an impressive .343, the same percentage he had reached in gaining last year's batting title.

Even more important news was reported that same day. It was announced that because Reiser was the sole support of his parents, as well as his four sisters and a brother, his draft status had been changed to 3-A. This would probably keep him from any uniform but a Dodger one for the remainder of the season.

There were several astounding performances by the young outfielder in early June that gave further evidence of his hitting prowess. It should be pointed out that it is essential to report in detail what this player accomplished in his second full year in the majors. Only then can one understand, and marvel, if you will, at his absolute batting brilliance, his straight-line consistency and his historic potential.

In a doubleheader victory against Chicago, he got six hits in nine at bats while knocking in three runs and scoring three more. His final hit of the day knocked in the winning run with two outs in the tenth.

In another doubleheader win, this time against Boston, Reiser got six more hits, this day in only eight tries. The hits included a double, a triple and a home run and, once again his hits knocked in three runs while scoring five for himself.

Two days later, he got five hits in five tries in a single game against the Pirates. His efforts that day included a home run and three doubles that batted in four runs in the Dodgers' winning game. By the end of that game, Reiser's batting average had risen to a soaring .366, and his team was six games ahead of the second-place Cardinals.

Sandwiched between these efforts was an accomplishment, a quite rare accomplishment in baseball, that years later would become a Reiser trademark. During a 3–3 tie game with the Cubs, the phenomenal young man found himself perched on third base with two out and the weak hitting Alex Kampouris at the plate. As the pitcher, left-handed Johnny Schmitz, went into his stretch, his back to the runner, Reiser took off like a streak of lightning. Before a throw could even be made, Reiser slid into home safely, carrying the winning run across and leaving players and spectators with their mouths open.

This man, or so it seemed, could do everything. His masterful performance the previous season was perhaps simply a prelude to unimagined greatness.

Not long after this, Reiser proved this sort of thievery was no accident. Arthur Patterson described the action in his account of this 4–3 victory over the Cards in *The New York Herald-Tribune.*

"The larcenous Pete Reiser stole home for the third Dodger run," wrote Patterson. "As a matter of fact, Reiser stole his way around from first to home with a bit of aid on the part of Harry Walker, Dixie's brother, who cavorted in center field for the opposition."

Reiser had opened the inning with a single to center but looked for more. "When he made a false motion to second on this blow," Patterson continued, "Walker unleashed a throw which was finally run down on the brink of the dugout by Jimmy Brown. By this time Reiser wasn't faking. He was at third. White then proceeded to fan Medwick and Camilli. Eventually he also fanned Rizzo, but Reiser didn't wait for that eventuality. He made a few false starts for the plate and then took off, surviving under White's pitch."

By the end of that game, the Dodgers had pulled to a six-and-a-half-game lead over the losing Cardinals and Reiser was leading the league with a .351 batting average.

All through June, Brooklyn continued to add to its lead over St. Louis. Reiser, too, clung to his lead in the race for the batting title, keeping his average drifting between .350 and .365, stratospheric air for any batter.

The Dodger fortunes were also being propelled by a lengthy 27-game

The relaxed Reiser at home, reading a novel rather than chasing fly balls (courtesy of Shirley Reiser Tuber).

hitting streak by Ducky Medwick, strongly disputing the oft-repeated supposition that the veteran slugger was washed up. Hitting more than .400 during the run, Medwick for a while threatened Reiser's batting lead and, for a couple of days, led the young center fielder by several points.

An article late in June by Arthur Patterson in the *Herald-Tribune* declared how immense the Dodger performance was over the team's first 60 games. "One must go all the way back to John McGraw's base-stealing phenoms of 1912," wrote the reporter, "to discover a National League club with a greater record over its first sixty games. The Dodgers, with forty-three victories and seventeen defeats, have topped everything the senior circuit has seen since that club, breezing to McGraw's fourth pennant, won forty-nine while losing eleven in the same span."

There was, however, a word of warning couched in this sanguine piece. One other club, Patterson pointed out, Bill Terry's 1935 Giants, could challenge the Dodgers present seven-and-a-half-game lead. "And it is a duty to warn exuberant Flatbush," Patterson continued, "that Bill Terry's 1935 team, which on the morning of June 22 led the St. Louis Cardinals by seven lengths, eventually blew the championship when they were blasted four straight by the Chicago Cubs in September."

Nonetheless, the Dodger onslaught continued. By the time of the All-Star game on July 7 the Dodger lead over the Cardinals had increased to nine and a half games. Reiser's batting average by then had surged to .361, 18 points ahead of the trailing Medwick. In a doubleheader win over the Phillies, just preceding the All-Star game, Reiser got five hits in seven tries, including a double and the game deciding home run, the young slugger's sixth of the season.

Seven Dodgers were named to the National League team that year, the most in the league. Three of them, in fact, were in the starting lineup. The starters were Vaughan, Medwick and, of course, Pistol Pete Reiser. The other Dodgers named were Wyatt, Herman, Reese and Owen.

In Reiser's second appearance in an All-Star game, this one played at the Polo Grounds, he did somewhat better than in his previous try. He collected one hit in three at bats in what turned out to be a tight pitcher's duel. The Nationals lost again, however, 3–1, with all runs coming by benefit of homers. Lou Boudreau and Rudy York hit theirs, all in the first inning, to give the junior circuit an insurmountable 3–0 lead. Mickey Owen, at least, brought some pride to the Dodgers by homering in the eighth for his team's lone score.

In tribute to former players now in uniform, the winning American League team played an All-Star team of servicemen, led by Bob Feller, on the following night in Cleveland. Once again the Americans won, this time by a score of 5–0.

Once the midseason interleague festivities were out of the way, the Dodgers continued their march toward their Promised Land. They won three out of a four-game series with the Reds at Cincinnati, two out of three from the Pirates at Pittsburgh, and two out of three from the Cubs at Chicago. Reiser missed a couple of these games with an ankle injury he suffered in the All-Star game, but he returned with a ferocity at Pittsburgh and Chicago.

The young slugger got three hits in the doubleheader with the Pirates and another three in the single game that followed. In that game, each of his hits was instrumental in the five runs the winning Dodgers earned. So, in fact, were his two stolen bases. Evidently, if he couldn't beat you one way, he would beat you another. Then there were times he would beat you both ways.

The next day he got three for three, including a double, two runs scored and another knocked in as the Dodgers destroyed the Cubs, 10–5. By this time, Reiser was batting .364 and his team was seven and a half games ahead of the Cards. Besides leading the league in batting at this point, he was leading in doubles and stolen bases and was second in hits and runs scored.

At about this time, players and writers began touting Reiser as the next .400 hitter. Ted Williams had amazingly managed .406 the previous season, and that was a feat that had not taken place since way back in 1931, when Bill Terry hit .401. To this day, it should be added, no one has accomplished it since.

During one of Reiser's batting surges, his average had gone as high as .381, and suddenly the .400 mark seemed quite conceivable. This was, after all, only his second year in the majors, and he had already jumped to another level. Even Reiser believed he could do it.

"I was just starting to get warm," he later told writer Donald Honig. "Just starting to get the bead on everybody. I could've hit .400 that year. No doubt in my mind about that."

Certainly by this time, only 23 years old and in his sophomore season, Reiser was the most outstanding player in the National League, if not in all of baseball. He was leading all players—Ted Williams, Joe DiMaggio, the rookie Stan Musial—in batting, and his startling combination of talents couldn't be matched by anyone. His sensational fielding ability, his powerful arm, his unrivaled speed on the base paths, his gutsiness and drive in every aspect of his play. This was without a doubt baseball's man of the moment.

After splitting a doubleheader with the Cubs, the Dodgers moved into St. Louis for an important four-game series with their closest rivals, now eight games back. Because of earlier rainouts, the four games were to be played as a pair of doubleheaders on consecutive days. The first pair was split, the Cards taking the initial game, 7–4, and the Dodgers coming back with a 4–3 win. Reiser, who had remained hitting-hot since his recovery from the ankle injury, had a hit in each game. He had smashed a homer in the first and a single in the nightcap, stretching his current consecutive-game hitting streak to 13 games.

On the morning of Sunday, July 19, things for the Dodgers looked as shiny as the hot St. Louis sun. Lose the pair today, and they still would be six ahead. Win just one and they would move out with the same eight-game lead they brought in. Win them both, and they could start thinking about printing those World Series tickets.

The Cardinals in those days played in old Sportsman's Park, a relic of a ball field that had been constructed a good ten years earlier than Ebbets Field. St. Louis' stadium was built back in 1902, a year before Mr. Ford introduced his Model A and Orville and Wilbur Wright took a Flyer to Kitty Hawk. The seating capacities of Sportsman's Park and Ebbets Field were within three or four thousand of each other, and the field configurations were also quite similar. A fielder could circle under a fly ball in one field and almost believe he was doing it in the other. At least, in Sportsman's Park, he knew he had more room in center field.

The St. Louis field was a little shorter in left field, a little longer in right and about 20 feet deeper at its deepest corner in center field. The walls, like those in Ebbets Field, were solid concrete. Great for leaning against and nothing more. This would be the home field for so many crucial Cardinal-Dodger matchups over the years, so many pitching duels not over till the final out, so many moments that would decide pennants and change baseball history.

But this day, which would begin with a torrid St. Louis morning and would end with the shirt-drenching mugginess of the city's twilight, a baseball moment would take place that would burn forever in the memories of those who watched and would drastically change the fortunes of the man it most effected.

The first game promised to be one of those great pitching duels between the Cardinals' Mort Cooper and the Brooklyn ace, Whitlow Wyatt. It wasn't. Neither man had it that day, but Wyatt had it less. The 35-year-old Dodger right-hander, who had pitched 12 shutouts over the past two years, gave up seven runs in less than three innings.

By the time the Dodgers went up to bat in the fourth inning, the score was already 7–0, and pretty much out of reach. The Dodgers ended up with five runs, knocking out Cooper finally in the eighth inning, but ultimately losing the game, 8–5. Reiser, too, had a losing effort at bat, going hitless in five tries. This ended his 13-game hitting streak, but by the time the second game started, he was ready to begin a new one.

Kirby Higbe and rookie sensation Johnny Beazley were the two starters in the second game. Higbe, who along with Wyatt had amassed 22 wins in 1941, had by this time taken nine games. The 24-year-old Beazley, in his first National League season, had a stunning record of 11–4.

Higbe lasted until the third inning, Beazley until the fifth. This steamy day was certainly not conducive to pitching. By the end of the fifth inning, the game was a 6–6 tie, with Curt Davis now on the mound for Brooklyn and Max Lanier, well known as a Dodger killer, going for the Cards. Reiser managed a single, and, by dint of that hit and a walk, had scored two of the Dodger runs. But that wasn't nearly enough.

The game continued without another run through the next five innings. The Cardinals had picked up only two hits during that time, the Dodgers three. The pitching duel that had been promised all day had finally arrived. But night was coming fast, the heat had barely let up, and the players were running out of play.

It was now the 11th inning, the start of the day's 20th inning, and there wasn't a dry or clean uniform on the field. Very few of the 34,000-plus fans in the stands had left. Most sat there hungering for the Cards to win and reduce that commanding Dodger lead to a less-dominating six games.

Lanier did his part in the Dodger 11th. The Dodgers went down without a threat. Curt Davis had gone out for a pinch hitter in the top half of the inning, and Johnny Allen, fresh and ready to go to work, came in to pitch for the Dodgers. Enos Slaughter was the first batter up. A solid .300 hitter since his second year for the Cards in 1939, he was close to that defining mark once again. Slaughter, however, hadn't done much in this second game, not a hit in four official at bats. He was about to make up for it.

The count went to one and two when Slaughter sailed into Allen's fast ball and smashed it far and high toward the center field wall. Reiser, playing deep for the slugger, raced for it like a tiger after its prey.

"It's a line drive directly over my head," Reiser later told Donald Honig, "and my first thought was that it could be caught. Which is pretty much the way I felt about any ball that was hit. I used to stand out there in center field and say to myself, 'hit it to me, hit it to me.' Every pitch, I wanted that ball."

"Well, if this ball isn't caught, it's a cinch triple," Reiser pointed out. A triple to open the inning and probably lead to the winning run.

His eyes glued to the ball, his legs churning for all their worth, he kept going and going, racing relentlessly for the ball and toward the danger of the impending wall. Just as the ball fell safely into his glove, he smashed his head and shoulder against the solid, unyielding concrete of the center field wall. "It was like a hand grenade had gone off inside my head," he said later.

Then, because of that horrendous impact, the ball popped out of his glove. The stunned Reiser immediately realized it and quickly picked it up.

"I relayed it to Pee Wee," he remembered. "How I did that I'll never know, but we just missed getting Slaughter at the plate. Inside the park homer."

That was the game, and the Cardinal crowd went wild. For ten maddening minutes, *The New York Times* reported, cushions were thrown onto the field and randomly tossed from section to section in the ball park as crazed fans celebrated this important doubleheader victory. The frenzied party continued despite frantic appeals from the public address system, pleading with people to stop.

And while this was taking place, Pete Reiser lay in a heap in center field. His manager, Leo Durocher, rushed out to see how he was and was relieved to learn that he was conscious and, with help, would be able to walk. Between Durocher, right fielder Frenchy Bordagaray and Reese, they were able to walk him to the clubhouse.

There Reiser, who short moments ago had stood on top of the world, immediately collapsed.

14

Nice Guys Finish Last

"I have never, ever blamed Leo for keeping me in there. I blame myself. He wanted to win so badly it hurt, and I wanted to win so bad it hurt. I've heard a lot of guys knock Leo for all sorts of things, but I've always said this about him: If you don't know him, you hate his guts, but if you do know him, you love him. He was the best."
—Pete Reiser

The name of Leo Durocher's second book of memoirs, published in 1975, was *Nice Guys Finish Last*. This was a phrase he made famous, that he was known by, and it was obviously a credo that he believed in. His earlier book, *The Dodgers and Me*, published in 1948, promised a more placid, politer appraisal of his life and attitudes.

But by 1975, the secret, if it ever was one, was out. Certainly he had revealed this belligerent frame of mind in his playing days for both the Yankees and the Cardinals. He was, after all, Mr. Gas House Gang himself. He might have been called scrappy or fiery or pugnacious or gritty or some other euphemism, but most of the players he played with or played against knew better.

From his earliest days in the Massachusetts slums, he was a hell-raiser, a troublemaker and a two-bit crook. Thrown out of school for his disruptive behavior in the ninth grade, he had barely been familiar with the word "nice." Remember, he had stolen money from his own teammates in Hartford, and while he was with the Yankees, he had purportedly swiped Babe Ruth's watch. He had alienated players everywhere, had passed rubber checks without conscience and had drunk and gambled with infamous racketeers. Now that he was a pennant-winning manager, delirious with desire to win a second time and then go on to take the whole baseball of wax, he was ready to show the world what the hell "unniceness" was all about.

And he would have more than enough help from the man who was his boss, general manager Larry MacPhail.

After the doubleheader loss to the Cardinals, Durocher and the rest of the Dodgers took a train out to Pittsburgh for a scheduled night game. But Reiser, his head heavily bandaged, had to be left behind in St. John's Hospital in St. Louis. Several newspapers had called his injury "a slight concussion" that would keep him out for a few days. *The New York Herald-Tribune* was only slightly more alarming.

"Pete Reiser, Brooklyn Dodger outfield ace," said the *Tribune*, "will be out of action a week to ten days as a result of the moderate brain concussion received yesterday."

But it really was a great deal more serious.

This was, after all, the second time in consecutive seasons that the young center fielder had crashed into an outfield wall while chasing a fly ball. To be more exact, this center fielder was not originally a center fielder. Reiser was originally an *infielder*, and an infielder of superb defensive ability, who would be allowed to become a regular on this ballclub only if he would learn to play center field, the most demanding position in the outfield. In May of the past year, he had smashed into the iron center field gate of Ebbets Field catching a ball off the bat of Cardinal Enos Slaughter. Incredibly, it was the same Enos Slaughter whose long fly ball one year later had led to Reiser's awful encounter with the wall in Sportsman's Park, this one of concrete.

The doctor attending Reiser was Robert Hyland, a noted St. Louis physician who was the Cardinal team doctor as well as Reiser's personal one. He was a highly respected orthopedist who was constantly sought out by other major league teams, including the Dodgers themselves, for difficult medical problems and injuries.

He diagnosed Reiser with a severe concussion and a fractured skull. "Look, Pete," he told the injured player, "I'm your personal friend. I'm advising you not to play any more baseball this year."

General manager MacPhail went predictably insane when he heard this. "He began screaming that Hyland was saying that just to keep me out of the lineup," Reiser later told Donald Honig. It was all a St. Louis plot, MacPhail deduced, manufactured by Branch Rickey himself so that the Cardinals could win the pennant. Forget the diagnosis, he told Reiser. MacPhail would have his own doctor take a look at him.

Reiser later said that lying in the hospital was not his cup of joy. "The injury occurred on a Sunday," he told Honig, "and on Tuesday I left the hospital. I wasn't supposed to, but I told Dr. Hyland that I had to get back to Brooklyn. I insisted on leaving, whether they liked it or not. I was kind of bullheaded. Probably still am."

Reiser remembered that the room began to spin when he first got up. But it didn't deter him. They took off his bandages and he walked out of the hospital.

The Dodgers had begun to win again while they awaited the return of their injured star. They took four straight games—from the Pirates, the Reds and the Cubs—and increased their lead over the Cardinals to seven games. During this time, news items continued to chronicle the supposed recovery of the Brooklyn star.

"Pete will leave at six o'clock tomorrow night for New York," said the *New York Times* on July 21, just a day after the report of his accident. "If the doctor's advice is followed he will rest for two or three days."

The next day's issue declared Reiser "was reported enroute to Brooklyn. He will probably sit out the next few games."

And on the following day, the rival *New York Herald-Tribune* stated that "Pete Reiser, the injured center fielder, took batting practice and said he could pinch-hit if they needed him. He also said his arm hurt more than his head after the crash in St. Louis Monday night. The arm scraped the wall."

Two days later, on July 25, just six days after the accident in St. Louis when his doctor advised him to take off the rest of the season, Pistol Pete Reiser was back in the Dodger lineup as the starting center fielder.

The Dodgers lost the game to the Pirates, 4–1, and that, combined with a Cardinal win, brought them back down to a six-game lead. But Reiser, surprisingly, got two hits in four tries. One of them knocked in the lone Brooklyn run, and a fielding gem, his shoestring catch of a low line-drive hit by second baseman Frankie Gustine, saved another. Almost lost in the excitement of his apparently successful recovery was a report by the *Times* saying that "Reiser played but suffered more dizzy spells."

The next day, the Reiser did even better. So did his teammates, defeating the Pirates in a doubleheader, 3–2 and 5–3, and moving their lead back up to seven games. Reiser played a huge part in the Dodger offensive, getting three hits, including a double, in seven at bats, scoring three runs, knocking in one and, for good measure, stealing a base.

Was it possible that Dr. Hyland had spoken too quickly?

Reiser was showing little if any effect from his collision with the wall in Sportsman's Park. And with him back in the lineup, the Dodgers continued to thrive. They beat the Cards two games out of three and the Cubs three games out of four to increase their league leading margin to nine full games.

In one game, Reiser's three-run homer providing the winning margin. In another, his long fly ball with one out in the tenth brought in Reese with the deciding run. In still another, he got three hits, including a double, in five official at bats. At one point, he had even upped his league-leading batting average to .353.

Suddenly, however, Reiser disappeared from the lineup for more than a week. It wasn't until the fifth day that a reason was given for this. "Pete Reiser wasn't in uniform," reported *The New York Herald-Tribune*. "He is suffering from headaches and is under the care of a physician."

Three days later, the same newspaper said, "Pete Reiser, still under doctor's care, wasn't with the Dodgers."

Over the years, Reiser spoke a good deal about his condition after the dreadful accident in St. Louis. "I was dizzy most of the time," he said, "and I couldn't see fly balls. I mean balls that I could have put in my pocket, I couldn't get near."

These intermittent dizzy spells and headaches were there from the start. Later came episodes of double vision, when, indeed, he would see two pitched balls coming at him while he stood at the plate.

While the press and the public were kept in mystery about Reiser's condition and his whereabouts, he had been brought to Peck Memorial Hospital in Brooklyn. After considerable examination, the doctors there concurred with Hyland's diagnosis. "The doctors," said Reiser, "suggested that I not play anymore that season."

But with Reiser out, the Dodgers had begun to lose. "MacPhail blasted the team," Reiser remembered, "accusing them of complacency. He's willing to bet that we're going to blow it. What he was trying to do, of course, was jack us up."

MacPhail, as a matter of fact, staged a conference in the Press Club room at Ebbets Field, with all his 25 players in attendance as well as the Dodger correspondent from every newspaper in New York. "One of the most unusual meetings in the history of big league baseball," *The Herald-Tribune* called it.

With this crowded room before him, MacPhail angrily berated his players for their terrible batting slump, commending only six of them for, as he put it, "carrying a glove."

The six he named were Mickey Owen, Peewee Reese, Joe Medwick, Curt Davis, Hugh Casey and, of course, the still out of action Pete Reiser.

"The Brooklyn club has paid $5,944.26 for bats," he ranted at his captured audience, "and if you fellows can't get any better use out of them than you've been getting lately maybe I could use them as fence posts on my Maryland farm."

As Reiser said, he was only trying to "jack us up." He did such a good job on Reiser that the proud and vulnerable young man volunteered to play. From his boyhood days, he had given his all when playing baseball. His all, and at any cost. That was the only way he knew how to play.

When he was still in the Cardinal organization, Branch Rickey called him into his office and took young Reiser's dogma one step further. "Young man," he told the impressionable kid, "you're the greatest young ballplayer I've ever seen, but there is one thing you must remember. Now that you're a professional ballplayer you're in show business. You will perform on the biggest stage in the world, the baseball diamond. Like the actors on Broadway, you'll be expected to put on a great performance every day, no matter how you feel, no matter whether it's hot or cold. Never forget that."

Reiser believed that Rickey was the smartest baseball man he had ever known. Of course, he would take this to his bosom and to his heart. His manager wasn't one to release him from such rules.

An incident Reiser later told about Durocher reveals how the second part of the Dodger managerial tandem worked on him. While lying in a hospital, bleary-eyed Reiser could just about make out the figure standing next to his bed. It was Durocher, who asked, "You awake?"

"Yep," answered Reiser.

"How do you feel?" asked the manager.

"How do you think I feel?" answered the suffering Reiser.

"Aw, you're better with one leg and one eye than anybody else I've got," smiled Durocher.

"Yeah," responded Reiser, "and that's the way I'll end up—on one leg with one eye."

So hungry for winning a second pennant and perhaps a World Series championship, neither Durocher nor MacPhail was going to restrain himself. Not just for the sake of this player, whose eagerness and pride had no limits, who had shown that, literally, he would attempt to crash through a wall for you. But also for their supposedly beloved Dodgers, who had a lifetime contract on this incredible player and wanted him there at his best for all his playing days.

Reiser was only 23 years old at this time, and his rashness, if not brainlessness, might be understood. He was sitting on top of the baseball world and must have felt as invincible as a Clark Kent in a Dodger uniform. As for MacPhail and Durocher, well, that's another thing.

An article in the *Tribune* at this time pointed up what Reiser's loss had meant to the team. "Drop in Brooklyn's fortunes laid to Reiser's absence," read the headline. The story said, "The recent drop in Brooklyn's fortune accentuated the value of Two Gun Reiser to the champion's forces. The men who have taken his place, Augie Galan and Johnny Rizzo, have gone 10-for-0 in these losing games and Dixie Walker, although on a hitting streak of ten straight games, is not as forbidding in the Number three spot as is the powerful Pete."

But the reporter, as well as the players on the team, hadn't the faintest idea of Reiser's real condition.

In any case, Reiser returned immediately to the lineup. Fortunately for the Dodgers, though they had won only one game while their star was out, they hadn't lost much ground. The Cards were having troubles of their own winning ball games. So by the time Reiser returned to the lineup on August 10 in a game with the friendly Phillies they were still eight games ahead of their rivals.

The Dodgers responded immediately to the return of their injured star. As the *Herald-Tribune* noted the next day: "Pete Reiser hopped back into the lineup in yesterday's dusk at Ebbets Field and the Dodgers dipped into black ink again. Pete's aid in this snipping of a three game losing streak was strictly on the morale side, Kirby Higbe's four hit pitching coming under the heading of manual labor."

Brooklyn beat the Phils, 6–0, and though Reiser failed to hit in three tries, he still had the fastest legs in baseball, and these drove him around the bases for two runs. With the Cardinals being idle, the Dodgers upped their lead to nine games.

Two days later, they won again. This time it was a 1–0 shutout against the Phils, with Larry French on the mound for the Dodgers. Reiser managed only a bunt single in four at bats, but he saved the shutout and the game on the strength of his arm. With a man on second base and two out for the Phils, he fielded a single in center field and with a great throw from his position caught the runner trying to score. "By the proverbial mile," declared the *Tribune*.

It got even better. The Dodgers took three straight games from the Braves to give them a five-game winning streak since Reiser's return. And Reiser's play was significant in each of these games. During this short run, he hit his ninth and tenth homers, a double, another bunt single, and knocked in three runs.

"Remember when way back last week when the team was in a slump?" said the *Tribune*, as it noted the Dodgers present nine-and-a-half-game lead.

Reiser went without a hit the next two games and the Dodgers without a win. The player and the team woke up in the next game as Reiser got three hits, including a double, knocked in two runs and scored three as the Dodgers trounced the Braves, 11–1. It certainly seemed that, once again, as goes Reiser, so go the Dodgers.

This game also marked the first time that Reiser batted right-handed in the major leagues. In his last at bat in the eighth inning with a south-paw pitching for the Braves, he turned around his stance and smashed a single through the middle. With the score being what it was, this might simply have been a hopeful taunt to say he was back and as good as ever.

He slammed an impressive triple against the center field wall in the next game, a 2–1 victory against the Giants. Though he still led the league in batting, his average had drifted down somewhat since his return, and was now at .338. The Cardinals, on the other hand, were drifting up. Their almost continuous winning ways brought them to seven games behind the Dodgers.

Brooklyn won three more games from the Giants, giving them a solid five game win streak with the Eastern teams. Reiser hit well in the first two of these games, before being blanked in the third one. He had three hits, including a triple, and managed to score four runs. The Dodgers, as well as Reiser, appeared ready for the coming and quite crucial four-game series with the charging Cardinals in St. Louis.

It was now late August, with only 35 games left to play in the regular season for these first-place Dodgers, six and a half games in the lead. But St. Louis, a deadly war zone, had been sheer hell for the Brooklyn club this season. It wouldn't get any better this time.

In the first game of the series, the Cards crushed the Dodgers, 7–1. Reiser batted only twice, being relieved halfway through the game, and for no announced reason, by reserve outfielder Frenchy Bordagaray. The second game was even more telling.

This was one of those many great pitching duels between Whitlow Wyatt and the Cardinals' Mort Cooper. The game was scoreless for 12 long, exhausting innings. The Cardinals finally won in the 14th inning, 2–1, with Cooper having pitched the entire game. This reduced the falling Dodger lead to a slender four and a half games.

Reiser went hitless in six tries, and more significantly, plate umpire Babe Pinelli decided during the game to confer with Durocher about Reiser's apparent physical condition. "You'd better get him out of there," he told the manager, "because he's not seeing them. I know he's not seeing them."

"I was seeing two baseballs coming up there," he later told writer W. C. Heinz. "Babe Pinelli was umpiring behind the plate, and a couple of times he stopped the game and asked me if I was all right."

Neither Durocher nor Reiser paid heed to the umpire's warning. Reiser played the rest of that game.

But Reiser was missing the following day when the Dodgers lost again to the Cards, another 2–1 losing effort, this one going ten innings. The *Tribune* explained it this way: "Durocher had to rest Pete Reiser because of his bad leg."

The Dodgers finally won the last game of the series, 4–1, and moved themselves back to a five-and-a half-game lead. Reiser, incidentally, played and went hitless in two official tries.

Brooklyn then moved on to Chicago, where they won a single game against the Cubs while the Cards won twice against the Phils. This reduced the margin between them to five games. Reiser started the game but came out after his first at bat, an unsuccessful one, and Augie Galan took his place.

Taking note of this, the *Tribune* wrote, "Pete Reiser, removed in the second inning because of his injured leg, is in the worst slump of his career. (Fifteen for 0 at this writing.)"

"Injured leg?" Was that the official Dodger euphemism for double vision?

What was surprising, however, and should also indicate how much better Reiser had been hitting than the rest of the league players, was that despite his slump, he still led the league in hitting. Though his average had come down to .328, he still led his closest pursuer, Enos Slaughter again, by four points.

The next day, the Dodgers lost to the Cubs, 4–3, and lost another game of their lead as the Cards beat the Phils once again. Reiser did not play that day, and the *Tribune* reported, "If Pete Reiser's injured leg doesn't enable him to get back into the lineup soon, he will be shipped to Johns Hopkins for an examination by Dr. George Bennett."

St. Louis crept another game closer the next day, the last day of August, as they took a doubleheader and the Dodgers split their two games with the Pirates. By now, the two teams were only three games apart, and Pistol Pete Reiser, it was reported, was on his way to see Dr. Bennett in Baltimore. Those glory days of June, July and much of August—as well as those of the young center fielder—seemed to be fast disappearing.

However, as September began, the Dodgers picked up a half game on the idle Cards while beating the Pirates, 5–4, and hope sprang anew. Durocher promised he'd still win the pennant if the Dodgers could return to Ebbets Field after Labor Day with as much as a one-game lead. "Nobody'll catch us then," he vowed, pointing out the statistics that showed the team nigh to unbeatable at home.

Reiser continued to be absent. Now he was reported to be resting at Larry MacPhail's farm, and according to the *Tribune*, "He should be as strong as a bull when he rejoins the Dodgers." Five days later he would return, and on this Sunday before Labor Day, it would appear that Durocher got his wish.

Though losing to the Giants, 7–6, the Dodgers were three games ahead of the Cardinals, two more games than the manager had requested, and with only 22 still to be played. On his return to action, Reiser managed a double in his three at bats, and, amazingly, still held the lead in the batting race at .328, five points ahead of Slaughter.

Reiser's hitting, however, continued to deteriorate. In his next 18 times at bat, he got only four hits, three of them, all singles, coming in one-half of a doubleheader. Prior to those hits, he had gotten just one in his last 26 times at the plate. His batting average had dropped to .323, six points behind the new leader, catcher Ernie Lombardi, then playing for the Boston Braves.

Perhaps it should be deemed a miracle if he could hit one pitch for a base hit when his head was spinning and his eyes saw two baseballs being thrown at him.

The Dodgers had better luck. Winning three times in five games against the Giants and Pirates, they still maintained their three-game lead, and now there were just 17 to be played.

They lost a game of their lead the next day as they were trounced by the Cubs, 10–2, while the Cardinals beat the Giants. Reiser played only the first two innings of the game, not getting a hit in his one at bat before being relieved by Augie Galan.

The Cards were now coming into Ebbets Field for a truly crucial two-game series. The teams were only two games apart, and these were the last games they'd play against each other that season. The Dodgers would need to win at least one of these to maintain their lead. They didn't. It was a disaster. The Cards took them both, and the Dodger chances by this time seemed razor slim.

The first Cardinal victory was a 3–0 three-hit shutout, pitched by their powerful ace, Mort Cooper, in another of his great duels with Whitlow Wyatt. St. Louis followed that with another masterful pitching performance, this one by left-hander Max Lanier, as the Cards won, 2–1. Reiser, evidently suffering badly from headaches and dizziness, played neither game. Even the management, it seemed, sometimes knew when to stop.

The two teams were now tied, the first time in 144 days that the Dodgers were not the sole possessors of first place. But all the momentum, for certain, was with the Cardinals. As their team's president, Sam Breadon, gloated, "I think we're in. We've won twenty-eight out of thirty-three games and those fellows have lost five of their last eight."

"Those fellows" surely looked lost, and they got loster and loster.

Pete Reiser gave it another try in a doubleheader with the Reds on the following day, and in each game he managed a hit in four at bats. It didn't help much. The Dodgers lost them both, 6–3 and 4–1. The Cardinals, by winning one of their two games, gained a full hold on first place. The Dodgers were now one game behind, resting meekly in second place.

Two items in the *Tribune*'s coverage of these games also bore out what Reiser later said about his dizziness having caused inadequacies in his fielding. "Tipton was credited with a triple," said the *Tribune*, "as Pete Reiser, fearful of a collision with Walker, let the ball drop out of his glove after a long run."

The paper also described "a knockout three run double by Walters, the ball carrying past Reiser in right center."

Before this, very few balls went past this sterling outfielder, and still fewer, without benefit of a collision, had popped out of his glove.

The Cards continued to increase their lead with two victories over the Phillies while the Dodgers were idle. A day later, the Dodgers, as well as Reiser, showed some life. Brooklyn beat the Pirates, 10–3, and Reiser looked like the Reiser of old. He got three hits, including a double, in five tries. He knocked in two runs and scored three—accounting for half the Dodger total—and as an added dividend, he stole a base.

Evidently, his dizziness occurred intermittently. This, however, did little to dispel the verdict of the two doctors who recommended he give up playing the remainder of the season to ensure his complete recovery.

For the moment, and for the day, his performance raised Reiser's steadily declining batting average to .321, now second in the league race to Ernie Lombardi's .332. It is interesting—and painful—to note that of the five leading batters that day, four would go on to the Hall of Fame. These were Lombardi, Stan Musial, Enos Slaughter and Joe Medwick. Only Reiser would miss that honor.

But the Cardinals, it seemed, had forgotten how to lose. Even as the Dodgers beat the Phils, 5–4, in 11 innings on September 19, St. Louis had a two-and-a half-game lead with little more than a week to play.

The win over Philadelphia was an all–Reiser show. His clutch single with the bases loaded in the second inning had knocked in the Dodgers' first two runs. After he fielded a single in the tenth, his throw had cut down the potential winning run as the base runner tried to score from second. And his walk with the bases loaded in the 11th knocked in the winning run.

Yet, even with the Dodgers ending the season with an eight-game winning streak, they would get no more than a half game closer.

Reiser would have only three more Reiser-like games that season, and all on consecutive days. He would get a pair of hits and two runs batted in in a 9–8 win over the Giants and follow that the next day with three hits, including a double and two batted-in runs as the Dodgers beat the Phils, 6–0. Once again the next day he would get a pair of hits and a stolen base while knocking in one run and scoring another as the Dodgers beat the Braves, 5–3.

But he finished the season without a hit in his last 14 attempts, and his once lofty batting average, which had thrived for awhile in the .380's, had dwindled to .310. This was still high enough to be fourth in the league, but miles away from what could have been. Since his crash with the Sportsman's Park wall, he had hit less than .200. And this accomplished with chronic headaches and intermittent bouts with dizziness.

He did, by the way, lead the league in one department that year. Reiser's 20 stolen bases, perhaps minuscule in comparison to those swiped in later years, was enough to make him the National League's champion.

The Dodgers, though winning their last eight games and amassing an amazing 104 victories for the season—more than any previous Dodger team had ever won—lost the pennant to the Cardinals by two games.

The dream had burst back on July 19 with Reiser's vain and valiant effort to save a ball game. And with the foolishly stubborn resistance of Durocher and MacPhail to removing their once-in-a-lifetime prize from the lineup.

Branch Rickey was once asked what he thought of MacPhail's handling of Reiser during these times. "That character," he said, "should never have been entrusted with anything that fine."

That seemed perfectly evident. What wasn't certain was whether this young star could return to his previous greatness?

15

Men of War

"Pete Reiser may have been born to be the best baseball player that ever lived, but there never was a park big enough to contain his effort."
— Red Smith, *Los Angeles Herald-Examiner*

Once the pennant race was deemed over in 1942, Larry MacPhail was in a rush to get out of Brooklyn. Actually, there were still three games left to be played—and, mathematically, at least, the Dodgers were still alive—when MacPhail resigned as general manager and president of the Brooklyn baseball club. In an announcement before a roomful of reporters, he said that he had volunteered his services to the United States Army and was awaiting his commission.

During World War I, MacPhail had been an officer in the Army as well as a bit of a misguided adventurer. Soon after the Armistice had been declared, he headed a group of fellow officers who attempted to kidnap the German Kaiser, who had by then taken refuge in The Netherlands. Fortunately for everyone, they failed. Success could have earned MacPhail a court-martial and caused the Western World a nasty international incident.

Actually, MacPhail's group almost succeeded. They got as far as the castle, where the former German leader had been staying, but, thank goodness, Kaiser Wilhelm wasn't home at the time. MacPhail took a souvenir for these efforts, an ashtray stamped with the Kaiser's seal, which he always displayed prominently on his desk.

As for MacPhail's rejoining the Army, it appears the Dodger management had moved first. The executives of the Brooklyn Trust Company had already informed MacPhail that his contract would not be renewed.

They were simply letting him save face with the preemptive announcement of his enlistment. Before this, the owners had decided they were tired of his inordinate spending and were disenchanted with the unstable ways he had been running the club.

The final blow, it seems, had been MacPhail's purchase late in the season of Bobo Newsom for $25,000 from the Washington Senators. Newsom, a veteran pitcher who had played for more teams than a clubhouse has lockers, was supposed to ensure the Dodgers' winning of the pennant that year. He had managed for Brooklyn a mediocre 2–2 record that certainly brought no pennant.

Peter Golenbock, in his book *Bums*, suggests that MacPhail's firing had more to do with his not showing enough profit for his expenditures. "The Age of the Bottom Line was slowly eating away at the business of baseball," Golenbock wrote. "Stockholders were the ones calling the shot, and the bottom line in Brooklyn was that, because of MacPhail's extravagant spending, they were not getting big enough dividend checks."

In any case, once the season was over, MacPhail went off to the Army as a colonel, and troops of players soon followed his lead. The rosters of many teams would be depleted by the following season. Wartime baseball, of much inferior quality with overage players and others still in their teens, would slowly take over.

Gone by the start of the 1943 season were such important stars as Ted Williams, Joe and Dom DiMaggio, Tommy Henrich, Cecil Travis, Enos Slaughter, Johnny Mize, Phil Rizzuto.

The Dodgers had lost Cookie Lavagetto the season before, but this year, as expected, Pee Wee Reese would be gone. As was not expected, so was Pete Reiser.

He should never have been drafted. Much later on, Reiser explained to writer Donald Honig the strange string of mishaps that had gotten him into the Army. Soon after the season was over, Reiser had tried to enlist in the Navy and was declared 4-F, ineligible for health reasons. Because of his many baseball injuries, including several concussions, he was told that "no induction center in the country" would accept him.

For Reiser, who had been deferred earlier as the sole support of his parents and his siblings, this had to have been welcome news. He now had a new bride to support, too, and this might be the first year he could earn a substantial paycheck. His physical condition, of course, would make it impossible for him to serve in any combat or overseas capacity.

But by mid–December, the Army called him, and he reported to an induction center for his exam. He was given a complete physical and then led to the area where the rejects were placed. Reiser sat there for about an hour till he heard his name being called.

"Is there a Harold Reiser here?" a captain shouted out.

"Yes, sir," Reiser responded, expecting that he was about to be given his release.

"Goddamn, boy," exclaimed the captain, "why don't you use your right name when you come into this man's army?"

"What are you talking about?" responded Reiser.

"Aren't you Pete Reiser, the ball player?" asked the captain.

"Yes, sir," said Reiser.

"Goddamn," the captain repeated. "Your papers have Harold Patrick. So you're trying to pull a fast one, are you? At a time like this, with a war going on, you came in here under a false name. What do you mean giving your name as Harold Patrick Reiser?"

"Pete's my nickname," Reiser tried to explain, and the captain stared at him suspiciously.

"What are you going to do if we let you go?" asked the captain finally.

"Play ball," said Reiser.

The captain turned around and spoke to a nearby sergeant. "Sergeant," he said, "fingerprint this guy and induct him."

On January 13, 1943, Reiser, who should never have been in service, was inducted into the Army and sent to Fort Riley, Kansas. "First two days there," he told Honig, "we're put on a 50-mile forced march, full pack. It's fifteen below zero. I catch pneumonia. I don't know where I'm at and care less."

Reiser awoke in an Army hospital, and a doctor, who had been studying his record, came by to speak to him.

"How long you been in the Army, son?" the doctor asked him.

"Three weeks," Reiser answered.

"How'd you ever get in?" the puzzled doctor asked.

"They told them to fingerprint me and induct me," said Reiser.

"You'll be out in two weeks," the doctor said and walked away.

With Reiser's luck, of course, he wasn't. One day soon after this, while waiting for his medical discharge, a voice roared out his name over the public address system and ordered him to report to camp headquarters.

Reiser followed orders and found himself at the desk of an officer. "He tells me who he is," Reiser explained to Honig, "Colonel so-and-so, graduate of West Point. I don't know why he's telling me all this. Then he says, 'One of the greatest things in my life is that I'm a sports fan. I've followed all sports, but my love is baseball.'"

By this time, Reiser knew he was in trouble.

"You wouldn't happen to be related to Pete, would you?" the colonel then asked.

"Yes, sir," Reiser answered.

"You're not Pete, are you?" said the wide-eyed colonel. And by now Reiser knew he was in very big trouble.

"You know," the colonel smiled, "I've always wanted to meet you."

"Thank you," replied Reiser.

"I've got your papers right here," the colonel went on, glancing down at Reiser's discharge papers sitting on his desk. "They want to discharge you. It's up to me to sign them or not. Tell me, what happens if I sign?"

"I'll probably play center field for the Dodgers," Reiser answered.

"I was looking forward to having a hell of a ballclub here in Fort Riley," said the colonel. "Now do you really want to go back to Brooklyn? The war's going bad, you know. I think it would be a shame if you left the Army. No, I'm not going to sign this."

He picked up the papers and, right in front of the young man's face, he tore them to pieces. Years later, Reiser said that he could still hear the sound of the awful tearing of those papers. "You don't like that, do you?" the colonel said to Reiser in a self-satisfied taunt.

"I didn't say anything, did I?" said Reiser stoically. "Just tell me what I'm supposed to do."

There was nothing for Reiser to do. The colonel would take care of everything. And if he had to be in service, Reiser was granted an ideal way of serving. He was given a private room in the barracks with no Army duties to perform. He was given a pass that would allow him to go anywhere he chose. And he was given, without tryout, the center field position on the Fort Riley team.

For two years he played for this team, which included such players as Joe Garagiola, Lonnie Frey, Frank Crespi, Harry Walker, Alpha Brazle, Murry Dickson, Rex Barney and Ken Heintzelman. At one time, in fact, there were 17 major leaguers on the club. The National League's Near-All-Stars, it would seem. And, according to Reiser, "We whomped everybody we played."

The team scheduled four games a week, playing at night and usually for war plant workers in the Wichita area. In their first year, they took the national and semipro titles. Finally, however, this Fort Riley team was so overwhelming in beating the other teams in the tournament that an order was given by Washington to break up the club.

While Reiser was still at Camp Lee, his wife, Patricia, gave birth to their first child, a daughter named Sally. Once the baby was born, he was granted leave to return to St. Louis, where Patricia was staying with her parents. There the family reunited, if only for a few days, to enjoy this joyous event.

It is ironic to note that the Reeses had their first child, and also a daughter, at just about this same time. Apparently, the Gold Dust Twins were still connected as if by some invisible cord.

"Considering what a lot of other guys did in the war, " Reiser later told writer W. C. Heinz, "I had no complaints. But five times I was up for discharge, and each time something happened. From Riley they sent me to Camp Livingston. From there they sent me to New York Special Services for twelve hours and I end up in Camp Lee, Virginia."

Reiser expected that there he would at last be discharged. By this time, it was May 1945, the European War was over, and the one in the Pacific was in its final days.

Reiser was immediately called in to speak to the camp general, who greeted him with a warm smile and an effusive hello. "Reiser, I saw you on the list," he told him, "and I just couldn't pass you up."

"What about my discharge?" asked the weary young man.

Reiser being carried off the field, a regular occurrence in his major league career as well as during his years in the Army (National Baseball Hall of Fame Library, Cooperstown, N.Y.).

"That will have to wait," answered the general. "I have a lot of celebrities down here, but I want a good baseball team."

This was a team that included the Yankees' Johnny Lindell and the White Sox's Dave Philley, and Reiser was the third man in that outfield. Even during his days in the Army, Reiser couldn't keep away from the outfield walls. Several times he crashed against Army field fences, but these, at least, were made of wood. But during a game at Camp Lee, he chased a foul fly ball from his left field position, broke through a wooden fence and tumbled down a 25-foot hill.

"I came to in the hospital," Reiser recalled, "with a dislocated right shoulder."

The commanding general came in to visit him. "That was one of the greatest displays of courage I've ever seen," he told Reiser, "to ignore your future in baseball just to win a ball game for Camp Lee."

It didn't matter where or for whom or for what reason, Reiser proved once again that this was the only way he knew how to play the game. And this injury, in the service of Camp Lee, would come back to haunt him, and haunt him incessantly.

Finally, the war was over and Reiser was still at Camp Lee. "By this time, I've got enough points to get out," Reiser told Honig. "I don't need a medical discharge."

But by this time, servicemen were being selected as entertainers for the overseas troops in Europe, and Reiser was chosen as one of them. For this assignment, Reiser did need a physical.

"I walk in," remembered Reiser, "and there's a colonel sitting at a desk going over my papers. He's got a chestful of medals and ribbons and battle stars. He's been through it all. I look at that chest, and I figure I'm gone."

The colonel looked at Reiser, turned again to his papers and finally blurted out, "How the goddamn hell! For three years you've been putting up with this crap?"

Reiser remained stone silent.

"You come with me," he ordered him.

"I went with him," said Reiser, "and he signed some papers and said to a sergeant, 'I want this man discharged in twenty-four hours.'"

Reiser was out the next day. It was January 1946, and this ordeal was over. After the unleashing of MacPhail and Durocher and a veritable war council of narrow-minded, baseball happy Army officers, Reiser must have felt like the biblical Job in baseball regalia. He had been through it all and had more or less passed muster. His body had been badly bruised, his head had been battered, but his spirit was alive and he was still kicking.

Now he would finally be going home and back to the Dodgers, where an important change had taken place. Branch Rickey, the man who had first uncovered this baseball treasure and had done his best to have Reiser returned to him, was now running things for the Brooklyn club.

Was it time, at last, for retribution?

16

The Men Come Home

"Here was a man who was once hailed as 'a second Ty Cobb.' It's an extravagant superlative that is constantly misapplied. But in the case of Pistol Pete, it came close to being justified."
—Arthur Daley, sports columnist
for *The New York Times*

The Dodgers didn't fare well during baseball's war years. Unlike the Cardinals, who lost Enos Slaughter and Terry Moore and kept almost everyone else including Stan Musial, the Brooklyn veterans couldn't keep up with the traffic. Actually, neither could any of their youngsters. The Cards, too, still had their remarkable farm system infusing them with new blood that, in many cases, was superior to the old. They won the pennant in 1943 and 1944, and barely lost out the following year to the Cubs, when Musial finally entered service.

On the other hand, Brooklyn finished in third place on two occasions, and in 1944, in a dismal seventh, just a game and a half ahead of the cellar-dwelling Phillies. Thank goodness for Dixie Walker during those years. He gave Brooklyn a modicum of dignity. He led the league in batting in 1944, hitting .357, ten points ahead of Musial. Walker hit over .300 the other two seasons and along the way became the Dodgers' favorite player. "The Peepul's Cherce" is what they called him, and he would retain that name for the rest of his days as a Dodger.

It is fascinating to note that in the American League in 1944 the pennant was won by the St. Louis Browns, baseball's perennial weakest link. This was the only time the team ever managed to win the flag, and it was primarily because of an obvious bit of circumstance. The Browns enjoyed baseball's largest number of 4-F's, those deemed ineligible for service, and they eked out the pennant by a single-game margin over the Tigers. There were 18 4-F's, by the way, on that team, and one of them even hit .300.

By 1943, Branch Rickey had become general manager of the Dodgers and had introduced his methods of running a ballclub, so different from MacPhail's. MacPhail had been a checkbook executive while running the Dodgers. He would search other teams' rosters, then refer to his checking account, or at least to the line of credit the Brooklyn Trust Company had granted him, and purchase the ones whom he had money to buy. But just like old suits, these soon would be past their prime and ready for disposal.

Rickey built from the bottom up. He had developed the best farm system in baseball for the Cardinals and was pledged to do much the same for Brooklyn. That would take some doing, of course, but in time he would accomplish this. Later Brooklyn teams were by and large made up of players that came up through this newly constructed system. Like Duke Snider, Gil Hodges, Carl Erskine and Carl Furillo. And then with an assist from the Negro Leagues, such players as Jackie Robinson, Roy Campanella, Joe Black and Don Newcombe.

Soon after taking control of the team, Rickey began cleaning house of the older players MacPhail had corraled. Joe Medwick, Dolf Camilli and Johnny Allen, in two separate trades, were sent to the Giants, though Camilli refused to report and decided to retire instead. Whitlow Wyatt, at the age of 37, was sold to the Phillies and, within half a season, also chose to retire.

But in 1946, the Dodgers, like the rest of the teams in both leagues, waited passionately if not patiently for their stars in service to return. Pete Reiser, Pee Wee Reese, Cookie Lavagetto, Billy Herman, Mickey Owen and Kirby Higbe would all be back from wartime duties and on the Dodger roster. In the National League, such players as Johnny Mize, Enos Slaughter, Terry Moore, Hal Schumacher, Johnny Vander Meer and Babe Young would all be trading their service uniforms for those of their baseball clubs.

The American League had an equally impressive group. Joe DiMaggio, Ted Williams, Dick Wakefield, Joe Gordon, Bobby Doerr, Johnny Pesky, Luke Appling, Bill Dickey, Tex Hughson and Stan Spence would all be back with their teams. Hank Greenberg, who had been inducted as early as the start of the 1941 season, had come back in midseason in 1945, and had led the Detroit Tigers to the American League pennant and their subsequent World Championship against the Cubs.

This, finally, would be a return to prewar standards, erasing from memory the freakishness of the past three years. No more midgets at the plate seeking bases on balls, no more 16-year-old shortstops, no more one-arm outfielders.

The boys were back!

The Dodger training camp in early February 1946 was held in Sanford, Florida. Leo Durocher, who had remained as field manager of the team all through the war years, was still at the helm and in a much different relationship with his general manager. Instead of the whiskey-guzzling, belligerent MacPhail, Durocher was now dealing with the Bible-toting and, yes, Bible-quoting Branch Rickey.

In his book *Nice Guys Finish Last*, Durocher tells of a discussion he had with Rickey about one of their carousing minor league pitchers. Rickey, who had been defending the man, said, "Luke. Chapter Fifteen, verse eleven. 'A certain man had two sons...'"

Durocher sat there stunned as Rickey quoted the entire parable of The Prodigal Son, presumably about this pitcher, but, as the manager really knew, actually pointed at him.

"Like most good men," Durocher wrote, "he wanted other men to be better than they were. Unlike most good men, he found it unthinkable to intrude upon another man's private life."

As Durocher might say, this was a helluva difference from the other guy.

The Dodger camp opened with a good amount of optimism. One hundred fifty-eight players reported to camp that season, most of whom were former servicemen. Several of the new players, most of them nurtured by the expanding Rickey farm system, caused a lot of excitement and a lot of press.

One day there was a Marvin Rackley who caught the eye of some writer and the lip of Leo Durocher. Another day it was a Stan Rojek. Still another it was a pitcher named Johnny Van Cuyk or his brother Chris or a lefty named Paul Minner. None of whom, by the way, would much help the Dodger cause that year.

There was also much talk in camp about the newly discharged players, stars and superstars of 1942 who would be donning their Dodger uniforms again. Several had signed contracts and had shown up early. A few others had not signed and, apparently, were unreachable at their various homes.

Pee Wee Reese, who had been in the Navy, signed and delivered himself early. He had played considerable baseball as a shortstop on a team managed by Yankee star catcher Bill Dickey and had then gone on to manage a Marines squad of his own in the Pacific. Dickey, in fact, had been quoted as saying that Reese was even better now than he had been back in 1941 when the Yankees played against him in the World Series.

Most of the holdouts didn't faze the Dodger management. "I have only one player," said Rickey, "with whom I may have difficulty in getting him to sign." *The New York Times* speculated as to who that might be. "That man is Pete Reiser," said the newspaper, "who is still in his home in St. Louis."

Two quite spectacular events became the talk of that spring-training year, both in a way precipitated by the end of the war and the return of players from service. A rival Mexican League was started by a pair of Mexican multimillionaire brothers, Jorge and Bernardo Pasquel, who were purported to be worth well over sixty million dollars. Between their money and that of a group of other very wealthy Mexican investors, there was said to be over a hundred million dollars supporting this venture.

Several of their agents searched through the major league camps that spring in an attempt to lure players south of the border to join this upstart organization. More money—and, in many cases, *much* more money—than the players' major league salaries was offered as means to entice their move.

The two brothers had some early success. They got one of the Dodgers' best hitters of the war years, Luis Olmo, Puerto Rican by birth, to make the jump. He was soon joined by Brooklyn's All-Star catcher, Mickey Owen, once he had been released from the Navy. At that time, Vern Stephens, a standout shortstop for the St. Louis Browns, was perhaps the biggest name to be recruited. He had led the American League in home runs the past year and had hit close to .300 in each of the four years he had been in the league.

One of the brothers' most interesting acquisitions was hard-throwing pitcher Sal Maglie, who had first entered the major leagues, as a 28-year-old with the New York Giants in 1945. Four years after this, he would be a brilliant pitcher for the Giants and later for the Dodgers and would eventually pitch for all three New York teams.

In 1946, the Mexican League seemed to pose a very dangerous threat to baseball. In an attempt to counter this, the commissioner, Albert B. "Happy" Chandler by then, announced that baseball would welcome back all players who returned before the start of the season. Those who stayed away beyond that time, he vowed, would be banned for five years.

The Mexican League remained a threat to major league baseball through all of that season. This, even though several American players, like Stephens and Owen, quickly returned to the United States. Many of these players—or their wives or their children—found living in Mexico not all they had hoped it to be. Others, however, like Maglie and Olmo, decided too late and were banned from major league baseball for years afterward.

The more significant, more permanent and certainly more historical happening that spring was the addition of Jackie Robinson and pitcher John Wright to the roster of Brooklyn's Triple A farm team, the Montreal Royals. These would be the first Negro players since early in the 20th century to be considered as candidates for a major league team. Defying any unwritten agreement—its existence, of course, denied with straight face by anyone connected with baseball—Branch Rickey dared to overturn this rotten applecart

This first step to erase baseball's racial barrier was being met by surprising and quite nasty resistance, which was indeed an omen of what was to come. Five games that spring training season were called off because of the presence of these players on the Montreal squad.

A game with Indianapolis at Deland, Florida, was cancelled supposedly because "a test of the lighting system revealed that repairs, involving digging up of the cables under the field, would take two days to complete."

"That's the reason they gave," said General Manager Mel Jones, of the Royals, "but you can interpret things to suit yourself."

Other cancellations were much more honestly explained, if not also more offensively so. Three games were called because so-called "mixing of players" was not legally allowed in that area. This hardly stalled Branch Rickey, who marched on with his mission.

It is worthwhile to note that the Pasquel brother saw what was happening with Robinson. In mid–March, they offered $6,000 to the young shortstop, probably a lot more than his Dodger contract had called for, to join their league. But Robinson turned them down. "There's too much at stake for me right here," said Robinson. "I wouldn't accept an offer that involved as much money as they offered Ted Williams." (An offer, by the way, that was put at about $150,000.)

On April 4 it was announced that two more Negro players were assigned to the Dodger farm system. These were Don Newcombe, a 22-year-old pitcher from Elizabeth, New Jersey, and Roy Campanella, a 25-year-old from Philadelphia, who was said to be the best catcher in the Negro Leagues. They were assigned to the Nashua, New Hampshire, minor league team of the Dodgers.

It is significant to note that two of the first four Negro players signed, Robinson and Campanella, went on to being named to the Baseball Hall of Fame, each after significantly illustrative careers. A third, Newcombe, if not for some significant drinking problems during his playing days, would most assuredly have also been elected. Three times he won 20 or more games, once as many as 27, and in a fourth season he won 19.

But the historic process all began back in the 1946 spring-training season. This, too, taking place while the Dodger club of that year attempted to assimilate its returning stars with its young rookie hopefuls and its wartime veterans and meld them into a contending ballclub.

There were, indeed, several significant rookie players who emerged that year. Three young outfield hopefuls, Carl Furillo, Gene Hermanski and Dick Whitman, all seemed important prospects, and Furillo, certainly, would become a Dodger star for long years. Pitcher Joe Hatten, a hard-throwing left-hander who had built a reputation for himself while in service, was a vital addition to the Dodger pitching staff. And Bruce Edwards, who came up to the team in midseason, would be an All-Star catcher and later an infielder for Brooklyn for many years.

The Gold Dust Twins, Reese and Reiser—Reese still only 28, Reiser a year younger—were certainly the two most important returnees. Reese had already won Durocher's heart with his early signing and his magnificent play in spring training. Almost 15 pounds heavier than when he went into the Navy, Reese was also swinging a much heavier bat. "I don't know if my weight has anything to do with my hitting," he said, "but I hope I can keep it up."

Many observers believed Reese was the equal of the two supposed standouts at his position, Marty Marion of the Cards and Eddie Miller of the Reds. Durocher believed Reese was superior to either of them. To Durocher, Reese was the best shortstop in all of baseball.

The other half of this dynamic duo, Pete Reiser, however, remained unsigned most of that spring. As late as March 7 *The New York Post* reported, "Pete Reiser brooding furiously on his Missouri farm." But Reiser did not brood alone. His fatherly boss, Branch Rickey himself, went out to see the disgruntled young man and obviously soothed his wounds. Rickey soon returned, Reiser's signed contract clutched in his fist.

By March 12 Reiser reported to camp in Daytona Beach. "The big bat that conceivably can pace the Dodgers to their second pennant in twenty-six years," wrote the *Post*'s reporter Arch Murray, "was back in the Brooklyn rack today after three long years in the Army. Pete Reiser came back in the fold last night, his stubborn holdout siege ended and his sights trained on the batting championship he won in 1941."

"Reiser's return," the writer went on, "comes at a time that finds the Dodger attack at a low ebb, held to a total of fifteen hits in losing three straight exhibitions to the A's, Giants and Phillies. He promises to supply the punch that has been missing down here in the grapefruit glens."

A few days later a far more optimistic story by that same reporter appeared. "Reiser still clouts them" read the headline. The story began,

Pete Reiser (left), Dixie Walker and rookie Carl Furillo in a rare snapshot of the Dodger outfield of 1946 (courtesy of Shirley Reiser Tuber).

"It looked as though he'd never been away three years in the Army, had added no rust to his rhythmic swing nor taken any of the quicksilver from his flying spikes. Pete Reiser, making his postwar debut in his Dodger flannels, was his old ball-busting self all over again."

Murray became even more expansive. "The box score," he continued, "revealing a perfect day at bat, tells only part of the answer. There was the grace and ease that cold figures never show and the sure-handed touch of the professional. In the flick of an eyelash one could see why he was rated one of the greats of the game before he was siphoned into the maw of GI life."

Leo Durocher added the manager's two cents. "Predictions are a dime a dozen this time of the year," said Durocher, "but I think Pete is a great bet to win the batting championship. He's certain to hit between .335 and .360. If he's closer to the latter figure he'll likely wrap it up."

Reiser elicited these paeans after only three days of practice. In a single day's work, he smashed three solid hits, coaxed three walks and stole a base under a hot Georgia sun. It sure looked like he was on his way back. All the way back.

But a few days later it suddenly didn't appear that easy. In a game at Orlando, Reiser suffered a separation of the clavicle and sternum while swinging a bat. It was expected that he would be out of action for from ten days to three weeks. What most distressed the Dodger trainer, Doc Wendler, was that this was the same injury Reiser suffered while in the Army when he crashed through a fence and rolled dangerously down a hill at Camp Lee.

"He may never be able to throw as hard as he did before the war," the Dodger trainer warned.

Durocher tried to sweep away all concern. "He won't have to at third," reasoned the manager. "That's one of the reasons I'm putting him there. He'll be in the lineup even if he can't throw a lick."

There had been talk that spring about just where the returning slugger would play. There were, after all, the three outfield prospects—Carl Furillo, Gene Hermanski and Dick Whitman—as well as the still well-functioning Dixie Walker and Augie Galan.

The infield was where problems seemed to lie. Reese, of course, was set at short, but an injury to the third baseman, Cookie Lavagetto, was expected to keep him out of action for weeks. Speculation arose as to whether Billy Herman or Reiser would play third, with the other going to second. Now that Reiser was back, the team had enormous flexibility.

As opening day drew near, predictions for the pennant race began to appear. Eddie Dyer, the new Cardinal manager, believed the Dodgers were the team to beat. "Most people are picking the Cubs (pennant winners of 1945) as our chief stumbling block," said Dyer, "but I don't agree with them. The Cubs have pretty much the same team as last year's war-time outfit. But the Dodgers have three good pitchers—Kirby Higbe, Joe Hatten and Ed Head—as well as a couple of pretty fair ball players named Reese and Reiser. My scouts tell me they also have some good looking youngsters."

The nationally syndicated columnist Jimmy Cannon said, "I like the Dodgers. If Pete Reiser's arm holds up and they get a catcher, I can't see how you can keep them out of second place. They won't make trouble for the Cards, but they'll do all right for themselves."

Leo Durocher, who declined most years to make a prediction, made one at the start of this season. "If Pete Reiser's arm enables him to play every day and we can add a little heavy power to the batting order," said Durocher, "we can beat the Cardinals and win the flag."

Eventually, he said, he wanted to "play Lavagetto at third, Herman at second and put Reiser back in center field where he belongs."

Then it was time to play ball, and time to see whether Pistol Pete Reiser—wherever he would eventually play—would be the Pistol Pete Reiser of golden memory.

17

Home Is for the Stealing

"Young man, you're the greatest young ball player I've ever seen."
—Branch Rickey to Pete Reiser

The Mexican League didn't go away as quickly as many had expected, or to be more precise, as major league owners had hoped. For too long during the 1946 season, it loomed large like a 16-armed monster, ready to scoop up a premier star from one team or another. Every now and then, the monster seemed less dangerous as an American player, once caught up in its enticements, grew disenchanted and grabbed the next plane back home. Still the money that was offered, and there were tons of it, was far more attractive than the Yankee dollar. Or, for that matter, the Dodger or the Cardinal dollar.

In mid–April, Rud Rennie, one of the newspaper's foremost reporters, wrote an article in *The New York Herald Tribune* evaluating the league and its threat. "Mexican baseball," he wrote, "is equivalent to that played in— Oh, maybe a Class A league here in the States. That's probably giving them a little the best of it."

The ballparks, he said, "are as primitive as our own minor league parks which are made of wood." Rennie also pointed out that the air in Mexico is so thin that a baseball hit by one of our sluggers would simply keep on flying for as much as 700 feet.

He indicated that the Mexican League's present method was not to develop its own players or to get youngsters from our country that it could slowly develop into stars. Instead, it was fixed on the moment and on acquiring some of the best and more established of the American stars.

146

But so far, said Rennie, the Mexican League had "not been able to acquire the finest quality."

However, he concluded, the league did have over one hundred million dollars at its disposal and, "if they can get one top player, at $125,000, they'd have a chance."

Many wondered as that season began if the Mexicans would get their wish.

In the Dodger camp, much wondering was over the fate of Cookie Lavagetto and his ailing arm. The Dodgers' returning third baseman would be operated on, and he would therefore be sidelined for the season's first six weeks. Performing the operation would be none other than Dr. Robert F. Hyland, the noted bone surgeon from St. Louis.

This was, of course, the same Dr. Robert F. Hyland whom former general manager MacPhail refused to believe when the doctor suggested that Reiser take the rest of the 1942 season off after his harrowing crash against the wall in Sportsman's Park. MacPhail had shamelessly called Hyland an agent for the Cardinals. The Dodger general manager had suggested that the hiatus he had prescribed had been merely a plot to keep Reiser off the playing field and help the Cards win the pennant. What a difference a general manager makes!

But for all the talk as to where Reiser would play that year, the young man did not start at any position in the first game of the season. Utility infielder Lew Riggs was at third base, Billy Herman was at second base, and the rookie Carl Furillo patrolled center field. The Dodgers, incidentally, lost inauspiciously to the Braves in Boston, 5–3.

Reiser, however, made his first start, and that at third base, in the very next game. He batted cleanup, got a pair of hits, and the Dodgers this time beat the Braves, 4–2, behind the pitching of Hank Berhman, one of the team's benchful of rookies. This began an eight-game winning streak—and what a superb trail of games these were—that vaulted them into first place, a game ahead of their expected rivals, the St. Louis Cardinals.

In a victory over the Giants, Reiser stole three bases, including a daredevil swipe of home. "Which Reiser stole with ease," reported *The New York Herald-Tribune*, "after faking (Jack) Brewer into a false sense of security by running halfway down the line on a previous pitch."

Reiser's swipe of home, this rather rare feat, proved just the first of a marvelous string of steals of home he accomplished that season. What other speedsters had done once or twice in a career, he would turn into a magnificent habit. No one ever before had dared to steal this elusive base—squarely in front of the pitcher's eyes and in direct conflict with his pitch to the plate—with the consistency of Reiser.

This was yet another bit of artistry in his arsenal that would awe the baseball public into utter disbelief. What this did to the opposing pitcher and his teammates was something else. There was tension and trouble in the air when Reiser was on first or second. Now on third, he was the devil incarnate.

Several days later, Reiser was once again instrumental in the Dodger cause, as they beat the Braves, 5–4, in ten innings. Reiser got four hits that day, including a pair of doubles, one of which knocked in two runs to tie the score in the ninth inning. There was another stolen base in his totals which, by this time, gave him the early National League lead in that department.

There was a major outbreak of joy in Flatbush one day later. Ed Head, the promising young right-hander, newly back from service, pitched a brilliant no-hitter against the Braves, winning 5–0, with much hitting and fielding help from Reiser. This was, incidentally, the first no-hitter for Dodger pitching since 1940, when Tex Carleton had thrown one against the Reds.

"My biggest scare," He said afterward, "came in the eighth inning when (Whitey) Wietelmann lined to Pete Reiser. I figured it was all over. I didn't think Pete had a chance to make the catch."

Reiser made the catch, saving the no-hitter, and had added a pair of hits that scored one run and knocked in another.

Reiser hit his first home run of the season in the very next game to score the Dodgers' first run in a runaway romp over the Phillies. He added a double to his totals that day, and it appeared that Reiser was very much the Reiser of old. He was hitting, he was fielding, he was stealing bases as never before, and he was sparking the Dodgers in an early run for the pennant. By the end of April, he was hitting over .400, and the scars of all those injuries seemed almost to disappear.

Meanwhile, the Pasquel brothers and their upstart Mexican League had struck again. And soon, and quite suddenly, it began hitting home in Brooklyn. Catcher Mickey Owen, who had earlier jumped to the Mexican League and then had decided to return home, changed his mind once again. Fearing that his days with the Dodgers were about to be ended, he accepted the Pasquels' money and flew back to Mexico City.

Two New York Giant pitchers, Ace Adams and Harry Feldman, both veterans of five seasons, made the same journey, joining a rather large contingent of ex–Giants already there. Each of these players was reported to have been given $15,000, tax free, plus all moving and living expenses, for his change of allegiance.

Then, on May 4, it appeared that they might have snatched that all-important great player who, as Rennie had suggested, would give them a chance. It was reported that superstar Pete Reiser, the Dodgers' most important player, was considering an offer of $100,000 to join the Mexican League.

Two Dodgers, in fact, were considering offers from the Pasquels, Reiser, of course, the more important one. Infielder Stan Rojek, a sensation during spring training and purportedly being paid $4,500 that season, had been offered $10,000 as a signing bonus and a yearly salary of $8,000 for three years.

Reiser was being offered a bonus of $20,000 for signing and a contract of $15,000 per season for five years. In addition, *The New York Herald-Tribune* reported, "The Mexican League, or the Pasquel Bros., Inc., would pay all taxes on the bonuses and salaries and would assume both players' living costs."

"The lost of Reiser would practically eliminate the Dodgers from the pennant race," concluded Bob Cooke in the *Tribune*. "Despite three years in the Army, Brooklyn's golden boy has been hitting with more ferocity than ever, and his ability to play either in the infield or the outfield enhanced his value to the club."

"Considering Reiser's caliber," the writer continued, "it must be reported that he has been drawing a peasant's wage. He was the Dodgers' most stubborn holdout in spring training and finally signed a conditional contract for $9,000 until he proved his physical fitness. Rickey was supposed to increase the salary if Reiser started to produce. Despite the fact that he has been producing, Rickey isn't certain than he'd get more than $13,000."

Who could blame the young man for weighing such options?

It didn't take Branch Rickey long to get with his star. Down in Fort Worth, Texas, where he had been checking out the Dodgers' minor league team in that city, he immediately chartered a plane and flew to St. Louis. He huddled with Reiser—and later with Rojek—for an hour the next day, perhaps quoting biblical chapter and verse, in his attempt to talk him out of this adventure. Finally, the general manager's appeals prevailed, though Rickey insisted that Reiser would remain affixed to the terms of his signed contract.

Whatever it took, and it is not clear what, both Reiser and Rojek rejected their Mexican offers. Before leaving St. Louis for Pittsburgh, the next stop in Brooklyn's western trip, Reiser told reporters that he believed he had done the right thing in remaining with the Dodgers.

Meanwhile, the Cardinals and Dodgers had renewed the two-team race for the pennant they had fought in both 1941 and 1942. Through most of this season, they would remain just a few games apart. And Reiser, as in both those previous seasons, was in the forefront of the battle. If he had not as yet come all the way back to his prewar greatness, he certainly was fast approaching it.

In two consecutive days, his home runs beat the Braves and then the Phillies. The second one, an inside-the-park clout, was described by the *New York Herald-Tribune* as a "titanic blast which ricocheted off the wall in center field with such momentum that Reiser was able to circle the bases." It was calculated as a hit that traveled 410 feet in the air and an additional 50 feet by the power of the carom.

Several days later, his steal of home—his third so far that season—helped Brooklyn to its win over the Phillies. What made this even more notable was that Reiser was the lead runner in a successful triple steal that would eventually bring in the other two runners behind him.

His fielding prowess, now being exhibited primarily in left field, constantly brought accolades from the press. "Reiser proved that he is in a class with the Cardinal fly chasers," raved the *Tribune*, "after he bounced against the right center field wall and ricocheted with Ken O'Dea's long fly."

These, to be sure, were not single-time events. He hit still another inside-the-park home run, this one with two men on, to put the finishing touches on a win over the Pittsburgh Pirates. And he managed yet another steal of home, this one his miraculous fourth of the season, after tripling in two runs and racing in with a third. His defensive play, too, was constantly being noted and praised. Reiser's powerful throw from center field cut off a Phillie runner attempting to score in the 11th inning of a game to seal the Dodger victory. And this in a contest in which he had hit a double and a home run.

How much better could he have been before? This Pistol Pete Reiser could beat you in more ways than a baseball has stitches.

In addition to the extraordinary National League pennant race in 1946, the season was one of constant turmoil in several ways. The Pasquel brothers and their Mexican League would disappear from headlines for only short periods of time. When it seemed that their cause was all but lost, they would suddenly come forth with a piece of threatening news. One day, they were in talks with Stan Musial and Enos Slaughter. Another day, they were promising to snatch a new contingent of Giant players. Finally, near the end of May, Bingo!

A trio of Cardinals, including star left hander Max Lanier and the fine young second baseman Lou Klein, took the money and ran south of the border. Lanier was reputed to have been paid $200,000 for his jump, which

Reiser's first steal of home in 1946. He would steal home six more times that year and establish a new major league mark for the rare feat (National Baseball Hall of Fame Library, Cooperstown, N.Y.).

came roughly to $10,000 a mile for his trip down. This, everyone agreed, was a portentous event, and several major league teams were shaking in their banks.

That wasn't the only peril that year to baseball's equanimity. A baseball union was being organized in Pittsburgh, a hotbed of union activity with all its many steel mills. Robert Murphy, the organizer of the American Baseball Guild, threatened to call a strike of the Pirates unless the team and the league accepted his union as bargaining agent for the players. This, too, hung over the league like a sword of Damocles, or perhaps better, the lethal bat of a Pete Reiser.

Finally, in early June, the Pirates held a secret vote to determine whether they would strike. It was held minutes before a scheduled night game with the Giants at Pittsburgh's Forbes Field. Just before the game was to start, and while opposing players and all of baseball's managements held their collective breath, the team marched out of the clubhouse and onto the diamond. Apparently, the Pirates had turned down the strike action.

However, a day later when the results of that balloting were announced, the Pirates had voted 20–16 in favor of a walkout. But this was four votes shy of the two-thirds majority they had agreed upon with management that would allow the union to be accepted as their bargaining agent.

"We played a dirty trick on Murphy," said infielder Lee Handley. "We let him down, and I was one of those who did it. We are not radicals. We don't want to be affiliated with any labor organization."

He went on to say that the players' concern for the club management and the team's fans had a lot to do with the way they voted. But then he made it clear that a giant step had been taken here, and that sometime in the future, important actions would have to follow.

"We do think ball players should be organized," said Handley, "to correct some of the abuses in baseball. We don't want strikes, but we would like some power to bring about a fair minimum wage, participation by a player in part of his purchase price and some sort of blanket insurance."

One of the sadder casualties of this aborted strike was the ex–Dodger infielder Pete Coscarat. Twice an All-Star while playing for Brooklyn and Pittsburgh, he was suddenly dropped from the team like the proverbial hot potato. Obviously punished for his support of the strike effort, Coscarat, at the age of 32, would never again play in the majors. He finished his baseball career, banished, if you will, to Portland of the Pacific Coast League, one year short of the ten-year requirement for a major league pension.

Between the strike action by the Pittsburgh team and the veritable declaration of war by the Mexican League, the club owners of the then 16 major league teams had to wonder whether their stranglehold on the game was beginning to loosen. By mid–July, the owners themselves answered with a softening of their own dominant position. In a historical disclosure, the president of the American League, Will Harridge, announced that a committee of players would be created, one player representing each of the teams, that would have a voice in all baseball affairs.

"Baseball's steering committee, meeting here (in Chicago) the last two days, has discussed the whole future of the game," said Harridge. "We felt that if some revisions are to be made it might be well to invite players to contribute their views."

"There have been stories written to the effect that players want this and that," he continued, "so we thought we'd like to have them join us in expressing just what they have in mind, including a minimum salary."

The war in the Pacific had been over for more than a year by then, but a new one, it appeared, was about to open on these shores.

Meanwhile, Pete Reiser had not escaped his Job-like plight. In a game with the Reds in late May he reinjured his bothersome throwing arm. The Dodgers "lost the services of Pete Reiser for an indefinite period," reported the *Tribune*, "when he injured his throwing arm after retrieving Grady Hatton's triple in the third."

"He tried to throw off balance," said the Dodgers' physician, Dominick Rossi, "and pulled a muscle in his right shoulder. I don't think he'll be out for more than a week, but you never can tell about these things. I think that warm weather will solve a lot of our aches and pains."

During the next several weeks, Reiser's arm and shoulder—originally hurt in his crash and fall at Camp Lee—remained a matter of great concern. He was in and out of the lineup many times, sometimes appearing only as a pinch hitter.

"Reiser may not play for three or four days," read one report in the *Tribune*. "The ache in his arm is now concentrated in the region of his right elbow. Doc Wendler, Brooklyn trainer, believes that a few sunny afternoons will supply a cure."

They were still praying for that solar care several days later, when that same newspaper reported, "Pete Reiser's ailing arm is still a matter of conjecture as far as the future is concerned. Reiser says he still feels as though a nerve is bothering him in the region of the elbow and if the sun ever shows for two consecutive days out here, he hopes that will be the cure."

Finally, by mid–June, during a Dodger series in St. Louis, Reiser went to see his friend and favorite doctor, Robert F. Hyland. "He told me he couldn't find anything wrong with my arm," reported Reiser, "after he took several X-rays. I asked him why the arm didn't feel strong and he said all I needed was a few days of hot weather."

The sun came out, and came out strong, as Reiser returned to the lineup to play a full game for the first time in two weeks. During this period, considering all, Reiser, as well as the Dodgers, had not fared too badly. The team was still leading the Cards, usually by from two to four games. Reiser was hitting in the vicinity of .320 and was stealing more bases than he had ever done before. And one day, after he threw out Ralph Kiner trying to score from third on a fly ball to center, one writer commented, "Reiser's sore arm is apparently not as sore as it used to be."

Even if his arm was still sore, Reiser's bat certainly wasn't. Meeting the next Western teams who moved into Ebbets Field—certainly the tougher division in the league—Reiser led the way as the Dodgers took five of the following seven games, including two out of three from their St. Louis rivals.

"The top third of the Brooklyn batting order," read the *Tribune*, in a game with the Pirates, "particularly Pete Reiser, supplied Higbe with five of Brooklyn's seven runs. Reiser drove in four with a pair of doubles, a single and an outfield fly. The Pirates would like to know if other teams ever get him out."

Just before the Cardinals came to town, their new manager, Eddie Dyer, explained why he liked to use his left-handers against Brooklyn. "Not that they're loaded with left handed hitters," he said, "but Reiser's such an important man to them and Dixie Walker is hitting better than he ever did. If we can hold these two to a minimum, I figure we get a little edge."

They didn't. At least, not in this three-game series. Reiser managed five hits in the set, knocked in several runs, stole a base and had raised his batting average to .329, fifth in the league standing. All games, incidentally, were played against left-handed pitchers.

The Dodgers continued their winning ways, and Reiser his hitting ways, all through the days preceding the All-Star Game on July 10. By that time, Brooklyn had increased its lead over St. Louis to five games and Reiser was hitting a solid .330. Near the end of June, however, it became obvious that his plaguing right arm was acting up again. The injured arm not only hindered Reiser's throwing ability but also made swinging a bat painful and difficult. So after three playing days without a hit, he was rested for several games.

In one of those games, he was brought in to pinch-hit in a late inning. The Dodgers were down by a run, but the bases were loaded and two were out. Unable to take a full Reiser swing, he topped the ball slowly along the infield and barely beat the throw to first to bring in the tying run in a game his team would eventually win. At least his feet were as fleet as ever.

Several days later, he returned and enjoyed a streak of six consecutive games in which he had two hits in each. In that period, he knocked in six runs, scored five and stole two bases. As the All-Star game was about to be played, the Dodgers appeared a solid choice to take the pennant from the Cards for the first time since 1941. And, yes, Pete Reiser seemed a good bet to once again win the batting crown.

Four Dodgers were originally chosen for the National League squad that year. Dixie Walker, who had been leading the league in batting average, pitcher Kirby Higbe, and the Gold Dust Twins, Pee Wee Reese and Pete Reiser. Days before the game, however, some of the gold seemed to be missing. Reese suffered a chipped bone in his neck and had to miss the All-Star Game and, perhaps more importantly, more than a week of games afterward. Reiser's arm troubles returned and he too had to be excused from the big game.

At about that time, a remarkable piece about Reiser appeared in *The New York Post*, by legendary columnist Jimmy Cannon. Under the headline, "Reiser is best in National," Cannon blasted forth with an accolade to a Pistol that had seldom been heard.

"Pete's the best," the columnist started. "Guys may hit a ball harder. Maybe, there's another who can journey farther for a fly ball. If anyone's faster, I haven't seen him. But don't show me the records because the book has nothing to do about it. It's my opinion that Pete Reiser is the greatest ball player in the National League. On my ballclub, Reiser is first pick and there isn't one close enough to make a real run at second money. Can you hear me good?"

It is important to remember that some of those other National League players that year were Stan Musial, Enos Slaughter and Johnny Mize, with Musial having one of his finest seasons.

"At the Polo Grounds yesterday," Cannon went on, "he came up ten times and was on the bases seven. He slammed a home run, a double, and two singles and walked twice. When Pete was on, spasms of panic ran through the Giants. He taunted them with his presence."

Cannon then dealt with Reiser not playing for the coming All-Star Game. "Without him," concluded the writer, "the All-Star game is a hoax."

Apparently it was Durocher who had appealed to the powers that be to have Reiser excused for the game. "I've asked Ford Frick (President of the League) officially to take him off," said the Dodger manager. "That three days' rest will be like three months' rest for him. I'm going to take him and his wife to Montreal with me."

"He's the best ball player in the league," a reporter commented . "He belongs on the All-Star team."

"Sure," agreed Durocher, "he's the best. Better than Stan Musial. Pete has more power. More speed. But I'm fighting for a pennant."

Reiser, who had been sitting across the room in the clubhouse where this conversation took place, said, "I'd like to play if I'm capable. But I go through torture out there now. Three days' rest may not do me any good, but it can't do me any harm."

"When does it hurt you?" he was asked.

"When I swing and miss and when I throw," he answered. "The other day I tried to throw. I thought I had everything on it. The ball went just ten feet in front of me. I'm scared to throw. We have a hell of a chance to win the pennant and I don't want to be the one to screw it up."

At this juncture, one other thing to bear in mind is that Reiser, then hitting .330 and winning games for the Dodgers with his bat, his fielding, his speed and, yes, his arm, was doing everything with a maximum of pain.

"What do the doctors say?" he was then asked.

"Some say to play it out," said Reiser. "Others say rest will do it good. Others say it never will be any good. It feels like it's coming off every time I throw. It has no strength in it when I throw. It takes twenty minutes or half an hour for the life to come back to it."

"The American League figures to win the ball game," Cannon wound up, "whether he's in there or not. But the Nationals won't have their All-Star team in Boston if Pete Reiser is up in Montreal."

Reiser did not play in that year's version of the game. Just as Cannon had said, it wouldn't have mattered if he had. Before a hometown crowd in Boston, Ted Williams had the greatest All-Star performance in game history, leading the winning American League to a 12–0 victory. All Williams managed was four hits, including two home runs, and five runs batted in, tying one record for his homers and establishing a new one for his runs batted in.

The rest, however, provided only temporary relief for Reiser. Coming out of the All-Star break, the Dodgers took only one of three games with the Cubs, as they began an extended Western trip. In the one game they won, 4–3, it was Reiser who played the decisive role. The Dodger outfielder got two hits, including a triple and two runs batted in.

Chicago pitching ace Claude Passeau was routed by Reiser's triple in the fifth inning. The hit came with two men on base and gave the Dodgers a 3–0 lead, which was never relinquished. But Reiser wasn't going to stay put on third. As the pitcher went into his stretch, Reiser danced cautiously down the third base line. Suddenly, he took off and slid, he believed, under the tag of catcher Clyde McCullough.

"You're out!" bellowed Umpire George Magerkurth, his thumb poked into the air.

Reiser looked up at him, stunned. "Then he dropped his voice," Reiser later revealed, "and told me, 'Goddamn, did I blow that! Called you out, kid. Sorry.'"

Reiser, who would end up that season with a record-breaking seven steals of home, should actually have had this eighth one.

That was the last good news for a while. From Chicago, the Dodgers took a train to St. Louis, four and a half games ahead of the Cardinals and Reiser still maintaining a .328 batting average. But just like the old days, St. Louis proved a hellhole for the team.

The Dodgers lost all four games in St. Louis, and Reiser, obviously hurting badly again, got only one hit in 14 tries. Brooklyn had lost all but a half-game margin over the Cardinals, and even that wouldn't hold.

By the time the Dodgers left Cincinnati—their next stop on this torturous road trip—where they lost two of a three game series, they were in a flat-footed tie for first with the Cardinals. Their slightly tarnished Golden Boy, Pete Reiser, who was still playing in extreme pain, managed only two hits in 11 at bats.

In their last stop on the trip, in Pittsburgh, the Dodgers returned to winning ways. They swept the three-game series but remained in a tie for first with the Cards, who had matched them game for game. Reiser, however, remained ineffective, having only two hits in his 12 tries. The .320 plus batting average he had earlier sported was now wavering in the .280's. Apparently, his shoulder injuries continued to take a nasty toll.

Back amidst the friendlier fans of Ebbets Field, the Dodgers did much better against the invading bloc of Western teams. Though Reiser's hitting continued to sag, the team took two from the Cubs and two again from the Pirates, while the Cards went on a rare losing streak. By the end of July, the Dodgers held a two-and-a-half-game lead over the second-place Cardinals.

As the Reds moved in, Reiser seemed to wake up. "An inside the park home run by Pistol Pete Reiser," crowed *The New York Times*, "was the blow that sank the Reds." After two were out and two were still on base, Reiser slammed the ball past the racing right fielder Lonnie Frey. Before the ball could be recovered, the speeding Reiser crossed the plate for his eighth home run of the season. This, his second hit of the game, gave the Dodgers a commanding lead that they never surrendered.

But two days later the impossible happened once more. The impossible that more and more was becoming the inevitable. Chasing a towering fly ball off the bat of Cardinal third baseman Whitey Kurowski, Pete Reiser crashed once again against the concrete wall of Ebbets Field. And, ironically, for a third time, it happened in a game with the St. Louis Cardinals, the team that had originally owned him.

"Disaster dealt the Dodgers a double blow yesterday," wrote Joseph Sheehan in *The New York Times*. "Not only did they drop the rubber contest of the three-game series with the Cardinals," he continued, "but they also lost the services for several days at least of Pete Reiser, their stellar left fielder."

In another daring, if misguided, attempt to catch an apparently uncatchable ball that eventually went for a double, Reiser crashed headfirst into the left field wall, cracking his head so viciously against the concrete that he once more had to be carried off the field on a stretcher. As several times before, he was taken to Peck Memorial Hospital, where he was diagnosed with a slight concussion and would remain for a few days.

It is astounding to think that no one, in what could be loosely called

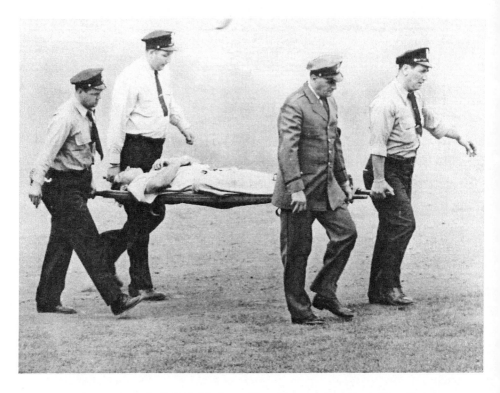

Reiser being carried off the field after still another crash against the wall, August 1, 1946. Once again, it was against the St. Louis Cardinals, this time at Ebbets Field (National Baseball Hall of Fame Library, Cooperstown, N.Y.).

the Dodger Brain Trust, would study this unusual—if not downright eerie—case of self-destruction and try to understand it. And if not understand it, to make a change that could reasonably safeguard against its further recurrence.

Was it simply Reiser's hell-bent way of playing? Was it possible that Reiser had a real and chronic problem of depth perception? Wasn't there a course of action that could keep him away from those outfield walls? Not even the fences in the service fields were immune to his battering.

Here was a man who had originally come up as a shortstop, had played second and third in the majors, and had performed at every outfield position. Each of these positions, mind you, with skill if not brilliance. Reds Manager Bill McKechnie had called him the best third baseman in the league. The Yankees had wanted to buy him and play him at third. A man with that much ability could play *anywhere*.

If his throwing was still a problem, why not simply move Reiser to first base? At that time, the Dodgers were alternating lefty Ed Stevens and right-handed-hitting Howie Schultz at that position, neither of whom would last. In 1947 the Dodgers would actually transform Jackie Robinson into a first baseman to begin his major league career. Unhappy with Stan Musial's throwing, the Cards had moved their star to first base that season. The Detroit Tigers had made weak fielding catcher Rudy York into a first baseman to get his bat into the lineup. This move had to be accommodated by also moving the Tigers' skilled first baseman, Hank Greenberg, into the outfield.

Changes of players' positions were being made constantly. Didn't this player deserve at least that? To insure the health, safety and physical capabilities of their best ballplayer—who so many considered to be the greatest player in the entire league—why didn't the Dodgers find another position for Reiser to play? Did they dare believe this would be the last time he would tangle with an outfield wall? He had thus far played three seasons as an outfielder in the majors, and in each of these three seasons, he had crashed against an outfield wall. He was an odds-on choice to do so again next year. If not, sadly, before then.

But, it would appear, the Dodgers had no intention of making such a change. Exactly one week later, Reiser was back in action with the Dodgers. In fact, in center field. Miraculously, he was also a one-man show as he led his team to victory.

"Pistol Pete Reiser is what they call him," read *The New York Times* the day afterward, "but yesterday at the Polo Grounds he developed all the power of a siege gun as he clubbed the Dodgers to a ten inning 3–1 victory over the Giants."

In the first inning, on the very first pitch thrown to him by Giant pitcher Ken Trinkle, Reiser slammed the ball into the right field stands for his ninth home run of the season. This gave the Dodgers a 1–0 lead, which the Giants tied several innings later. The score remained 1–1 until the tenth inning when Reiser came to bat with two men on and two out. This time, the returning slugger blasted a triple to right center, bringing home the two winning runs and accounting for all three Dodger runs that day.

A day later, this time against the Phillies, Reiser again batted in the only run of the day. In the eighth inning, with two out and Reese on second, Reiser's single to center field brought in the shortstop as the Dodgers, behind Higbe, triumphed, 1–0.

And the Pistol didn't stop shooting. In game after game he brought in the winning run for his team. "It was Pete Reiser," read one *Times* report, "whose single drove home the deciding point in last night's contest." Said another: "The dangerous Pete Reiser, not wasting any time, slashed a single to left and Furillo scored what became the winning run."

If he couldn't do it one way, he did it another. "Then the Dodgers struck back," began the *Times* on still another day. "Ed Stanky's single, Augie Galan's sacrifice and Reiser's single tied the issue. Two walks followed and Reese struck out, so that it appeared (Bill) Voiselle might escape."

"But Reiser, with Edwards at bat," the report continued, "stole home and gave the Dodgers a lead they never relinquished. Incidentally, this was Reiser's sixth steal of home this season and his twenty-sixth of the campaign."

Late in August, clinging to a two-game margin over the Cardinals, Brooklyn prepared for its fourth and last Western trip of the season. An article by Joseph C. Nichols in *The New York Times* explained that Dodger players and their manager, Durocher, were optimistic about their chances to win the pennant that year. "This optimism," said Nichols, "was based mainly on the fact that Reiser is back in action and smacking the ball with all his old-time power."

"In and out of the lineup all season," he went on, "Reiser now appears to be in the best of playing form, as attested by his showing on Sunday, when he rapped out a homer, a double, and a single against the Phillies."

"With Reiser in there," Durocher was quoted as saying, "this trip won't bother us any. All we have to do is come back with the same lead we leave Brooklyn with, and Pete will be fine insurance against our blowing that lead."

In that same day's newspaper, columnist Arthur Daley wrote, "The most heart-warming development (for the Dodgers) is the return to health of Pistol Pete Reiser, a lad who comes pretty close to being the best ball player in the National League. Pete not only wins games with his booming bat but also with his twinkling feet. Once he's on the base paths, he gives pitchers a severe case of the jitters and his value to the team as a whole is beyond any adequate measure."

During these days of rekindled hope for the Dodgers, major league baseball continued to face trouble and complication from the Mexican League. Dodger outfielder Augie Galan reported that the Pasquel brothers had "flooded every team in both leagues with offers to star players. And unless some of the owners realize what's coming up next year, they may wake up without ballclubs."

Phillies infielder Roy Hughes confirmed this and claimed that Ted Williams had been offered a signed blank check to play in the Mexican League the following year.

The St. Louis Star-Times reported that Jorge Pasquel, in a telephone conversation with the newspaper, had said, "We will redouble all efforts to encourage the biggest stars in major league baseball to come here and accept our large salaries."

All this occurring in the aftermath of Mickey Owen's latest turn-around. For a second time, the former Dodger catcher had decided that life below the Mexican border was intolerable and had packed his trunk and driven back home.

"The first time I saw the Nuevo Laredo Park," said Owen, "I had a feeling I'd seen it before. Do you ever have nightmares? When I have bad dreams, I dream about playing in places like that. Almost every game somebody limped off the field."

Now Owen was seeking his old job with the Dodgers. "I believe I could still help the Dodgers win the National League pennant," he said, "and I'd like to get a shot at the Boston Red Sox in the World Series this fall."

This, however, wouldn't prove that easy. Neither Baseball Commissioner Happy Chandler nor players from both leagues were welcoming him with open arms. The commissioner stressed that legal procedures would have to be followed. After all, he himself had proclaimed a five-year ban on all players who had joined the Mexican League. If there was something unique in this case, he'd have to be convinced of its validity.

The players representatives, recently elected to meet club owners to formulate a new contract, were particularly vociferous in their opposition to Owen. To them he was a turncoat who had deserted his fellow players for the promise of the bigger Mexican paycheck. They didn't want him back until he served at least a good part of the five-year suspension.

"Owen jumped his team to go down there for that big money," said Cardinal shortstop Marty Marion. "We would feel the same way about Lanier."

Max Lanier, incidentally, was the Cardinal pitching ace who had jumped to Mexico, but unlike Owen, had thus far remained there.

While these battles involving the Mexican League continued, the National League was having a bang-up skirmish of its own. That final trip out West for the Dodgers did not turn out the way Durocher had hoped. They did not return home with the same two-game lead they had started with. Losing six of the 11 games on this trip, the Dodgers limped home two and a half games behind the now first place Cards.

Perhaps even more troubling was the continuing unstable condition of Reiser. His shoulder, which affected his hitting as much as his throwing, was not healing. There were days, like one in Cincinnati, when his two-run homer helped them to a 5–4 win over the Reds. Or a performance in St. Louis, where his three hits, his daring base running, and his spectacular catch of a sure run-producing hit led the Dodgers to a win over the Cardinals.

"The Cards couldn't keep up with Reiser," commented *The New York Times* the following day. "He stole his twenty-ninth base in the first and advanced from first to second after Dixie Walker had fouled out in the second. Kurowski was so surprised to see Reiser enroute that he made no attempt to get him."

But for five of these games, he went without a hit, and too often his hitting was ineffectual. If the Dodgers were to win this pennant, it seemed, the injured outfielder would have to produce a lot more.

Instead, it would be less. As the Dodgers moved into the climactic month of September, Reiser was more and more forced to the sidelines. "Reiser withdrew in the sixth inning complaining of a back ache," read one report in *The New York Herald-Tribune*. "Pete Reiser was in uniform but didn't play because of a slight attack of pleurisy," read another. "Reiser, still suffering from the miseries, stayed out," was a third *Tribune* report.

One newspaper account even noted, "Reiser, who plans to have his shoulder operated on after the season, started throwing with his *left* arm in pre-game practice. He has been able to throw from either side since he first tossed a baseball."

Finally, on September 7, with the Dodgers still two and a half games out of first place, Reiser returned to action. Through he went hitless in three at bats, his stolen base led to an important run in Brooklyn's win over the Giants. Surprisingly, thanks to the pitching efforts of Kirby Higbe, Vic Lombardi, Joe Hatten and Hank Berhman, the Dodgers had kept themselves in the race with a string of five victories while playing the clubs of the weaker Eastern division.

Reiser had a banner day in the following game. Almost like the Pistol of old, he knocked in two runs, scored another two and stole three bases, including his seventh steal of home, in an 11–3 trouncing of the Giants.

Columnist Arthur Daley made some astute comments in *The New York Times* about Reiser's astonishing thefts of home. "Before Pete Reiser acquired the habit of stealing home with considerable regularity," he wrote, "he virtually had to educate the umpires to the peculiar slide he uses. In the beginning the ball would beat him to the plate and the Men in Blue would automatically call him out. It still beats him to the plate but Pistol Pete is usually called safe because the catcher can't tag him. He slides far to the right of the rubber and merely flicks it with his left hand as he flashes past."

Whatever way he did it, he seemed to be doing it again, and hope sprang once more in the hearts of the faithful and their scribes. "With Pete Reiser's flying spikes churning up the base bath dirt once again," wrote Arch Murray in *The New York Post*, "and their pitching getting better all the time, the Dodgers are well fortified for the last grim stand against the West."

"They never looked better," he went on, "than they did over the week-end as they swept a two game series with the cellar-bound Giants."

"We're hot and rolling now," agreed Durocher. "The pitching has been great and with Reiser back in there again, I'm not a bit worried about that two game bulge of the Cards."

The Dodgers did hang in there and slowly whittled down the Cardinal lead. Reiser, however, despite that brilliant effort, could only play intermittently and rarely with any exhibition of his real ability.

On September 25, with the Dodgers one game behind and with only four games left to play, *The New York Times* said, "Whether Pete Reiser will be able to play still is questionable. Pete's recurring miseries have been almost as painful to Durocher as they have been to Reiser. 'He makes such a lot of difference when he's in there,' Leo has said repeatedly."

Reiser played only two more games that year. In fact, only one more full game, in which he didn't get a hit in five tries, and the Dodgers lost unmercifully to the Phillies, 11–9. In the following game, before the Dodgers could finish beating the Phillies, Reiser walked—and fell—on the path of disaster once more. In the very first inning of that game, he was once again carried off the field and to a room in Peck Memorial Hospital. As one caption read, "For the last time this season."

This time it was a broken left leg, injured in his attempt to slide back into first base after taking a short lead. He caught his foot on the bag, causing him to severely wrench his leg as he completed his slide. The freak play caused a fractured fibula and, of course, finished him for the season.

As *The New York Times* wrote, this Dodger victory "was marred by the loss of Pistol Pete Reiser. The speed boy and powerhouse hitter plagued all year by sundry ills and injuries eliminated himself in the first inning."

"The Pistol has now taken the year's hard-luck crown away from the Giants' Walker Cooper and the Cubs' Andy Pafko," wrote Arch Murray in *The New York Post*. "In addition to the ailing shoulder which has bothered him all year, he has had a bad back, a twisted knee and a charley horse before yesterday's broken leg."

"It's the toughest sort of break for the Dodgers and for Reiser," the writer went on, "who in top shape is the same kind of star as the Cards' Stan Musial. But the Dodgers will carry on the fight without him, driving into that photo finish with all the scrap and hustle they have mustered all year."

Surprisingly, Murray was right. One game behind the Cardinals as they entered this game three days later, they finished the season in a flat-footed tie with St. Louis, the first time this had occurred in major league history. Each team at season's end had finished with 96 wins and 58 losses, and the pennant winner would be decided in a three-game playoff.

Thirty thousand Brooklyn fans lined up for tickets at 215 Montague Street, home of the Dodger offices. They and the rest of the borough went wild with excitement and solemn with prayers as they faced this season-ending tournament. Who could have imagined that a 154-game season could end this way? Just win two more games and it's a second pennant in only six years.

This time, however, Reiser's absence might certainly have mattered. The Dodgers went meekly before the favored Cardinals, losing 4–2 in St. Louis and 8–4 before their own hometown crowd. The season had once again ended with a murmur and a gasp.

Still, the old Dodger war cry of "Wait till next year!" seemed less hollow than ever before. "They'll be looking at the back of our uniforms," Manager Durocher vowed, speaking of the coming season.

He was thinking of the array of Dodger rookies who had come forth this past season—Carl Furillo, Gene Hermanksi, Bruce Edwards, Joe Hatten and Hank Behrman, being only a few. He was thinking of Jackie Robinson, who had been the International League's leading hitter as well as the foremost player in the recently completed Little World Series that the Montreal Royals had won.

And he was thinking, too, of Pete Reiser, who without injuries this past season would surely have led the team to its pennant. Because of these injuries, Reiser had missed more than 40 games this past year, and because of the chronic pain, he managed to hit only .277. Still, he had led the league with his 34 stolen bases, and he had broken all existing records with his amazing seven steals of home.

Plans had already been made to have Reiser's ailing shoulder operated on, and there was little doubt that his ankle injury would not slow him down. "It was a clean break," Reiser told reporter Murray, "and figures to heal perfectly."

Perhaps there was a lilt to the words of "Wait till next year!"

18

The Natural

"Reiser was proclaimed the reincarnation of Ty Cobb: he could hit and field and play with abandon, perhaps too much."
—Michael Shapiro, author of
The Last Good Season

It is widely accepted that the finest novel ever written about baseball is Bernard Malamud's *The Natural*. Sadly, perhaps, most people today know its surrealistic story more from the Robert Redford movie that was released in 1984 than from the classic novel itself, published more than 30 years before that.

But to really know *The Natural* and to know its hero, Roy Hobbs, one must turn to the Malamud novel. In a *New York Times* review of the book, Harry Sylvester wrote: "What he (Malamud) has done is to contrive a sustained and elaborate allegory in which the 'natural' player who operates with ease and the greatest skill, without having been taught is equated with the natural man who, left alone by, say, politicians and advertising agencies, might achieve his real fulfillment."

That observation, of course, can also describe the adventures and misadventures of Pete Reiser. This was a player and a man, after all, who was plummeted into his failures by the self-serving manipulations of his employers. Left alone, and left at his natural position in the infield, he probably would have achieved all that had been predicted for him.

More than that, one wonders whether Reiser himself was the real-life inspiration for Roy Hobbs. In Hobbs' adventures there are certainly elements of Eddie Waitkus, the Philadelphia Phillies first baseman who was shot in his hotel room by a female fan, and, of course, of Babe Ruth,

165

who pitched and hit with similar Hobbsian glory. But the essence and meaning of Roy Hobbs is Pete Reiser.

At the time this book was written, around 1951, he'd have to have been the baseball idol of Brooklyn-born Dodger fan Bernard Malamud. There was no one else who could have grabbed the fancy of a Dodger fan then, and the fictional abilities Hobbs was endowed with Reiser had in reality. No player, certainly to that time, was more a baseball natural and the epitome of baseball-playing totality and perfection than Reiser.

But whether he was *The Natural* or simply the natural, as the Dodgers began training camp in late February of 1947, their chances for the pennant that year seemed to depend solely on Reiser's ability to recover from his multiple injuries and to become again the Reiser of before.

The expectations, at least early on, were that he would. Reiser's shoulder had been operated on by Dr. Hyland during the winter, and the orthopedist had assured the player that he was recovering well and could begin throwing immediately. As for his left leg, fractured during the final days of the previous season, Reiser told *The New York Post*, "That's healed completely."

"I haven't run on it yet," he conceded, "but I've done a lot of skating and it hasn't bothered me at all."

Reiser seemed equally pleased with the progress of his healed shoulder. "I can comb my hair and shave for the first time in four years," he said, "without feeling any pain."

So almost newly armed, and armed with a new contract estimated at $20,000, he reported happily to training camp that season. "The Pistol," boasted *New York Post* reporter Arch Murray, "confident that his once ailing flipper will be its old powerful self this season, can be the National League's best ball player this year."

"The Dodgers need him," chimed in that newspaper's sport columnist, Leonard Cohen, "if they are to give the Cardinals real opposition."

That was the way it seemed to many that spring as the Dodger management and newspaper reporters covering the club began to assess the coming season. General manager Rickey believed the Dodgers would perform better the coming season than the pennant-tying club had done the previous one. "The younger players," he said, "have an extra year's experience and the squad as a whole is much faster afoot."

Manager Durocher believed that simply the return of third baseman Arky Vaughan "should make this a far better team."

"I look for the pitching," he went on, "to show definite improvement. Joe Hatten, Ralph Branca and Ed Head all figure to have much better years. Higbe should be a twenty-game winner."

"The big 'if,' though," he pointed out, "is Pete Reiser. If he's all all right, well…"

"Well" indeed. And almost everyone in camp that year held their collective breath on that. There was also much concern about the Dodger management itself that spring. Coach Charlie Dressen had been fired by Branch Rickey during the winter and had ended up as coach for the crosstown Yankees, now under general manager Larry MacPhail and field manager Bucky Harris. This also seemed to precipitate a strange battle of words and accusations in the commissioner's office between MacPhail and his former sidekick, Durocher. Apparently even now that they were apart, they couldn't stop brawling.

In his book *The Dodgers and Me*, Durocher said, "Larry MacPhail offered me the job as manager of the Yankees (in 1947). I told him it was my hope that I'd spend the rest of my career in Brooklyn."

"My refusal of his Yankee offer," Durocher declared, "embittered Larry MacPhail and he began to attack Laraine (Durocher's new wife, actress Laraine Day) and me. That led to a series of events which culminated in hearings at St. Petersburg and Sarasota before Commissioner Chandler."

What exactly led to this state of affairs is difficult to determine from culling news reports and evaluating various conflicting memories of these circumstances. Apparently, what first seemed a tempest in a teapot—MacPhail's outrage at Durocher's ghost-written name-calling in his columns for the *Brooklyn Eagle*—got out of hand and became a whirlwind that blew all the way to the commissioner's office.

There were MacPhail's accusations of Durocher, Durocher's counterclaims against MacPhail, Durocher's apologies for everything he admitted doing and for whatever they accused him of. All of this finally led to an astounding declaration unprecedented in baseball history. On April 9, just days short of the season's opener, the baseball commissioner suspended Leo Durocher as manager of the Dodgers for the entire 1947 season because of "conduct detrimental to baseball."

"Durocher has not measured up to the standards expected of managers of our baseball teams," said Commissioner Chandler. "As a result of the accumulated unpleasant incidents in which he has been involved, which the commissioner construes as detrimental to baseball, Manager Durocher is hereby suspended from participating in professional baseball for the 1947 season."

Whether this was caused by Durocher's gambling or his gambling chums—including his best pal, actor George Raft—or his trysting with Laraine Day while she was still married to her former husband. Or, as several have suggested, merely different rules for hirelings—like manager Durocher—and owners—like general manager and president MacPhail— who as everyone knew had similar friends and similar gambling habits. Who can tell?

Whatever its cause, this was a shocker for the Dodger team, suddenly stripped of their manager just as they were about to begin a race for the pennant. All of baseball—except apparently MacPhail—had been willing to put up with the shenanigans of Durocher for over 20 years. What really brought on this change of heart?

One more thing was about to happen, and one wonders whether a clue may lie in it. The Brooklyn Dodgers were about to inaugurate a new era in baseball by introducing a Negro player into the major leagues for the first time in the century. Jackie Robinson had more than earned his way onto the 1947 Dodger lineup by his great performance the season before in Montreal and his spectacular work in spring training this season. In seven games between Montreal and Brooklyn that spring, Robinson hit .625 and stole seven bases—all in a Royals uniform.

There was no way that Branch Rickey would be diverted from his goal of breaking baseball's racial barrier. He had found the man in Jackie Robinson who certainly had the ability, the will, the nerve and the disposition—whether manufactured or real—to take on this role. Trouble was expected, of course, and trouble had already begun. From opposing players, from Dodger players, from managers, from fans themselves. But nothing would deter Rickey. He had the full backing of Durocher and of his own playing personnel.

There was nothing anyone now could do to stop this from happening. But things could be done to make it difficult and overturn the applecart, even after it had started rolling. Removing the manager from the team just days before the season opened might certainly be one of those.

In Peter Golenbock's book *Bums*, the author wrote that sportswriter Joe Williams had "teamed up with Yankee owner MacPhail to snipe at Rickey whenever he could."

"At the end of the 1946 season," said Golenbock, "Williams asserted that Rickey had sold second baseman Billy Herman because he wanted to lose the 1946 pennant. That way, wrote Williams, if the Dodgers win in 1947 it would be a 'Negro triumph.'"

Another of Williams' "astute" remarks was that "Blacks have been kept out of big league ball because they are a race of very poor ballplayers."

MacPhail's chum Joe Williams, of course, didn't stand alone. Most club owners, including MacPhail, were dead set against removing the sport's racial barrier. As a matter of fact, in an article by Dan Daniel of *The New York World Telegram* on November 1, 1945, it was reported that MacPhail "didn't think it in the best interests of all concerned for the Majors to raid the Negro leagues for the few good players possessed by those organizations."

"Larry pointed out that, as landlord of Negro leagues," wrote Daniel, "those owning Major League parks could not afford to break up the Negro organizations. He said that the Yankees got $100,000 a year in rentals from Negro ballclubs, in New York, Newark, Kansas City and Norfolk."

In any case, while Landis was alive, there was no way that a Negro would play in the major leagues. When Chandler was elected to replace him—and elected with much thanks to MacPhail—it was expected that the former Kentucky senator would act the same as his predecessor. Chandler, however, fooled them all. But just as Rickey had gotten MacPhail his old Dodger job and demanded the hiding of Reiser as compensation, was it possible that Chandler was asked to repay MacPhail for his help?

In *Bums*, writer Golenbock concedes. "Leo Durocher's suspension, on April 9, 1947, the day before Branch Rickey brought up Jackie Robinson, compounded Rickey's problems. Without the right man running the team, Rickey knew his experiment might fail. He needed a manager with experience, whom he could trust implicitly and who would support Robinson."

And that wouldn't be easy.

By the time the season began less than a week later, Durocher was gone, coach Clyde Sukeforth, who had refused a permanent managerial role, was the day-by-day interim manager, Jackie Robinson was in and playing at first base, and Pete Reiser, it seemed, would be ready for action.

"Even Pete Reiser can be reported in top shape," reported Arch Murray in the *Post*. "He played the full nine innings for the first time yesterday and cut loose with his best throw since prewar days." Reiser had charged a sharp single to center and thrown a sizzling strike to third that froze the base runner at second and caused Reiser's manager to leap with joy in the dugout.

Having worried much of the spring about regaining the strength of his right arm, Reiser had even spent time practicing to become a left-handed thrower. "I'm beginning to get good at it," he had reported earlier. "At first the ball wobbled when I threw, but now it goes straight and true. I hope I won't have to make the turnover to southpaw, but I'll be ready for it if necessary."

Several days before the season opened, Durocher came by the Dodger clubhouse at Ebbets Field to say good-bye to the team he had put together.

"You've got a great ballclub," he told them, "great pitching and some of the finest kids I've ever seen and just enough veterans. You've got a great chance to win the pennant and my heart will always be with you. I may not be in uniform, but I will be with you in spirit every day of the season."

"Things pile up on a guy," he went on, "and then comes the last blow and the roof falls in on you. I'm going to be around here for three days and I'll be out to see you play from time to time all through the season. Good-bye and good luck."

Durocher would be gone for the rest of that season and then manage the Dodgers for only half of the following year. But unhappily for him, and for several of the players including Reiser, he would not be at the helm to share the history that was about to be made.

19

The Walls

"Pete Reiser just might have been the greatest player ever to hit the National League.... You name it and Pete could do it. Run, hit, throw, bunt, catch. Willie Mays might have been platooned if Pete Reiser played his position."

—Jim Murray, sports columnist

The story of the 1947 baseball season, in terms of this text, was very much the story of two walls. In one instance, it was the breaking down of a figurative wall, the barrier that had stood for long years keeping Negro players out of major league baseball. This deed was accomplished by Jackie Robinson, a man of immense athletic talent and perhaps even stronger will and determination, and Branch Rickey, a man of business and the Bible, who combined them both in this laudatory and historically significant achievement.

The second wall was a very real one. A tall, hard concrete wall that could not be broken by a man in a thousand attempts. In this case, it was the one that bordered the playing field in Ebbets Field, but it could have marked the outer edge of the seven other parks in the National League that year. None of them would have given way, and none of them would have escaped the blind daring of Pete Reiser.

The breaking of the racial wall occurred on the very first day of the season, April 15, 1947. Still without a permanent manager, Coach Clyde Sukeforth, in his role as acting manager, placed Robinson in the starting lineup, batting second and playing first base. History of some magnitude was being made that day that apparently muzzled the suddenly staid audience.

"A solemn crowd of 26,623 customers looked on," wrote Bob Cooke in *The New York Herald-Tribune* the next day, "none of whom could be accused of relationship to the normal Ebbets Field fan who is frequently guilty of conduct unbecoming to the other boroughs."

Brooklyn came from behind to win the game over the visiting Boston Braves, 5–3, but it was Pete Reiser who stole the show, not Robinson, the man most came to see. Reiser scored three of the Dodger runs and knocked in the other two, completely dominating the moment.

As Bob Cooke put it, "The Brooklyn Dodgers, still without a permanent leader, found an adequate one for their opener yesterday when they grouped themselves behind Pete Reiser, their winged foot outfielder, who encircled the Boston Braves with as much ease as he did the bases."

Columnist Red Smith added, "It was a typical Reiser day—two walks, three runs, a double and a single, two runs batted in and one splendiferous running catch."

Reiser and the Dodgers continued their good fortune in the second game of the season as Brooklyn crushed the Braves, 12–6, and Reiser got three more hits and scored two runs. This gave the rejuvenated outfielder five consecutive hits as a start for the new season before he was finally retired by a topped ground ball to the infield. Robinson also managed his first major league hit in this game, a well-placed bunt single down the third base line.

Rickey, meanwhile, had not given up on Durocher returning as his manager later that season. Still hoping to persuade Chandler to rescind his order, Rickey finally hired a manager, but hired him without benefit of a written contract. Three days into the season, 60-year-old Burt Shotton, who had gone into semiretirement as a recruiter of high school players for the Dodger organization, was finally given the job.

A former outfielder for both the St. Louis Browns and Cardinals for 14 seasons, Shotton had managed the Phillies for five years, as well as having piloted various Cardinal minor league teams under Rickey. He was a mild, gray-haired man, who sat on the bench in a business suit and managed the team in an even-tempered colorless manner.

"Shotton watched the game in a pearl gray hat, a topcoat, and spectacles," wrote Peter Golenbock in *Bums*. "Soft-spoken and subdued, he was the antithesis of Durocher. The players who had loved Durocher were disappointed with Shotton. Those who hated Durocher loved Shotton."

Outfielder Carl Furillo said, "That one was a prince…. He wasn't like Leo, and he didn't say, 'I want to be in front all the time.' He would say, 'Here's my ball players. Take my ball players.'"

Pitcher Ralph Branca didn't agree. "The man just wasn't competent enough to be a big league manager," said Branca, "except he was a friend of Rickey's." He then pointed out that the Dodger players "would sit on the bench, and we'd laugh at some of the moves Shotton made."

Dixie Walker, who had just begun his eighth year in a Dodger uniform, and all under Durocher's helm, said, "I don't think anybody yet realizes how much of a loss this is to Brooklyn. I've never seen anyone who could take a team by the seat of its pants and lift it up time after time the way Leo did."

Of course, Pete Reiser loved Durocher and was pained to see him go. But publicly at that time, his response was mild. "It sure is different with Shotton managing," said Reiser. "He never raises his voice no matter what happens. Even when the Giants hit all those homers against us at the Polo Grounds. I think we'll be all right when we get used to it."

Years later, in a taped interview with her son-in-law, Rick Tuber, Patricia Reiser added her thoughts. In answer to the question as to whether Reiser liked Shotton, Patricia Reiser turned the question on its head. "Shotton didn't like Pete," said Reiser's wife. "He had screwed up Shotton's prediction that Pete wouldn't make the big leagues. 'Go on home, kid,' he had told him. 'You're never going to make it.'"

She also pointed out that Shotton didn't approve of Durocher. "Not in any shape or form," she asserted, her tone suggesting that this alone had determined things for Pete. There was still something else she remembered. "He wore street clothes on the field," she said, "and Pete didn't approve of that."

But in street clothes he perched on the Dodger bench, commanding the team's fortunes with help from a coaching staff of Clyde Sukeforth, Ray Blades and Jake Pitler. In a *Daily News* article by Dick Young that appeared in early May, the writer stated, "For the first time in memory, a National League team was being guided by four men who didn't know filberts about their own loop."

Young submitted that the last time Shotton had coached in the National League was 11 years before when he had worked for the Reds. Sukeforth, he pointed out, "except for a brief back-slapping fling with the Brooks two seasons ago, had been out of touch with the league for ten years."

Blades, he went on, hadn't seen league action since 1940 when he last managed the Cardinals. And as for Pitler, he "had been away from the league for twenty-five years."

The employment of Shotton, however, didn't stop Rickey's pleas to Chandler for Durocher's reinstatement. Even MacPhail, who had started the whole thing, announced that he, too—whether with sincerity or not—was protesting the matter to Chandler.

A column by Red Smith at this time in the *Tribune* supported every protest Rickey would make. "He (Chandler) does not, whatever his decisions may suggest and whatever his opinion may be, work for Larry MacPhail," wrote Smith. "The fans are asking for a look at the record of the hearings which preceded the one-year suspension of Leo Durocher."

In asking for the opening of the books in the matter, this most respected columnist suggested that MacPhail's sinful past was the equal of Durocher's, that the Yankees' general manager had acted out of hand when he hired Dressen as a coach while the man was still signed to a Dodger contract, and that Durocher had certainly attempted to mend his ways. While Durocher was in spring training, said Smith, "there could be no doubt that he went out of his way to avoid gamblers there."

Finally, Smith asked, "Hey, Mr. Commissioner, was the decision based on the evidence or on what somebody else wanted?"

That "somebody," of course, was Larry MacPhail.

Sports columnist Stanley Woodward of the *Tribune* potently added his two cents. "In case any one is interested," he wrote, "it is this department's opinion that the suspension of Leo Durocher from baseball for one year by Commissioner Happy Chandler was the most colossal piece of injustice and bravado yet perpetrated. Knowing he was under fire for timidity, Chandler took refuge in overaction."

"There are few things that Durocher ever did," the writer continued, "to the detriment of baseball, such as assaulting citizens, talking out of turn, etc.—and we stand ready and willing to furnish particulars—which have not been done by his principal accuser, one MacPhail, who has turned out to be the greatest whistle-blower and cop-caller in our city."

Durocher himself weighed in on his own behalf. Supposedly still mystified by Chandler's ban, Durocher spoke about a conference he had had with the commissioner in Berkeley, California, during the winter. "When I saw the commissioner then," said Durocher, "he told me a number of things he didn't want me to do, people he didn't want me to be seen with, and all that. I went right down the line and agreed with everything he asked or suggested."

"He told me he didn't want me to get out of line," Durocher continued, "because if I got out of line too much it would be too late. So I got in line from then on and I defy the commissioner or anybody else to look me in the eye and say that I haven't traveled the straight and narrow since last November."

Durocher then pointed out that Chandler had thrown his arm around him as Durocher was about to leave. "I like you, Leo," Durocher reported him as saying, "and I'm for you."

While this turmoil persisted, the Dodger fortunes under Shotton and his coaching crew surprisingly flourished. By the end of April, the Dodgers sat happily in first place, a game ahead of the second place Cubs and five games in front of their expected rivals, the St. Louis Cardinals.

In the forefront of their attack was Reiser himself. Hitting like the master of old, though still a rather young man barely past his 28th birthday, the Dodger center fielder was hitting .400. Both he and Dixie Walker were leading their team, as well as the league, in batting. Dodger hopes, as always, spring eternal. That year at that moment, it seemed to make sense.

A curious thing was reported in one game that month, coupling these two player in an extraordinary way. "Walker is guarding Reiser like a mother hen this year," wrote Bob Cooke in the *Tribune*. "Every time Pete comes within crashing distance of a wall, as he did in the second inning while running for (Frank) McCormick's fly, Dixie's warning voice prevents him from making a hole in the concrete with his head."

(Which makes Dixie Walker, it would seem, baseball's first warning track, years before there ever was a real one.)

On that same day, Cooke wrote, "If it hadn't been for Reiser, Branca might have departed earlier in the afternoon. Pete roamed around center field picking line drives out of the air with a turn of speed that can't be matched by anyone else in the league."

This 1947 Dodger team was taking on very much of a Branch Rickey look. Veterans were being sold or traded and younger players were more and more being relied on. Billy Herman had been traded the year before, and Kirby Higbe and catcher Dixie Howell, together with a pair of inessential younger players, were traded to Pittsburgh for a ton of money, supposedly $250,000, and a pint-sized outfielder named Al Gionfriddo, who later would enjoy one golden moment.

The Dodgers seemed a solid ballclub that year, Reiser perhaps its only possible superstar. Reese was still getting better and better, and Dixie Walker looked like he had a bat that would manufacture base hits forever. Jackie Robinson, playing first base, was, of course, an experiment in the making and a star awaiting to happen. Ed Stanky had been a steady second baseman for the team since 1945 and a good leadoff man who could work pitchers for bases on balls as few before him. Spider Jorgensen, another of the Rickey youngsters, would beat out Vaughan and Rojek for third. At the third outfield position was Carl Furillo, a solid hitter in the mid .280's, who was a fine defensive player and owned an arm like a shotgun. And Bruce Edwards, just then only 24 years old, looked like the Dodger catcher of the present and the future.

The pitching staff was led by group of young hurlers with powerful arms. Ralph Branca, Harry Taylor and the two lefties, Joe Hatten and Vic Lombardi, were a potent quartet, and they were backed by Hugh Casey, still a premier reliever in the league. This was a solid team, if not a great one, but as Durocher had said earlier, "If Reiser's all right, well…"

Came the month of May, however, and the Dodgers started to falter. Walker's hitting slowed down, both Reiser and Reese went into batting slumps, and Jackie Robinson, pursued by the bigots who were out to prevent his playing, hadn't yet found his stride. The most flagrant attempt to protest Robinson's presence in a major league uniform came from Brooklyn's archrivals, the St. Louis Cardinals. In early May, a threat by a group of Cardinals to strike against the Dodgers was thwarted at the last moment by the team's owner, Sam Breadon. How ironic that this was the same team put together and run by Branch Rickey, who now set in motion the entry of Negro players.

As ugly and shameful as this attempted strike appears to our present thinking, it was hardly a singular event. Robinson was cursed from opposing team dugouts, spiked by runners coming into his base, brushed back by pitchers aiming at his head and constantly harassed by threatening mail. That he could play at all under this pressure was surprising. That he could play and thrive and grow into the outstanding star that he soon would become was indeed miraculous.

And it started to happen quickly. By the second month of the season, Robinson put together a 14-game hitting streak that brought his average up into the .270's. At the same time, his speed on the base paths and his ability to steal bases became apparent, and this talent became a major weapon in the Dodger arsenal.

Their former base-stealing champion, Pete Reiser, who had led the league the previous season with 34 swipes including seven historic thefts of home, was having a hard time of it. Reiser didn't steal his first base till May 29 in a game with the Giants, a month and a half into the season. He quickly followed that with his second steal, just two days later.

A week earlier, it was noted that he had been having trouble all year with his left ankle, stemming from the injury he had suffered at the end of the previous season. "Rest is the only cure," proclaimed Dodger trainer Harold Wendler.

But as Roscoe McGowen of *The New York Times* observed, "Reiser has not received any rest. On the contrary, he has played every game except one, running with almost his usual speed when necessary, but frequently limping on and off the field when merely walking or trotting."

This condition also troubled Reiser's hitting. After beginning the season with the heat of the past, he had cooled off in May. He awoke momentarily in midmonth, finally hitting his first homer of the season on May 10 and getting six consecutive hits over several days soon after that.

His two stolen bases came smack in the middle of a new batting surge, suggesting that the Pistol was back. His hits were now coming in bunches, and he was starting to bat with power once again.

The National League race, in the meantime, had turned into a tight eight-team affair, with the guys at the bottom always less than double digits away from the men at the top. By the end of the month, the Dodgers were two games behind the first-place Giants in a race that continued to seesaw.

In the last game of May, the Dodgers beat the Braves, 5–0, as Reiser's two-run home run clinched it for Brooklyn. A fascinating, if painful, statistic appeared in the notes of that game, published in *The New York Herald-Tribune*. Jackie Robinson, it was pointed out, was hit by Braves pitcher Mort Cooper for the second time that season in that contest. This made it an ungrand total of six times that the Dodger first baseman had been hit by pitches thrown by opposing hurlers. Quite an uncanny total for any batter at this point in the season.

Brooklyn continued its winning ways over the next few days, splitting a pair with the Cards and taking two from the visiting Pirates. Reiser was scoring runs again and hitting for extra bases, and the Dodgers by this time had climbed to just one game behind the Giants. On June 4, with a 9–4 victory over the Pirates, they actually tied the Giants for first place. But this game more importantly produced another historical disaster. One almost waiting, it seems, to happen. That is, to happen again.

The score was already 7–2 in the Dodgers' favor when outfielder Cully Rikard came to bat in the Pirate half of the sixth inning. The game looked easy from Brooklyn's perspective, with pitcher Ralph Branca, in the midst of his best season, coasting to his sixth victory.

Ebbets Field, always a cozy ballpark, was even cozier that year. General manager Branch Rickey had added boxes in the outfield, moving the left field wall 40 feet closer to accommodate the new seating, and the one in center a good 30 feet nearer. The center field wall, once 420 feet away, was now standing 390 feet from home plate.

Rikard took a hard cut on a Branca fast ball and sent it sailing high and far toward that center field wall. Patrolling the area like a cop on a mission, Reiser took after it, his eyes on the sky, his legs in a whir.

"Hell, this is an easy out," Reiser told Donald Honig years later. There was plenty of room behind him, plenty of space in which to snare that fly ball. "I'm going full speed," he continued, "and oh, my God!"

Reiser had forgotten that the wall was now 30 feet closer.

He gloved the ball just a moment before he crashed headlong into the concrete and collapsed unconscious on to the outfield grass. As Al Laney wrote in the following day's *Tribune*, "The crowd, which watched silently while Reiser was being carried away, did not know he had held onto the ball."

"Rikard circled the bases," Laney went on, "but Butch Henline, the umpire, who ran to Reiser, found the ball still in Reiser's glove…. Two outs were posted on the scoreboard after play was resumed. Then the crowd let out a tremendous roar."

Reiser was still unconscious when he was carried into the Dodger clubhouse. After a preliminary examination, the attending doctor feared the worst. A priest was hurriedly called and last rites of the Catholic Church were given to Reiser.

The young man came to for a moment and realized he couldn't move. He collapsed again, and this time he didn't awaken till 3 a.m. the following day in Swedish Hospital, a place that sadly had become by this time one of his homes away from home.

This was the fourth time in four consecutive major league seasons of play that Reiser had crashed into an outfield wall during a game. Add an additional one from his days in the service, when he crashed through a fence and toppled down a hill, and that brings the total to five.

Remember Robert Frost's words. "Something there is that doesn't love a wall," Frost wrote, "that wants it down." Young Pete Reiser, still in the prime of his life, apparently still did.

As to that catch of his, Gene Hermanski, who had played left field for the Dodgers that day, revealed quite a different story in a taped interview with Rick Tuber, Reiser's son-in-law. "I knew I couldn't get the ball," said Hermanski, "and I watched Pete as he kept rolling along."

"He *almost* made the catch," continued Hermanski, surprisingly. "He fumbled the ball in his glove and the ball trickled down the wall. His head then hit the concrete and he slumped down to the ground. The ball happened to fall between him and the wall and no one saw that but the people in the center field stands behind him."

"The first thing I did," the old-time Dodger outfielder said, "was to put the ball in his glove. Then I took his hat off and stroked his head. The umpire came out and saw the ball in his glove and said, 'You're out!'"

Whether Reiser caught the ball or was given the put-out by a kind and quick-thinking teammate, he deserved the catch. Heroism, even the foolhardy sort, justifies the reward.

This probably was Reiser's worst encounter with an outfield wall. "I almost died," he was quoted by Peter Golenbock. "When I woke up I couldn't move. For ten days I was paralyzed."

Newspaper accounts soon after the collision never suggested the severity of Reiser's injury. "Pete Reiser, who cracked his head against the wall Wednesday night," wrote the *Tribune* two days later, "suffered a concussion but not a fracture. He may be able to play again in ten days."

Two days later, that same paper said, "Pete Reiser, still recovering from his concussion in Swedish Hospital, received a number of teammates as guests yesterday. Reiser says his muscles ached but says there's nothing else wrong with him.

"'He wants to get up right now,' says Dr. Dominick Rossi, who attended Reiser. Dr. Rossi believes he is suffering from muscular shock more than anything else and predicted that Pete will return to the lineup during the next Western trip, beginning Thursday."

Two weeks after the collision, Reiser did join the team during its Western trip, while the Dodgers were in Chicago. But bad luck still trailed him. "I was out in the field during batting practice," he told Honig, "and Clyde King ran into me. We bumped heads. I was knocked out, but I didn't feel that bad."

That night, however, while he and Reese were sitting on the porch of their hotel, the shortstop looked at him strangely. "You all right?" Reese asked.

"Yeah, why?" Reiser replied.

"What's that big knot on your head?" said Reese, pointing to the large swollen protrusion on Reiser's scalp.

Reiser touched it and it felt the size of half a golf ball. "Maybe you'd better get the doctor," suggested Reese

"The doctor came," recounted Reiser, "had one look at me and called Mr. Rickey in Brooklyn. Next thing I know I'm being flown to Johns Hopkins in Baltimore to be operated on. I had a blood clot. I'd had it from the wall injury, and when King ran into me, that moved it. They told me I'd never play again."

"You're lucky," the doctor told him. "If it had moved just a little more you'd have been gone."

"Pete was unable to hold even a pencil," reported W. C. Heinz. "He had double vision and, when he tried to take a single step, he became dizzy. He stayed in the hospital for three weeks and then went home for almost a month."

While Reiser was enduring these relentless troubles, the Dodgers remained in the thick of that year's pennant race. This was very much a team effort, from a team made up mainly of new faces and very recent arrivals. Bruce Edwards, Carl Furillo, Ralph Branca, Joe Hatten, Vic Lombardi, a green Gil Hodges, a still greener Duke Snider, and, of course, Jackie Robinson.

Robinson was already becoming a star. It was almost as if the absence of Reiser, the basic electricity of the team, helped set off Robinson's surge. Through much of June and early July, the rookie first baseman went on another long hitting streak. This one was for 21 games, and it helped lift the Dodgers to the top spot in the National League and Robinson himself to the .300 batting mark. He also gained the league's lead in stolen bases, a place not unknown to Pete Reiser.

Robinson's breakthrough of baseball's racial barrier, as well as his almost immediate success, soon brought on several other signings of Negro ballplayers. The Cleveland Indians of the American League moved first. In early July, they signed the 22-year-old Larry Doby, who was then playing his second year with the Newark Eagles of the Negro National League, and would soon be roving the outfield for the Indians. Ultimately, of course, after an outstanding career, Doby would be inducted into baseball's Hall of Fame.

Less than two weeks later, the St. Louis Browns signed Willard Brown and Henry Thompson, from the roster of the Kansas City Monarchs of the Negro American League. Brown, 36 years old at the time, would play just a handful of games for the St. Louis team, but Thompson would enjoy long and successful years with the New York Giants. Playing mainly second and third, he would appear in two World Series for the Giants and be one of their stars in their championship in 1954.

This wall had been broken and, in a few years, would be demolished. But as to the other one…

In light of Reiser's latest collision, the one with the wall in Ebbets Field, a study of the Dodger box scores of that year points up the lack of foresight of the Brooklyn management. Robinson, a second baseman and shortstop, was playing first base. Gil Hodges, who later turned into the premier first baseman in the league, was a catcher. Carl Furillo, soon a right fielder, was in center. Shortstop Eddie Miksis was playing left field. Also playing left field on various occasions was shortstop and third baseman Arky Vaughan.

With all these shifts of positions having been made or soon to take place, why wasn't Reiser protected by returning him to the infield? Better yet, why didn't the Dodgers ensure themselves of a healthy Reiser for their future?

For the first time since Reiser's rookie season, he wasn't named to the National League All-Star team that year. Five Dodgers, however, were.

These were catcher Bruce Edwards, infielders Reese and Stanky, pitcher Ralph Branca and outfielder Dixie Walker—who together with his brother Harry, then on the Philadelphia Phillies, made for a rare brother combination on an All-Star team .

Strange, but probably predictable, was Jackie Robinson's absence on the National League team. The two teams were chosen by fans in write-in ballots that season, and by a look at the National League lineup, Robinson certainly warranted selection.

The National League lost again that year, 2–1, in a rare pitchers' duel, aided by Braves pitcher Johnny Sain's wild throw into the outfield on an attempted pick-off play at first base. This gave the American League its tenth victory in the first 14 All-Star games played.

But if Robinson didn't play for the All-Stars that season, he continued to play hard, strong and successfully for the Dodgers, who went on a seven-game winning streak immediately after the break. Brooklyn soon held a three-game lead in the league standing, and the team's forgotten star, Pete Reiser, was beginning again to see a modicum of action.

His return began slowly, in the opening game of a doubleheader with Chicago. It was July 12, almost five and a half weeks after Reiser's nasty collision with the Ebbets Field barrier back on June 4. His action that day was for only half an inning. Reiser relieved Vaughan in left field for the final outs in a sure Dodger win and made one of those put-outs himself. But as the *Tribune* reported, "He was received by the critical public of Flatbush with unanimous approval."

A day later, Reiser once again filled in for final outs in left field, this time in place of Eddie Miksis. And on the following day, he was sent in to pinch-hit for pitcher Vic Lombardi and grounded out. This was his first visit to the plate in a month and a half.

On July 15, he returned fully to action, playing both ends of a doubleheader that Brooklyn lost to the Pirates. But as Bob Cooke wrote in the *Tribune* the following day, "Pete Reiser started both games. He made two hits, a single and a double, and wasn't responsible for any of the day's woes."

On the next day, however, Reiser's two hits and two runs scored in three official at bats helped the Dodgers to a 10–6 victory over the Pirates and broke a three-game losing streak for the team.

Reiser continued to show signs of his old self over the next week. He won several printed plaudits for sparkling play in the field, these days mostly in left, and his hitting produced many long and timely hits. The Dodgers, too, kept their place at the top of the league's standing and began to increase their margin.

Was it really possible that Reiser could come all the way back? Once again, however, he didn't help his own cause. On July 21, in the first game of what turned into a doubleheader victory over the Reds, Reiser was injured again.

"The inherent recklessness of Pete Reiser," wrote Bob Cooke, "caused his withdrawal after four innings. Pete made a crash landing in an effort to intercept Young's inside-the-park homer and injured his left shoulder. Doc Wendler, Brooklyn's trainer, predicts he'll be back in the lineup in two or three days."

It kept him out twice that time. More than that, the injury added damage to a body that was reaching a point beyond repair. Ralph Branca, whose pitching that season was the saving grace of the team's staff, had some incisive comments about Reiser's build and that recklessness.

"I always marveled at Pete's build," said Branca. "He had sloping shoulders and his back muscles were like two tenderloins. His spine was about five inches deep because his back muscles were so strong."

"He played so hard," Branca continued, "even in batting practice. Pitchers would be shagging flies, and Pete would come out there, and a fly would go up, and Pete would take off. You'd have to yell, 'No, no, no,' because he would run into the wall in practice to catch a ball. The guy had no fear."

To his utter self-destruction, the guy had no fear.

When Reiser did finally return, the Dodgers were in the midst of a streak that would reach 13 straight victories and temporarily give them a ten-game lead as they stood in first place. And Reiser started to hit and score runs like he hadn't for a long while. Now mostly patrolling left field, in one doubleheader with the Pirates he got five hits in seven at bats, including a double, a home run and three runs batted in. In several other games, he had two- and three-hit performances. His batting average by now had risen over the .300 mark.

One report, in the *Tribune*, read: "Reiser looks more like himself at the plate every day. The oft-injured outfielder hit a double to left center in the fifth which bounced against the brick wall."

Even when the Dodgers went into a short tailspin after their long winning streak, his potent batting continued. Though one newspaper note gave warning. "Pete Reiser still suffering from dizzy spells," said the *Tribune*, "which caused his removal from last night's game, was in uniform but didn't play. Reiser isn't sure he'll be fit for tomorrow evening's battle with the Phillies at Ebbets Field."

But dizzy or not, he played. And he got two hits that day and three the following one as the Dodgers split the pair. Thus by mid–August, the

Dodgers held a four game lead over the Cardinals with less than 50 games to go.

Uncertain as Dodger fortunes had seemed when Chandler pulled the rug out from under them with his ban of Durocher, Brooklyn had prospered under the unlikely tutelage of Burt Shotton. But could this young Dodger team actually hold on and win its first pennant in six years? And was there still enough in Pete Reiser's battered body to lead that charge?

20

End Game

"Durocher played him before he was ready, the Dodgers lost the pennant and Reiser lost his chance at the Hall of Fame. Reiser, who would have been compared to Joe DiMaggio, Ted Williams, or Stan Musial, played at his superior level for exactly a half season before he was struck down."

—Pete Golenbock in *Bums*

The Dodgers held firm to their lead, slowly increasing it to seven and a half games by the end of August. Reiser, too, played well, hitting with some consistency and, on occasions, suggesting the player of his prewar years. There were times when he and Robinson appeared to make up a new Golden Duo. Several times they pulled off double steals together, and in one memorable outing with the Phillies, the two players came up with seven hits—four for Robinson, three for Reiser—and between them split four runs scored.

Reiser had also steadily climbed the hit parade of batting averages. During the last half of August and much of September, he constantly appeared amongst the top five batters in the league. On several occasions, he was as high as second-best to Harry Walker of the Cardinals, who would ultimately win the title. He was also high amongst the leaders in stolen bases. Robinson would win the title that year, with 29 stolen bases, but Reiser trailed him in second place.

Still, with all these impressive numbers, his efforts seemed lifeless and his presence inconsequential to this team. Rarely was he mentioned in newspaper accounts of the games, and his place as the engine that powered the Dodger machine was more and more being taken over by Jackie

Robinson. It was Robinson who was getting the key hit, it was Robinson who was taking the extra base, it was Robinson who was upsetting pitchers with his antics on the base paths, and it was Robinson who was even doing the undoable and stealing home, as Reiser had so often done.

The sad truth was that Reiser was still getting dizzy spells, still getting painful headaches, and, as he told Donald Honig years later, "I could feel myself getting weaker and weaker and weaker."

Back in early August, the doctor at Johns Hopkins had advised Reiser to skip the remainder of the season. "I want to play," Reiser had told him.

"I can't okay that," answered the doctor. "The slightest blow on your head can kill you."

So against doctor's advice and with his agonized head and body in constant pain, he was playing. What was most astonishing about all this was that under these incredible circumstances, when most others would never even dare to play, he was playing with some real success. And though he might not have been leading the charge, there he was miraculously hitting in the .300's and accruing the second highest number of stolen bases in the league.

Which only underscores the point: Imagine what he could have done if he had been healthy!

The race was all but finished in mid–September, during the Dodgers' last swing through the West. Going into St. Louis and into a three-game series, the Dodgers were only four and a half games ahead of the Cards. Lose the three of them and the pennant race would go down to the wire. But in three one-run games, Brooklyn took two of them, 4–3 and 8–7, while losing the middle game of the set, 8–7. This increased their first-place margin over St. Louis to five and a half games. The next day, the Dodgers took a doubleheader from the Reds, while the Cardinals over the next two days were trounced twice by the Giants. With only 11 games to play, the Dodgers were seven and a half games in front and a near certainty to win the pennant.

On September 22, while the Dodgers were enjoying a rare day off, the Cardinals lost a night game to the Cubs, 6–3. This squeezed every mathematical possibility out of the Cards' chances for the flag and gave the Dodgers the 1947 National League pennant. Early in spring, general manager Rickey had said that this would be the Dodgers' year. Despite the stunning loss of Leo Durocher as manager, Rickey's selection of Burt Shotton—if anything, Durocher's opposite—as his replacement, had somehow worked.

This youthful, well-balanced team, a club this season without an apparent superstar—though driven immensely by the *Sporting News*

The Brooklyn Dodgers of 1947, National League pennant-winners once again. Reiser is in the front row at the far left. Manager Burt Shotton, in hat and suit, sits close to the middle in the front row. Jackie Robinson is in the top row, third from the left (National Baseball Hall of Fame Library, Cooperstown, N.Y.).

Rookie of the Year, Jackie Robinson—had won the pennant by five full games over the Cardinals. They would now be facing their crosstown rivals, the New York Yankees, once again in a World Series. This time, the New York team was being managed by Bucky Harris and, strangely, run by the Dodgers' old boss, general manager Larry MacPhail.

The Brooklyn populace turned out half-million loud and strong to pay homage to their heroes. Just days before the opening of the Series, they congregated in huge throngs at Brooklyn's Borough Hall to cheer their players and party them on to battle.

"It was a great thrill when we won in 1941," spoke Dixie Walker to the crowd. "Now we've done it again in 1947. But we've never won a World Series. This time I think we will."

Other players chimed in with much the same voice, which the huge masses ate up like the famous Nathan hot dogs, native then to only Brooklyn's Coney Island. Then came the music, played by school bands from Brooklyn's Long Island University and Brooklyn Technical High School as well as Ebbets Field's own aggregation, the Brooklyn Sym-Phoney.

And then came the Series, and what a hell of a Series it was.

The opening game, played at Yankee Stadium, with former manager Leo Durocher rooting from a field box, looked promising for the Dodgers. They picked up a run in the first inning off rookie pitcher Frank Shea, while 21-game winner Ralph Branca pitched hitless ball for four innings. But things fell apart for Brooklyn in the fifth as Branca suddenly became wild and gave the Yankees five runs on three hits, three walks and a hit batsman. Brooklyn never quite got back into the game, losing finally, 5–3.

"Joe D started the fifth inning with an infield hit to deep short," Ralph Branca later commented, "and looking back my inexperience hurt me, because I started pitching in a hurry."

Branca pointed out that his brother, who had been sitting in the upper deck, told him, "You just started grabbing the ball and throwing. Nobody came out. No infielder came out to slow you down. Nobody came from the bench."

In retrospect, this was not unlike Hugh Casey's hurried pitching efforts after the third strike mishap in the fourth game of the 1941 Series.

The second game was far less of a battle. Behind Allie Reynolds, who struck out twelve Dodger batters, the Yankees belted Vic Lombardi and a trio of relievers for ten runs in an easy 10–3 victory.

Something more significant, however, happened in this severely one-sided game. Some things, perhaps better said.

In one instance, Yankee outfielder Johnny Lindell hit a triple past the glove of Pete Reiser. In a second, second baseman George Stirnweiss hit a line drive over Stanky's head into right center field, where Reiser deflected the ball into a triple. And, finally, third baseman Bill Johnson hit a high fly that went over Reiser's head in center field. First Reiser scrambled back for it, then he stumbled and fell down just as the ball was about to come into his hands. For a short moment he held onto the ball before he fumbled it and it dropped out of his glove.

"I lost it," said Reiser afterward, "but I found it again quickly enough. The reason I missed catching the ball was that I turned wrong."

"Pete Reiser," reported *The New York Herald-Tribune*, "had a bad day. He handled three triples one way or another, standing up and lying down. And he missed one grounder entirely, letting Bill Johnson take three bases on a single."

This would probably never have happened to a healthy Pete Reiser. By this time, his pains and his dizziness were wreaking havoc. He had gotten two hits thus far in the Series, but despite this, he was hardly in shape to play. Sadly, things would get even worse for him.

The Dodgers came home to Ebbets Field for the third game, which turned into a slugfest. But before the slugging took hold, Reiser, who had walked in the first inning, took off for second in an attempted steal. He was called out as he slid into the bag and collided with shortstop Phil Rizzuto. But more than that, he badly hurt his right ankle in the collision and had to be removed from the game one inning later.

The slugging began in the bottom half of the second inning as the Dodgers scored six times off starter Bobo Newsom and relievers Vic Raschi and Karl Drews. Before the day's beltings were over, the Dodgers ended up with a 9–8 win over the Yankees, and were back in Series contention.

Reiser's ankle was worse than surmised. It was X-rayed later that night and the doctor told him, "You've got a broken ankle. A very slight fracture."

"Boy, was I ticked off," Reiser told Donald Honig. "Did it have to happen right in the middle of a World Series?"

Reiser pleaded with the doctor to keep the break secret. "Just put a tight bandage on it," he told him, "say it's a bad sprain, and that I'm through for the rest of the Series."

Reiser was taking precautions for next season's contract negotiations. "I was afraid that if he said it was broken," he said to Honig, "Rickey would give me a dollar-a-year contract next year—meaning I would have to prove I was physically fit to play before I could sign a regular contract."

Astonishingly, Reiser got into the following game and at an important and historical juncture. The fourth game of the 1947 World Series was one of those games that will forever be remembered. The Yankees held a 2–1 lead going into the bottom of the ninth inning, but the game's story was much greater than that.

To that point, the Dodgers had not yet had a single hit against Yankee pitcher Floyd Bevens. They managed their lone run in the fifth inning on a base on balls, an error and a scoring fly ball. Bevens, in his first World Series effort, was on the verge of baseball history, three outs away from the first no-hitter ever recorded in a post-season game.

Bruce Edwards was the first man up for Brooklyn in the ninth, and he sent outfielder Johnny Lindell to the left field wall where he made a leaping catch of Edwards' drive for the inning's first out. One gone and only two more to go. Carl Furillo, the next batter, was walked, not anything new for Bevens that day. This was the Yankee pitcher's ninth walk of the afternoon, tying the World Series single game mark, established by Athletics' pitcher Jack Coombs in 1910. Al Gionfriddo, a pint-sized speedster, was sent in to run for Furillo, who had missed touching bases seven times that year. But Spider Jorgenson, batting eighth in the lineup, fouled out to first baseman George McQuinn for the second out. And now Bevens was only one out away from glory.

Pitcher Hugh Casey was due up and, of course, it was time for a pinch hitter. "Aren't you going to volunteer to hit?" Shotton purportedly said to Reiser. Reiser, who knew he couldn't run out anything but an out-of-the-park home run, shrugged and went to the bat rack. He was limping painfully and quite obviously as he strolled to the plate.

The first three pitches to Reiser were two balls and a strike, Bevens still having trouble with his control. "When the count got to 2–1," Gionfriddo later said, "I looked over at third base coach Ray Blades, and I see him going crazy trying to give me the steal sign. I took off for second, and I stole second headfirst. The throw came in a little high and the tag was a little late. The pitch to Reiser was ball three."

With the count now three balls and one strike, Yankee manager Bucky Harris ordered Bevens to put Reiser on. Purposely putting the potential winning run on base is unusual at any time, but doing so to a man who could barely walk was quite a tribute to that man's bat. Reiser walked slowly to first base, and Eddie Miksis was sent in to run for him.

Eddie Stanky was the next batter due up, and to almost everyone's surprise, Shotton sent Cookie Lavagetto in to pinch-hit for him. "I don't give a darn who's pitching," Gionfriddo later commented, "in a tight spot Eddie would get on. If anybody could break up a no-hitter, Eddie could, because he would foul off fifty pitches if he had to."

But up came Lavagetto in his stead. Two men on base, two men out and Bevens only one out away from a no-hitter. "I had never faced Bevens before," Lavagetto said later. "Didn't know anything about him, but you can observe for nine innings. I could see he was wild."

"Bevens was simply a fastball pitcher," Lavagetto had deduced, "so you go up there looking for it. And I know fastball pitchers pitch me up and in. They try to crowd me with the ball."

Indeed, the first ball was pitched in tight, and Lavagetto swung hard at it and missed. The next pitch was also a fastball, but this ball came over the heart of the plate. This time Lavagetto's swing didn't miss. He hit the ball solidly, sending it high and far in the direction of right fielder Tommy Henrich. Henrich, who in the inning before had made a great leaping catch of a drive by Gene Hermanski, sped back toward the soaring fly ball.

This time, however, the right fielder couldn't catch up with it. The ball slammed against the wall and caromed off of it and away from Henrich's glove. Before Henrich could retrieve it and throw it to first baseman McQuinn, who then relayed it to the plate, both Gionfriddo and Miksis had scored, and the Dodgers had won the game, 3–2. This was also, of course, the end of Floyd Bevens' no-hitter.

This was an electrifying turnaround for a team on the brink of disaster, and Lavagetto was the great hero of the moment. Had the Yankees won the game, whether on a no-hitter or something less, the Series would be all but over. A three-games-to-one advantage would be hugely difficult to surmount. But now this Series was tied at two games apiece, and there was still a game left to be played at friendly Ebbets Field.

But so much for friends. With pitcher Frank Shea, winner of the first game of the Series, going again for the Yankees, the New Yorkers won, 2–1, in a tight pitchers' duel. Rex Barney, the ultimate losing pitcher, led a quartet of Dodger hurlers in this fine, well-pitched game, giving up only five hits to Yankee bats. One of these hits, and the difference in the game, was Joe DiMaggio's fifth inning home run, his second of the Series.

Brooklyn's best chances came in the seventh when Bruce Edwards led off the inning with a walk. After Furillo flied out to DiMaggio and Jorgenson lofted one to Lindell, Vaughan came in to pinch-hit for pitcher Hank Behrman. Vaughan fouled off Shea's first pitch, then smashed the second one into the right field corner for a double, sending Edwards to third. Due up was Stanky and, once again, Shotton brought in the limping Reiser to hit for him.

But Bucky Harris would have none of him. Reiser still had one good leg, and as far as Harris was concerned, the best bat in the Dodger lineup. With two men in scoring position and his team only one run ahead, the Yankee manager once again chose to purposely walk Reiser and load the bases. Miksis, as per script, went in to run for him. But it all went for naught when, on a two-and-two pitch, Reese looked at a third strike.

The Dodgers had one more chance in the bottom of the ninth. Bruce Edwards led off the inning with a single to left, only the fourth hit off Shea in the game. Vic Lombardi went in to run for the catcher, and Furillo quickly sacrificed him to second base. There were still two outs left for the club, and the tying run was standing at second base. Spider Jorgenson was up next, but he flied to deep right center where Henrich was able to reach it and gather it in.

The Dodgers still had one out left, and up out of the dugout came Cookie Lavagetto, the hero of yesterday's magical victory, to hit for pitcher Hugh Casey. Was it too much to ask him to deliver again?

"I didn't get no butterflies against Bevens," Lavagetto later said, "but I sure got them the next day. Because now I figure, 'What the hell, I did it before. Everyone expects me to do it again.'"

"I had Shea two and nothing," Lavagetto went on, "he threw me a slider, and even though I was looking for it, I missed it. And then I had him three and one, and he threw me another slider … and I fouled that off. And on the three and two pitch he threw me a change of pace, kind of a slow curve, and I was so anxious to get a base hit that I miscalculated. I waited on the ball, but I wound up swinging and missing the damn thing. I still dream of that one."

The magic that day was gone.

Returning to their home in Yankee Stadium, New York brought back Allie Reynolds, winner of the second game, to pitch what they hoped would be the Series finale. But It wasn't.

"For in one of the most extraordinary games ever played," wrote John Drebinger of *The New York Times*, "one that left a record Series crowd of 74,065 limp and exhausted, Burt Shotton's unpredictable Flock fought the Yankees in a last-ditch stand at the Stadium yesterday and defeated them, 8 to 6."

The Dodgers started off with blazing bats. They scored a pair of runs off Reynolds in the first inning and sent the big right-hander to the showers in the third with another two. These runs were scored thanks to successive doubles by Reese, Robinson and Walker. But the Yankees were far from dead. They scored their four runs in a single inning, knocking out Dodger lefty Vic Lombardi in the bottom of the third, and the game was tied, 4–4.

For only an inning. On a disputed single by Yogi Berra, which the Dodgers loudly protested was foul, the Yankees added a run in the bottom of the fourth and took this 5–4 lead into the sixth inning. That's when the Dodgers really exploded. They crushed the superb Yankee reliever, Lefty Joe Page, and his relief, the ancient Bobo Newsom, with four runs in that inning, the last two coming via another clutch hit by Reese. The Dodgers were now in the lead, 8–5.

But it was hardly over. In the bottom of the sixth inning, with two out and two men on base, Joe DiMaggio blasted a long, high drive heading for the Dodger bullpen in left field and set in motion one of the greatest moments in world series history. (Yes, another one.)

Little Al Gionfriddo, all of five-and-half-feet short, was playing left field by then, having replaced Eddie Miksis, who had replaced starter Gene Hermanski. "I'm positioned between the 315-foot marker and the 415-foot marker," Gionfriddo later said, "which is where the bullpen was. I thought I was playing DiMaggio awfully shallow. With two on and two outs and Joe Hatten pitching, they were figuring him to pull, but that much?"

"So Hatten pitches," he went on. "and shit, DiMaggio hits the ball up the gap. I put my head down and ran, because I knew the direction it was going."

With his back to home plate, Gionfriddo ran like a hungry greyhound after the elusive rabbit, straight toward the Dodger bullpen, where the Brooklyn relievers hoped they wouldn't have to come in.

"I looked over my shoulder once," he said, "and I could see the ball was still coming, and I put my head down again, and I kept running and running, and when I got to just about where I thought the ball would come down, I reached out with my glove like I was catching a football pass over my shoulder, and I caught the ball. I was up in the air when I got it, and as I came down, I twisted a little bit to take the shock of hitting the fence with my ass instead of my stomach, and I hit that fence with my butt."

Gionfriddo, who would never play another season in the big leagues and whose name manager Shotton could never remember, had come up with one of the greatest catches in World Series history. On this day, this little man became a hero of gigantic proportions.

The Yankees could not catch up with the Dodgers that day, finally losing this sixth game, 8–6, and having to face a winner-takes-all seventh game.

The seventh game, after all this, was anticlimactic. Too much had happened before, and miracles had finally ceased to occur. The Dodgers, however, jumped off to an early two-run lead in the second inning, aided by Gene Hermanski's single to right being turned into a triple by the inadequate fielding of Yogi Berra.

The Yankees got one of those runs back in their half of the inning, on two walks and a single by Rizzuto. Two innings later, they added two more as well as gaining the lead on two singles by Rizzuto and Brown, a double by Henrich and a pair of walks. They added single runs in the sixth and seventh, but it was the sensational pitching of Joe Page that carried the day. The Yankee star reliever didn't allow a hit over the last five innings of play, facing the minimum 15 players to get the last 15 outs. The Yankees won, 5–2, and thus took the Series, four games to three.

As Arthur Daley put it in the following day's *New York Times*, "Once Page entered the fray, the handwriting was on the wall for all to see. The incredible Dodgers were done, their miracles and their magic at an end."

An added fillip to these proceedings was the announced retirement of Yankee general manager Larry MacPhail moments after the last out was made. This controversial figure, who had built championship teams in Cincinnati, in Brooklyn and here in New York; who had fought physically and verbally with his former manager, Leo Durocher, and did his best to have him banned this season; and who had prodded his young outfielder, Pete Reiser, to continue playing when doctors had strongly advised against it, was finally saying good-bye. At least, for the moment.

A bit of irony occurred during the Series that caused one to recall MacPhail's actions involving Reiser back in 1942. In the sixth game of the Series, outfielder Johnny Lindell, who had gotten two hits in his two at bats and had compiled an outstanding .500 batting average with nine hits, retired from the game because of a broken rib.

Lindell, who had sustained the injury in the game before, was castigated by MacPhail. "You're not doing the ballclub any good," ranted the general manager, "if you're out there not physically fit to play."

"I'm sorry, sir," answered Lindell. "I must disagree with you. I did have the interests of the ballclub at heart. The only reason I played was because I wanted my club to win this season. I thought I could go through with it, but I discovered when I swung at the plate, my side hurt as well as when I breathed."

Reiser, who had never fully recovered from that disaster in 1942, must have laughed through his tears at this sudden change of heart. Here he was again, hobbling on a broken ankle and still racked with pain and dizziness from his latest encounter with a wall, and wondering whether he had the strength to make a new effort next year. Though he was still being called the Dodgers' best player, they had continued without him to win three of five games and come innings-close to being the World Series winners.

He was only 28 years old, two months younger than Jackie Robinson and eight months younger than Pee Wee Reese, but was it all now behind him?

21

The Image Fades

"Maybe Pete Reiser was the purest ball player of all time. I don't know. There is no way of measuring such a thing, but when a man of incomparable skills, with full knowledge of what he is doing, destroys those skills and puts his life on the line in the pursuit of his endeavor as no other man in his game ever has, perhaps he is the truest of them all."
—W. C. Heinz, sportswriter for *The New York Sun* and five-time winner of the E. P. Dutton Award

Sally Reiser was born in St. Louis, on March 20, 1943, while her father was in his first months of service at the Army camp in Fort Riley, Kansas. Her mother, Patricia, was living with her parents in South St. Louis at the time, and her husband, Pete, was notified immediately of his daughter's arrival via the American Red Cross. He hurried home as fast as the Army would allow him, and the young couple, married for barely a year, were enthralled with the blessing of their first child, this beautiful young daughter that they were quick to christen Sally.

But the harsh realities of Sally's condition were only slowly evidenced during her early years. "I was only nineteen years old when she was born," Patricia Reiser pointed out in a taped interview with her son-in-law, Rick Tuber, long years later, "so it wasn't that easy for us to see. We knew she was probably three months behind other kids in walking and talking and things like that. We also knew she didn't like to play alone and certainly her attention span was a problem early on."

But not until Sally was ready for school and her physical and mental capabilities were tested did the family really understand the true nature of her condition. Sally was retarded, and her mental abilities would never go beyond those of a child at the second-grade level. This would remain an ongoing circumstance of life for the Reiser family, and one they would meet bravely, respectfully and with the fullest love. Sally would travel the baseball world with her parents, befriend her father's teammates, participate in many field activities, and always be treated as an equal member of the family.

Still, because of her affliction, she would also become an added financial and psychological obligation for Pete Reiser and his family at a time when they needed no further ones.

This realization of Sally's condition also closely coincided with Reiser's recognition of his own. Despite some valiant efforts and despite some hopeful assertions every now and then by baseball officials and columnists, the cumulative injuries had taken their devastating toll.

Pete Reiser's days of glory were over.

Reiser, his mother-in-law, Beatrice Hurst, and his two daughters: Sally, born in 1943, at the left, and Shirley, born in 1949 (courtesy of Shirley Reiser Tuber).

In early 1948, even as Branch Rickey had taken a first step in reformulating the structure of the Ebbets Field walls by adding one-inch foam rubber padding to protect against any further mishaps by Reiser, the Dodger general manager pleaded with Reiser to take the season off.

"He said he would pay me if I sat down all year," Reiser revealed to Donald Honig. "Being bullheaded, I said I wanted to play. But by that time all of those injuries were beginning to take their toll."

"Something was gone," Reiser went on. "It had always been so easy for me, but now it became a struggle. I was only twenty-nine, but the fun and the pure joy of it were gone."

Whether things could have been different if Reiser had acceded to Rickey's request and had sat out the 1948 season, no one could possibly know. But as Reiser admitted to Honig, his body had pretty much given way. It was probably too late for the caution that earlier could have saved an extraordinary career.

Durocher returned as manager of the Dodgers that year, his suspension at an end and Rickey's belief in the man as strong as ever. During the winter, Rickey had made some significant trades that would dramatically change the structure of the team Durocher was taking over. Ed Stanky had been traded to the Boston Braves, primarily for first baseman Ray Sanders, who would never play a single game for the Dodgers. This move was designed to open up second base to Jackie Robinson, whose defensive skills could better be utilized there.

Dixie Walker, along with pitchers Hal Gregg and Vic Lombardi, was traded to the Pittsburgh Pirates for Preacher Roe, Billy Cox and Gene Mauch. Walker, who, at best, had been a reluctant teammate of Robinson's, was already 37 years old and well past his most productive seasons. Roe and Cox would be significant additions to some of the finest Dodger teams in their history, Roe as one of the best left handed pitchers in the league and Cox as perhaps the league's outstanding defensive third basemen.

New, young players were also being brought in from Brooklyn's burgeoning minor league system as well as from the Negro Leagues. Catcher Gil Hodges was transformed into a first baseman to take the place of Robinson and became one of the foremost fielders at that position for long years. Roy Campanella, in turn, came out of the Negro Leagues to become baseball's premier backstop and ultimately the Dodgers' cleanup hitter. Bruce Edwards, their former All-Star catcher who had been touted as their catcher of the future, was turned into an infielder, but not with much success. There was also a rash of young outfielders, led by Duke Snider, George Shuba and Marvin Rackley, that would be contending for Walker's place in the outfield.

Where then could Reiser play?

In *Nice Guys Finish Last,* Durocher declared that Rickey wanted Reiser to play first base "to keep him from running into any more fences."

"So we sent Pete to Macon to work out under the guidance of George Sisler," wrote the former Dodger manager. But before the great Hall of Fame first baseman could work his magic, Durocher had discovered someone else.

"I put a first baseman's glove on our rookie catcher, Gil Hodges," continued Durocher, "and told him to have some fun. Three days later I looked up and—wow—I was looking at the best first baseman I'd seen since Dolf Camilli."

Even if Reiser had been given this chance, it would surely have been too late to change matters. Years before, it might well have resurrected Reiser's career and placed him back on his course to legendary greatness. But now, hardly. This was offering an aspirin to a man ravaged with cancer. Dizziness and headaches were still consuming him, and his body could never again perform as once it did. By this time, Reiser was a shell of what he once had been, and he never again would perform as a full-time player.

Neither his pride nor, yes, his financial obligations—considerably worsened by his daughter's condition—would allow him to walk away. Besides, a crippled and battered Reiser was still a player to be reckoned with. Remember, that twice in the past World Series, when Yankee pitchers were faced with a hobbling Reiser, barely able to walk on his broken ankle, Manager Bucky Harris had ordered him purposely walked.

In the 1948 season, still crippled by that bad ankle and suffering from dizziness and body wear and tear, Reiser was reduced to being a part-time player. He appeared in only 64 games—half of that as a pinch hitter—was at bat only 127 times and managed a woeful .236 batting average.

The Dodgers slipped to third place that year, seven games behind the pennant-winning Braves and a game back of the second-place Cardinals. Brooklyn was going through an immense transition that season with, as indicated, new players everywhere. No full-time player hit .300 that season, no one hit more than 15 home runs, no one knocked in more than 85 runs, and no pitcher won more than 15 games.

All this was done, in fact, under two different managers. Durocher remained for only half that season, being suddenly released by a disenchanted Rickey, who believed his reclamation project had gone back to his old ways. Durocher was immediately signed by the rival Giants, where he'd remain for many years and come home with two pennants. In Durocher's stead returned Burt Shotton, who would win another pennant in 1949 and manage this team until 1951.

But Reiser had had enough midway into the 1948 season. Once Durocher was gone and Shotton was back managing the Dodgers, he had asked permission to take his battered body elsewhere.

"I got permission from Rickey to make a deal," he told John McMullan of *The Miami Daily News*. "But every time I thought I had something lined up Rickey's price was too high. I was a great ball player when he was trying to sell me, but when I talked salary terms with him, it was another story."

He was finally granted his wish in the winter of 1948, when he was traded to the pennant-winning Braves for outfielder Mike McCormick, who would never accomplish much in a Brooklyn uniform. Much was still expected of Reiser, now garbed in the uniform of the Boston Braves.

"Reiser is the greatest young star the National League has known in many years," wrote the celebrated sportswriter Grantland Rice at that time. "Injuries, illnesses and fallacies cut him down. Reiser is still a potential star. A part of his hurt has been physical. A smaller part has been mental. If anyone can bring him around, it is Billy Southworth (the Braves manager at that time), a smart, keen understanding man in every way."

"It is up to Pete Reiser," the nationally syndicated columnist went on, "to prove that he still belongs in baseball. If he belongs in baseball, it must be in a big way. And if he is what he should be, the Braves are a pennant cinch."

Reiser was glad to be out of Brooklyn. He was delighted to be playing under Southworth, a man whom he had always admired, and was feeling much safer playing in Boston's player-friendly Braves Field. "They have tin, not concrete fences, in Boston," he told McMullan. "And they also have a cinder path in front of the fence. An outfielder can tell when he's getting close to trouble."

"I'm in the best shape since 1941," he boasted, "and I think I can help the Braves."

Dr. Robert Hyland, who had treated more of Reiser's ills than a hospital of doctors, assured the Braves that their new acquisition was sound. "I've found that Pete's arm is perfect (he's had right shoulder trouble for three years since crashing into the Ebbets Field wall) and his ankle is now normal," said Hyland.

"He shouldn't suffer any more dizzy spells," he continued, "since his new bridge has corrected the trouble of his upper and lower teeth meeting improperly. There is another angle to the Reiser situation which is just as important. His mental outlook has changed."

Early on, during the team's spring training in Florida, Reiser seemed to be playing like his old self. Perhaps too much like his old self.

"At one time," wrote Roger Birtwell in *The Sporting News*, "Reiser—standing in center field—raced deep into left field and hauled down a fly at the wall of the Braves' clubhouse, 385 feet from the plate."

"I thought he was going right through that clubhouse wall and wind up in the shower-bath room," commented one of the watching Braves.

"Ten minutes later," continued Birtwell, "Pete was playing a normal center field when a batter poled a terrific drive toward a clump of trees that obscured the 435-foot mark in deep center. Reiser again was away like the wind and hauled down the fly as it whistled toward the miniature forest."

"I thought he was going to land in one of those pine trees," commented one of the writers.

He didn't that time, but Reiser couldn't keep away from fences or from injury in two hapless years in Boston. Twice he collided with fences there and twice he dislocated his left shoulder while making diving catches on difficult fly balls. Nor, despite the dental treatment that Hyland believed would end Reiser's dizzy spells, did they stop.

Reiser played 84 games in 1949 for Boston, only two-thirds of them playing defensively, and managed to hit .271. He didn't hit with much power that season, and he stole only four bases. By that time, Pete Reiser during his abbreviated playing times had become a quite ordinary performer.

His wife, Patricia, gave birth to their second daughter during the season, when Shirley was born on July 11, 1949, a day before the All-Star game, which was played that year in Brooklyn. Years later, Patricia told her son-in-law, Rick Tuber, that she had suffered "nine months of agony" waiting for Shirley's birth, fearful of another retarded child.

"The first thing I asked," she continued, "was had she ten fingers and ten toes." Shirley did, and Shirley was a normal child who turned into an extraordinary young woman with a face so reminiscent of her father's.

According to her mother, "Pete was always the optimist," and didn't appear concerned about Shirley's birth. "Pete was positive about everything," she added. "Everything would turn out okay."

The Braves that year fell to fourth, two games ahead of Durocher's Giants. The pennant winners in 1949 were the Brooklyn Dodgers, who beat the Cards by the slim margin of one game. This was the start of the great Brooklyn teams of the late '40s and '50s, starring four Hall of Famers—Robinson, Campanella, Snider and Reese—as well as Gil Hodges and Carl Furillo, two of the finest players of the era.

That season they were led by Jackie Robinson, who led the league in batting with .342 and was selected as the National League's Most Valuable

Player. The parade had sadly passed Reiser by, and the kind of dominating and complete player Dodger management had envisioned in him was now appearing, if to a somewhat lesser degree, in Jackie Robinson.

Reiser's second season in Boston was a further step down. Twenty-four of his 78 at bats in 1950 were in pinch-hit roles. He hit a mere .205 with just 16 hits, only three of them for extra bases.

He was released by the Braves at the end of that season and found his way to a job with the Pittsburgh Pirates as a utility player and pinch hitter. Once again, he hit .271, and actually hit with some occasional power. He was a valuable pinch hitter, with 11 hits in 33 tries, but managed, all told, only 140 chances at the plate.

Reiser's final season as a player in the major leagues was for the Cleveland Indians, in 1952. For him it was a foreshortened one of only 34 games, in which he batted a dismal .136 and was released in midseason. Reiser was offered a chance to play on Cleveland's Indianapolis farm team but declined.

Painfully, it was time to go home.

At that time, Pete Reiser was barely 33 years old.

22

Aftermath

"Pistol Pete Reiser flashed across the heavens like a blindingly beautiful meteor. For one brief moment, his dazzling brilliance illuminated the baseball world. Then he was gone, and only a memory remained."
— William F. McNeil, *The Dodgers Encyclopedia*

Pete Reiser collided with outfield walls seven times in his career, collapsing unconscious after five of them. The other two collisions resulted in a dislocation of his left shoulder and a fracture of his collarbone. While running the bases, he suffered fractures of both ankles, wrecked the cartilage in one knee and ripped the muscles of a leg. Two times he was beaned while wearing the most primitive and useless of batting helmets. All told, he was carried off the playing field 11 times.

In June 1952, the awful counting had finally stopped. With his playing days behind him, Reiser went home to St. Louis and wondered what he wanted to do next. One of his closest friends there was Glen Schaeffer, whom he had known in the Army and with whom he had since kept close ties. Schaeffer had been the general manager of a Plymouth-DeSoto automobile dealership on South Grand Street in St. Louis since 1949 and offered his friend a job.

"I asked him if he would like to get into the automobile business," Schaeffer told Rick Tuber, Reiser's son-in-law, in a taped interview many years later. "Using his name, we would be able to advertise a lot and be able to bring people in."

"I paid him a salary, but it wasn't much," Schaeffer conceded. "But if he brought people in, we'd give him a percentage."

Prompted by the chance to meet the ballplayer—and to buy a car from him—people immediately started coming in and, indeed, buying cars. "This is where the idea of a batting tee came in," continued Schaeffer, "right there at South Grand Motors. I had never heard of the damn thing, and as far as I know, Pete's the guy who created it."

As a promotional event for the dealership, Reiser came up with the idea of a batting school day. He and a couple of local ballplayers would offer tips to kids on how to better their baseball swing. This would be accomplished with the aid of a raised tee that Reiser would construct and that could be raised or lowered to fit the kid's height.

By placing a plastic Whi°e ball on the tee, he could work with a kid to adjust and improve his swing as he attempted to bat it off the tee. Thus the batting tee was born, and a step later, tee ball.

"I didn't think it would go," said Schaeffer when he heard the suggestion. "I didn't think there'd be fifty kids who'd show up."

"Let's give it a whirl," said Reiser, and they did.

"Damn it," exclaimed Schaeffer, "there were five hundred, a thousand kids who showed up with their parents that day. There were so many that showed up we had to call the police to control things."

The event was so successful and received so much publicity that they held a second one with much the same results.

Soon after this, the two men decided to open their own business, a used car lot in a nearby community, that they called Pete Reiser Motors. "We did pretty good at first," said Schaeffer, but their timing turned out to be terrible.

"The automobile market for the first time I ever heard of," said Schaeffer, "went bust."

That was early 1953, and car agencies all over St. Louis were going out of business. Pete Reiser Motors was no exception. This time, at least for Reiser, the timing was good.

"We were at the dealership one day," explained Schaeffer, "at about two o'clock, when a call comes in for Pete from Buzzy Bavasi, the general manager of the Brooklyn Dodgers."

Reiser grabbed the phone and jumped right out of his chair when he heard what Bavasi had to say. "Pete," asked Bavasi, "how would you like to come back in to baseball?"

"Yes, sir!" Reiser screamed into the phone.

"How much would you want to come back in?" said Bavasi.

"You pay me what you think I'm worth," replied Reiser,

The small taste of the automobile business was enough to show Reiser that he did not want to be there. Even with the possibility of successful days. He was born to play baseball and to live baseball, and Bavasi's phone call proved that in a moment. Thus began a long, successful and happy career for the former ballplayer. He became a coach and manager in the minors, and beginning in 1960, a coach, a scout and an instructor for various major league teams, including the Dodgers, the Chicago Cubs and the Los Angeles Angels.

He rose up through the Dodger chain of minor league clubs, winning accolades from executives and players alike, until achieving his greatest success in 1959 by winning the Texas League pennant with the Victoria Rosebuds and by being named Minor League Manager of the Year. Reiser went from Dodger-owned teams at Thomasville, Georgia, to Kokomo, Indiana, to Green Bay, Wisconsin, to Victoria, Texas, to finally the big club itself. In 1960, he became the third base coach, under Manager Walter Alston, for the Los Angeles Dodgers, who had moved to their westward home two years before.

During those years with Dodger teams, he had worked significantly in teaching and coaching such major stars as Frank Howard, Tommy Davis and Maury Wills. Wills, in fact, named Robinson and Reiser as his two greatest idols and dedicated his biography, *It Pays to Steal*, to Reiser.

In a copy of that book given to Reiser, Wills wrote: "To Pete Reiser, 'My Guiding Light,' who is responsible for what measure of success that I've been able to realize."

In a chapter titled just that, "Pete Reiser—My Guiding Light," Wills goes much further. Describing a time back in 1960, the ballplayer's second season with the Dodgers, Wills says that he was ready to give up on himself. "I couldn't buy a base hit," wrote the great shortstop and base stealer. His four terrific months of the season before "were about to be washed down the drain."

Recognizing the greatness of Reiser's hitting ability, he decided to turn for help to the former batting champion, then in his first year as a Dodger coach. Surrendering his free time, Reiser worked with Wills for two hours every afternoon in the torrid pits of Dodger Coliseum. Starting almost from scratch, for 13 consecutive days, he taught the young ball player the fundamentals of hitting.

"Almost like a manager would do with a nine-year old Little Leaguer," wrote Wills. Reiser convinced him to use a lighter bat, changed his batting stance and his swing, taught him to hit to the opposite field, and gave him back the confidence Wills had lost in the terrible mire of his slump.

Reiser also helped him with his base stealing. "Taking Reiser's advice," wrote Wills, "I took greater leads, more liberties with specific pitchers. I assumed a positive attitude toward stealing bases."

"This approach paid off," he continued, "because by the end of the season I stole thirty-two more for a grand total of fifty—more stolen bases than any Dodger had piled up in thirty-seven years."

Before Wills had turned to Reiser, the shortstop was batting .204. By season's end, he was hitting .295 and would finish his 14 major league seasons with a lifetime average of .281. Along that glorious way, Wills, of course, would break Ty Cobb's single-season base stealing record with an incredible 104 stolen bases and lead the league in that category for six consecutive seasons.

This was hardly a single-success story for Reiser as a coach. On his road upward, he gained the reputation of being a tough and inspiring leader who drew out the best from his players with strict discipline and the building of pride.

"You had to give him one hundred percent every day," related Carl Warwick years later in a taped interview with Rick Tuber. Warwick had played for Reiser at Victoria, and he credited Reiser with helping him rise to the majors.

"He didn't allow you to loaf," Warwick continued. "You had to run, you had to hustle. If we lost a few games because of mental or physical errors, he'd immediately get you on the field and make you work out. But he'd make you do it till you learned to do it right."

Warwick related an incident involving that Texas League team to illustrate Reiser's methods. The team had driven in its bus all night from a game in distant Amarillo and had come back into town tired and bedraggled. Though still leading in the pennant race, the team had just blown several games because of careless play and mental lapses. Warwick recalled that their wives were waiting for them as the players drove into town, but Reiser wouldn't let the players off the bus.

They were taken to the team's clubhouse, told to don their uniforms and ordered onto the field, where Reiser worked out with them for two long hours. "Now, at least," said their manager, "when you get home you'll really be able to sleep."

Tuber wondered if this hadn't made Reiser less popular with the players. "With Pete," Warwick answered, "they understood what it was. He was saying that if you guys don't have enough pride in your playing, I'll show you how to get some pride."

Warwick pointed out that Reiser was at the same time a father figure to his players "If anybody had any problems," said Warwick, "he was always there to help. Pat (Mrs. Reiser) was always there to help, too. He tried to make the team a big family."

"He managed the way he played," Warwick concluded, "and the way he lived. When you finished playing for him, you knew you'd played to the best of your ability."

Reiser was always an intelligent and articulate man with a sly sense of humor, which had to have made him an ideal coach. Early in Reiser's career, Tom Meany wrote a piece for *Collier's* that spoke strongly of this unappreciated side of him. "He can be more articulate than the average ballplayer," wrote Meany, "and would be a meaty subject for interviewers if any took the trouble to draw him out."

Meany then described Reiser's appearance in Chicago when he was presented with a special award. "He rather surprised the Chicago baseball writers," remembered Meany, "with his speech of acceptance. Pete talked pleasantly and easily. Those who had watched him go quietly about his business on the ball field expected him to mumble, 'Thanks, fellas,' and sit down."

The writer also pointed out Reiser's excellent ability to mimic and his surprising sense of humor. "He does an imitation of the contortionistic wind-up of Coach Fred Fitzsimmons," Meany continued, "which is a reasonable facsimile of Fitz's work when he was an active pitcher with the Dodgers. In pepper drills, Pete clowns extensively, handling the ball with the dexterous skill of a prestidigitator. He expresses himself in pantomime, rarely making any wisecracks."

His extraordinary knowledge of baseball combined with his eloquence and his sense of humor made him an ideal coach and teacher for younger players. So many of them, surprisingly, had little idea of what he had accomplished as a player himself.

But even during these years, injury and catastrophe never let Reiser alone. In a memorable and devastating article, W. C. Heinz chronicled his own adventures in discovering Reiser in various tragic situations over the years, both during his playing years and later during Reiser's days as a coach.

While Reiser was managing the Dodgers' Class D Kokomo team, Heinz "found him moving and talking slowly and suffering chest pains." The doctor had just told him that he should be taken to a hospital immediately.

"What are you planning to do?" asked Heinz.

"I'm going home to St. Louis," Reiser replied. "My wife works for a doctor there, and he'll know a good specialist."

"How will you get to St. Louis?" asked Heinz.

"It's about three hundred miles," said Reiser. "The doctor says I shouldn't fly or go by train, because if anything happens to me they can't stop and help me. I guess I'll have to drive."

Heinz then offered to drive him, and he did. They drove for eight and a half hours in Reiser's seven-year-old Chevy as Heinz kept him occupied with baseball reminiscences. With each town they passed, Heinz had a fear that Reiser never would make the next one.

Several years after that, while Reiser was coaching for the Cubs, he was carried off the field after a fight in Candlestick Park between the Giants and his team from Chicago.

"There was a big scrap at home plate," Reiser remembered, "and I went up to separate (Bobby) Bonds and (Randy) Hundley. Somebody gave me a karate shot. Broke my collar bone. Somebody hit me on the head. Knocked me out. I went down and got spiked. I think that's what broke up the fight. They saw I'm on the ground, and they're stepping on me."

One more foolish decision to endanger his body, one more hospital visit, and one more, thank goodness, recovery.

Years later, while Reiser was working for the Chicago Cubs in St. Petersburg during spring training, Heinz tried to reach him at the motel he was said to be staying at. Instead the writer found him in the city's St. Anthony's Hospital.

"He had a small private room at the end of the hall," wrote Heinz. "The head of the bed was elevated, and he was in one of those hospital gowns, a sheet up to his waist. He was bald and heavier under the sheet and the oval face was fuller and he needed a shave."

Reiser had bronchial pneumonia and his breathing was heavy. "I can't breathe," he told Heinz. "I had an attack in 1970 in Palm Springs. In spring training. I been getting them on and off once a year. Now three times a year. This is the third. They're worried because each time the heart murmur shows up. That time in Kokomo it was a strained heart muscle. In '64 I had a heart attack. I also got a hiatus hernia. I can't make quick moves anymore."

An oxygen tube was standing at the side. Reiser asked Heinz to plug it into the outlet on the wall. "I can hardly breathe," he told the writer.

Reiser used it for little more than a minute then handed it back to Heinz. "If I leave it in too long," he told him, "my sinuses get worse."

Several days later, Heinz called Reiser, who by this time was back at his home in Palm Springs, California. His wife, Pat, answered the phone and told Heinz that Reiser was feeling better. When Reiser himself got on, Heinz told him to take things easier.

"Yeah," Reiser answered, "I guess from now on, with everything I got wrong with me, I'll have to."

But there was too much wrong with him by then. Trouble with his heart for over 25 years, his body brutally battered by baseball walls and wars, lingering dizzy spells from cumulative concussions, and, finally, from a history of inveterate smoking since his teen-age years, a severe case of emphysema that wouldn't let him breathe.

He had been working as a scout for the Chicago Cubs when he realized he didn't have the strength to continue. "I think I'm going to retire," he told his wife, Pat. The playing, the coaching, the scouting, the life of baseball had taken its toll.

Two days later, on October 25, 1981, at the age of 62, Harold Patrick Reiser at last reached the boundary of his life. This final wall had threatened him for a long time. But just as with all the others, it would not give way.

The Dodgers and the Yankees were playing the sixth game of the World Series that day, a Series in which the Dodgers would eventually win, four games to two. That was in New York.

In Palm Springs, California, Reiser died peacefully at his home, leaving the world that would remember the legacy of Pistol Pete.

23

An Imperfect Appraisal

"Pete Reiser was the greatest ball player I ever saw."
—Lonnie Frey, All-Star second baseman and shortstop of the Dodgers and the Reds for 14 years

There is no easy way to gauge how good Pete Reiser really was. There is no esoteric mixture of statistics that would apply, no way of reading his complete records to appraise the player, no easy way to determine his ultimate value. That is, unless you were lucky enough to have watched him play or to study the accounts of those who did. And even those appraisals may have been seen through subjective eyes.

Lonnie Frey is one of those who did watch him play. Usually from the field of opposing teams or from the vantage point of opposing dugouts, or, for several years, as a teammate on various service squads. Frey, who had also been born in St. Louis nine years before Reiser, started his baseball career in a Brooklyn uniform in 1933. But most of his playing days were spent with the Cincinnati Reds, primarily at second base, in a long and successful career that lasted 14 seasons and included several stints as an All-Star.

He is firm in his appraisal of Reiser. "Pete Reiser was the greatest ball player I ever saw," said Frey in an interview with the author in early 2002. "I didn't see Hornsby and I didn't see Cobb, but of those I did, Reiser would be my pick."

"He could do everything," he went on. "And if I was picking a team, he'd be my first choice. It would take the talents of a dozen players to match what this man could do."

Frey, an intelligent and articulate man despite his 90-plus years, also described Reiser as "the best kind of man," who never once blamed any of his bosses for his short-changed career. But Frey did. He believed that the Dodger management was responsible for his friend's injuries and his fore-shortened career.

"This was the worst management in baseball," he declared. "They should have moved him back to the infield the first time he hit the wall."

Frey doesn't stand alone in his thinking. Certainly not in his estimate of Reiser's playing talents. This book is strewn with quotations from base-ball management, fellow players, sportswriters and columnists that are astounding accolades to his abilities. Two others should be cited.

The first is a 1942 article in *Collier's* magazine by Tom Meany, a fore-most sports reporter of his day, titled "Pistol Pete—National Leaguer No. 1." Written prior to the start of the 1942 season—a season, mind you, that till Reiser's collision with the wall in Sportsman's Park was superior to his rookie year—it already calls Reiser the best player in his league, if not in all of baseball.

"There are competent judges—executives, managers, umpires and players—who will tell you Pete is the best player in baseball today," wrote Meany.

He then quotes writer Garry Schumacher as saying, "Reiser has reduced baseball to its simplest elements. The other guys throw the ball— he hits it. The other guys hit the ball—he catches it."

According to Meany, Schumacher expounded "the astounding the-ory that Reiser was so perfect mechanically that he probably could go to bat blindfolded and hit safely once in every three attempts."

Meany pointed out that "even now, when Pete gets hold of one, you'll hear somebody in the press box sing out, 'Blindfolded!' It has become a fairly frequent war cry in National League press coops."

The writer then went into the previous season's pennant race when the Dodgers and Cardinals fought tooth and nail down to the wire. "There was some question," wrote Meany, "as to how the untested Reiser would stand the gaff. He answered by hitting safely in twenty-nine of the last thirty games the Dodgers played, batting more than .400 for the month of September."

As to his fielding? "His exceptional speed," concluded Meany, "enables him to challenge even Terry Moore for ground-covering honors, while his steel arm ranks with those of the throwing DiMaggios."

That was Tom Meany's appraisal. Even more was said in a second piece, an article by John Lardner for the *North American Newspaper Alliance*, dated July 31, 1942. Lardner writes here about "the Carey system of rating baseball players." Devised by Max Carey, the Hall of Fame outfielder of the early 1900s for the Pirates and Braves, who had led the league in stolen bases ten times and in several other departments on various occasions, it was his method of evaluating baseball greatness.

"He divides the game into three departments," wrote Lardner, "hitting, fielding and base-running, with each player rated on a point basis. Five points represents perfection in each department—or as near perfection as Homo Sapiens can be expected to get on that green footstool."

"It occurs to me," Lardner goes on, "that Mr. Carey, shu°ing through the roll call of present day ballplayers, would have to stop at the name of Harold Patrick Reiser and award the ribbon there and then. Reiser, Brooklyn center fielder, comes as close to excellence by all three Carey specifications as anyone now in business."

At the time this article was written, Reiser was leading the league in hitting, in stolen bases, in doubles and in runs scored. "He is undoubtedly one of the six best defensive outfielders in the National League," observed Lardner, "with one of the two or three best throwing arms."

Lardner then made a guess that Carey would award Reiser 5-4-4, the five for hitting, each of the fours for fielding and base running. On that same scale, Lardner thought that Ted Williams would deserve a 5-3-2 or 5-2-2 or 5-3-1. Or four to five points less than Reiser.

DiMaggio, Lardner guessed, would be a 5-4-3 or a 5-5-3, still one or two points shy of Reiser. And, finally, he calculated the numbers on the Carey scale for Ty Cobb and Babe Ruth. Cobb was given 5-3-5 and Ruth a 5-4-2. Thus, only Cobb, according to Lardner's interpretation, could be considered on a par with Reiser.

How much do these considerations mean all these years later? These men had not then witnessed the playing days of Willie Mays, Hank Aaron, Mickey Mantle or the rest of the great players that came later. This was also projected on the belief that Reiser's career had just begun. None of them could dare imagine that it would be so painfully shot down in midflight. One thing more. Neither they nor any of us could calculate that given the chance, Reiser's career could have possibly been much, much greater.

There is something else to resolve. So much has been written and said about Reiser's acceptance of all responsibility for his disasters. "That's the only way I knew how to play," he often declared. He also exonerated Durocher for any wrongdoing after his collision with the wall in St. Louis, in 1942. "I have never, ever blamed Leo for keeping me in there," said

Reiser. "I blame myself. He wanted to win so badly it hurt, and I wanted to win so bad it hurt."

(Never, by the way, did he once exonerate MacPhail for his role in that matter.)

That, at least, was the public Reiser. His conditioning on the tough streets of St. Louis and his tutoring by the hell-bent Durocher wouldn't allow him to blame anyone but himself. He had brought it all on himself and, what's more, he would do it again.

This same kind of *hubris* also wouldn't allow him to beg off any undertaking. To "chicken out," if you will, of the role assigned him. As stupid and as self-destructive as that role might be. If he was given the job of a center fielder, that's where he would play. If he was asked to return to the lineup while still dragging a leg or not seeing clearly, he would play and play the best he could.

He would do that and never once complain. The code of the street wouldn't allow him to do otherwise.

But in a tape he recorded with his son-in-law, Rick Tuber, he indicated something else. Referring to the attempt by the Yankees to trade for him back in 1939, Reiser said, "If I had played with the Yankees, I would have never gone into a wall. I wasn't going to beat DiMaggio out. I wasn't going to beat Charlie Keller or Tommy Henrich out. Red Rolfe, yes."

And as Yankee manager Joe McCarthy had indicated to him, third base was where he would have had him play. "I could have played third base till I was fifty years old," Reiser said to Tuber.

Had the Cardinals been able to retain him, Reiser again would have played at third base. Enos Slaughter and Terry Moore were fixtures in center and right. In left, whether it was Medwick, Ernie Koy, Johnny Hopp, or later, Stan Musial there, the position was well-defended. During those years, third base was a Cardinal problem.

"I could have played third base," Reiser reiterated. "I was a heck of a third baseman. Bill McKechnie told me I was. He told me I was the best third baseman he'd ever seen."

"Who can I sue?" Reiser asked his son-in-law in a voice that told you he rued his fate.

Of course, he did. But someone else would have had to step in and take charge. If only someone had...

If only the Cardinals had been able to keep him. If only the Yankees had been able to trade for him. If only the Dodgers had guarded their treasure and forced him to sit out the remainder of the 1942 season. If only they had realized that those walls would always haunt him and that this infielder belonged in the infield. If only Reiser had had the foresight and the courage to say, "Not till those walls are padded and a warning track borders them will I play out there."

If only…

Then we all might have seen the plaque that David Markson imagined really hanging in Baseball's Hall of Fame.

Or, who knows, one that celebrated even more.

Chapter Notes

Preface

"where the games's...": Donald Honig, *Baseball When the Grass Was Real* (Coward, McCann & Geoghegan, 1975), p. 282

"the most naturally...": William F. McNeil, *The Dodgers Encyclopedia* (Sports Publishing, 1997), p. 92.

"For 727 days...": ibid.

"Without heroes...": Bernard Malamud, *The Natural* (Farrar, Straus, and Giroux, 1952), p. 141.

1. The Brooklyn Dodgers

"called the Excelsiors...": Ellen Snyder-Grenier, *Brooklyn! An Illustrated History* (Temple University Press, 1996), p. 222.

"named James Creighton...": op. cit., p. 223.

"suffered a tragic death...": op. cit., p. 224.

"His body lies at rest...": ibid.

"officially called the Brooklyns...": op. cit., p. 232.

"known as the Bridegrooms...": McNeil, p. 6.

"the owner of the Baltimore Orioles...": Snyder-Grenier, p. 234.

"simply transferred several of his key players...": McNeil, p. 6.

"the newly formed rival American League...": ibid.

"the development of a farm system...": op. cit.

"ramshackled Washington Park...": op. cit., p 4.

"fittingly called Pigtown...": Peter Golenbock, *Bums* (Putnam, 1984), p. 2.

"40 different owners...": ibid.

"Why don't you call it...": ibid.

"its cost of $750,000...": Snyder-Grenier, p. 236.

"the new ballpark...": op. cit., p. 238.

"He hired as manager...": McNeil, p. 7.

"In 1920, Brooklyn...": ibid.

"Brooklyn's 37-year-old outfield star...": ibid.

"Known as the Daffiness Boys...": Snyder-Grenier, p. 239.

"Twice in one season...": Golenbock, p. 4.

"carried lit cigars...": op. cit., p. 5.

"didn't goof alone...": op. cit., p. 6.

"a Bonehead Club...": op. cit., p. 4.

"he would play Dickie Cox...": ibid.

"a player named Clyde...": op. cit., p. 6.

"the permanent attachment of the Dodgers...": McNeil, p. 8.

"where did the name Dodgers...": op. cit., p. 5.

213

2. Larry and Leo

"owed the Brooklyn Trust Company...":
Golenbock, p. 11.
"tiptoed into the office of...": ibid.
"conferred with Branch Rickey...": ibid.
"Leland Stanford MacPhail...": ibid.
"went to Cincinnati...": op. cit., p. 13.
"kayoed the team's owner...": ibid.
"MacPhail had his own way...": op. cit.,
p. 12.
"There is no question...": Leo Durocher,
Nice Guys Finish Last (Simon & Schuster, 1975), p. 105.
"stemmed from Shylock profits...":
Golenbock, p. 11.
"I'll take the job...": op. cit., p. 13.
"If I can't do business...": ibid.
"Is this all there is?...": ibid.
"He modernized Ebbets...": op. cit., p. 14.
"a good-looking hustler...": op. cit., p. 15.
"Thrown out of high school...": McNeil,
p. 122.
"he was caught red-handed...": Golenbock, p. 16.
"We have a chance...": ibid.
"stole from and alienated...": op. cit., p. 18.
"He loved me like a father..." Durocher,
Nice Guys, p. 35.
"to go fuck himself...": op. cit., p. 50.
"Sidney Weil, the owner..." op. cit., p. 55.
"As Durocher has written...": op. cit., p.
67.
"a name, in fact...": Golenbock, p. 21.
"When he came to St. Louis...": op. cit.,
p. 20.
"his first baseball coaching job...": ibid.
"he's afraid you're after...": Durocher,
Nice Guys, p. 97.
"The old Bambino...": Golenbock, op.
cit., p. 21.
"How could that baboon...": ibid.
"Grimes claimed that...": op. cit., p. 22.
"The traveling secretary...": op. cit., p. 23.
"Durocher placed their first...": op. cit.,
p. 24.

3. A Pistol Is Fired

"He was the best...": W. C. Heinz, Once

They Heard the Cheers (Doubleday,
1979), p. 392.
Reiser admitted to his own...": Honig,
p. 285.
"This was a working-class family...":
Lonnie Frey telephone interview,
March 12, 2002.
"My Dad pitched...": Julia Reiser telephone interview, April 4, 2002.
"When I was twelve...": Honig, p. 283.
"I'm fifteen years old...": Pete Reiser taped
interview with Rick Tuber, circa 1979.
"Well, Dad, I guess...": Honig, p. 288.
"'You see,'" explained Reiser...": Pete
Reiser taped interview.
"But Reiser was still...": Honig, p.
288–289.
"In answer to this punishment...":
Golenbock, p. 25–26.
"I was a shortstop...": Honig, p.
289–290.
"Though Reiser was now...": op. cit., p.
290–291.
"They had a guy down there...": op. cit.,
p. 291.
"But there was one play...": ibid.
"One day during spring...": op. cit., p.
292.
"What have I got here...": Golenbock, p.
25.
And he didn't stop...": Honig, p. 292.
"Joe McCarthy walks up to me...": ibid.
"The deal the Yankees...": W. C. Heinz,
"The Rocky Road of Pete Reiser," from
Best American Sports Writing of the
Century (Houghton Mifflin, 1999), p.
238.
"Meanwhile, Branch Rickey...": Golenbock, p. 26.
"MacPhail called Reiser...": Honig, p.
293.
"A fistfight took place...": Golenbock, p.
296.
"I never did...": Durocher, Nice Guys, p.
110.

4. Hidden Away

"I didn't see the old..." Heinz, Rocky
Road, p. 237.
"But I did...": Honig, p. 294.
"Reiser was informed...": ibid.

"I know you're not...": ibid.

"a call from Bill ... Reindeer Bill had ridden to the rescue": op. cit., p. 294–295.

"There were two things...": op. cit., p. 295.

5. Dem (Not Such) Bums

"They'd lynch me..." Golenbock, p. 50.

"It was a sportswriter...": Snyder-Grenier, p. 239.

"the highest Brooklyn...": Durocher, *Nice Guys*, p. 111.

"We had an outfielder...": Leo Durocher, *The Dodgers and Me* (Ziff-Davis Publishing Company, 1948), p. 49.

"However, at spring training...": op. cit., p. 51–52.

"The first time Durocher...": Durocher, *Nice Guys*, p. 114.

"Phelps also wouldn't go near...": op. cit., p. 59.

"In a game...": *New York Times*, June 2, 1940.

"A 19-year-old shortstop...": op. cit., June 5, 1940.

"This transaction, too...": Honig, p. 295.

"When Rickey is willing...":Durocher, *Nice Guys*, p. 115.

"I know Joe will be..." *New York Times*, June 12, 1940.

"Flatbush in fever...": ibid.

"On the following morning...": Durocher, *The Dodgers*, p. 55.

"He dropped like...": Durocher, *Nice Guys*, p. 116.

"There were fights...": ibid.

"Though there were 32...": Durocher, *The Dodgers*, p. 56.

"The most important occurrence...": Durocher, *Nice Guys*, p. 117.

"Leo Durocher, in his...": Durocher, *The Dodgers*, p. 58.

6. Finally

"In my estimation...": Golenbock, p. 165.

"the House that...": *The New York World*, April 19, 1923.

"There was an informal...": Golenbock, p. 39.

"Perhaps most famous...": op. cit., p. 44.

"Five rabid musical...": op. cit., p. 40.

"I felt great ... not exaggerating": Honig, p. 296–297.

"July 23, 1940...": *New York Times*, July 24, 1940.

"A short item...": ibid.

"Reiser may be...": op. cit., August 3, 1940.

"Manager Durocher made...": op. cit., August 4, 1940.

"Reiser hit his first...": op. cit., August 22, 1940.

"When regular third basemen...": Honig, p. 298.

"You're the best third...": ibid.

"I still think...": Durocher, *The Dodgers*, p. 59.

7. A New Shopping Spree

"The pitcher they ... a legal mandate": Durocher, *Nice Guys*, p. 118–119.

"This was in no...": Durocher, *The Dodgers*, p. 72.

"The New York Giants...": Durocher, *Nice Guys*, p. 119.

"Still afraid to fly...": Durocher, *The Dodgers*, p. 73.

"to smash baggage...": op. cit., p. 75.

"I hollered for Billy...": op. cit., p. 79.

"This was another...": op. cit., p. 79–80

8. Coming Into His Own

"Out in Los Angeles..." Heinz, *Rocky Road*, p. 236.

"I figured I could ... change his mind": Honig, p. 298–299.

"Young Peter ... Pete's victim": *New York Times*, March 4, 1941.

"He announced the use ... use it": op. cit., March 9, 1941.

"One story in...": op. cit., March 21, 1941.

"Another said...": op. cit., March 25, 1941.

"He [Medwick] was overshadowed...": op. cit., April 5, 1941.

"Three times...": op. cit., March 22, 1941.

"Only one ball was hit…": op. cit., March 21, 1941.

"Durocher was already…": op. cit., March 19, 1941.

"I wouldn't trade him … he's kidding." *Brooklyn Eagle*, April 1, 1941.

9. Rookie of the Year

"Any manager in…": Heinz, *Rocky Road*, p. 241.

"As Hy Turkin … week or two": *Daily News*, April 24, 1941

"Of course, General Manager…": ibid.

"In an interview with…" Heinz, *Rocky Road*, p. 241.

"A reliable source…": *Daily News*, April 25, 1941.

"I was a little worried…": *St. Louis Star-Times*, February 15, 1942.

"Young Pete Reiser…": *New York Times*, May 5, 1941.

"MacPhail, trying to release…": op. cit., May 8, 1941.

"He even knew…" op. cit., May 8, 1941.

"An injury to Pete Reiser…": op. cit., May 9, 1941.

"A month ago…": op. cit., May 26, 1941.

"There is a conflicting story…" Heinz, *Rocky Road*, p. 241.

"Years later, Reiser said…": Honig, p. 102.

"I don't want him…": *New York Times*, June 14, 1941.

"The committee…": op. cit., June 15, 1941.

"Without sufficient time…": op. cit., June 23, 1941.

"Werber singled in…" op. cit., June 22, 1941.

"Pete Reiser's speed…": op. cit., June 25, 1941.

"First Reese beat…": op. cit., June 26, 1941.

"Reiser exhibited…": op. cit., July 1, 1941.

"Pete Reiser, the spirit…": ibid.

"In an interview … baseball more": *New York Herald-Tribune*, July 1, 1941.

"Wonderful gent … Brooklyn flagpole": *New York Times*, July 10, 1941.

"Homer by Reiser … around the bases": op. cit., August 19, 1941.

"The game ended…": op. cit., August 23, 1941.

"The Dodgers have … in considerable doubt": op. cit., August 15, 1941.

10. Down to the Wire

"How many guys…": Heinz, *Once They Heard*, p. 407.

"Reiser decides nightcap…": *New York Times*, August 19, 1941.

"Ike Pearson … it was played": Honig, p. 299–300.

"Walker, running…": *New York Times*, September 9, 1941.

"At the end … for the final out": Durocher, *Nice Guys*, p. 125–128.

"Two-Gun Pete Reiser…": *New York Times*, September 19, 1941.

"The outcome of the game…": *New York Herald-Tribune*, September 22, 1941.

"Approximately 18,000 loyal…": ibid.

"The longest and closest…": op. cit., September 26, 1941.

"I had just thrown…": op. cit., September 28, 1941.

11. Three Strikes and Yer—

"He could do…": Golenbock, p. 164

"They climbed … it will last": *New York Herald-Tribune*, September 30, 1941.

"The Dodgers, apparently … Keller": *New York Times*, October 1, 1941.

"It's the crowd…": ibid.

"Incredible as it…": op. cit., October 3, 1941.

"In this interesting…": ibid.

"as freakish a mishap…": op. cit., October 5, 1941.

"threw his bread-and-butter…": Durocher, *Nice Guys*, p. 139.

"Before the first…" *New York Times*, October 6, 1941.

"When Owen did not…": Durocher, *Nice Guys*, p. 139.

"I did nothing…": op. cit., p. 140.

"But when those…": Pete Reiser taped interview.

"DiMaggio mumbled something...": *New York Times*, October 7, 1941.

"DiMaggio had told him...": Pete Reiser taped interview.

12. The Gold Dust Twins

"It's my opinion..." *New York Post*, July 5, 1946.

"In personality...": *Collier's*, April, 1942.

"I didn't know a baseline..." *International News Service*, September 19, 1942.

"The first day ... girl after that.": *St. Louis Star-Times*, July 2, 1942.

"look for good hitters...": *New York Times*, February 18, 1942.

"If you're watching...": op. cit., April 10, 1942.

"He can storm...": op. cit., February 20, 1942.

"I've got just...": ibid.

"I'm not picking...": op. cit., March 3, 1942.

"If I were picking...": *New York Herald-Tribune*, March 3, 1942.

"There are some ... on the pitchers": *New York Times*, March 29, 1942.

"Reese and Miss Dorothy..." *New York Herald Tribune*, April 2, 1942.

"Pete Reiser, Brooklyn's...": op. cit., April 5, 1942.

"While announcements were...": op. cit., April 6, 1942.

"I kept hearing ... Dodger uniforms": Golenbock, p. 57–58.

"Having been denied...": op. cit., p. 58.

"It was awful...": Durocher, *Nice Guys*, p. 153.

13. A Season to Remember

"Some people...": Gene Hermanski taped interview with Rick Tuber, circa 1985.

"Pledged to carry on...": *New York Times*, April 14, 1942.

"We weren't very near..." Dottie Reese telephone interview, June 16, 2002.

"The larcenous Pete..." *New York Herald Tribune*, June 20, 1942.

"One must go ... Cubs in September": op. cit., June 23, 1942.

"I was just starting...": Honig, p. 284.

"It's a line drive...": op. cit., p. 285.

"It was like a hand...": Golenbock, p. 59.

"I relayed it to...": Honig, p. 285.

"For ten maddening...": *New York Times*, July 20, 1942.

14. Nice Guys Finish Last

"I have never...": Golenbock, p. 60–61.

"a slight concussion." *New York Times*, July 22, 1942.

"Pete Reiser, Brooklyn..." *New York Herald-Tribune*, July 22, 1942.

"Look, Pete ... probably still am": Honig, p. 303.

"Pete will leave...": *New York Times*, July 21, 1942.

"was reported enroute...": op. cit., July 22, 1942.

"Pete Reiser, the injured...": *New York Herald-Tribune*, July 23, 1942.

"Reiser played but...": *New York Times*, July 26, 1942.

"Pete Reiser wasn't in uniform...": *New York Herald-Tribune*, August 7, 1942.

"Pete Reiser, still under...": op. cit., August 10, 1942.

"I was dizzy...": Heinz, *Rocky Road*, p. 244.

"The doctors...": Honig, p. 304.

"One of the most ... Maryland farm": *New York Herald-Tribune*, August 13, 1942.

"jack us up.": Honig, p. 304.

"Young man ... never forget that": Heinz, *Rocky Road*, p. 237.

"An incident ... with one eye": W. C. Heinz, *The Cheers*, p. 401.

"Drop in Brooklyn's...": *New York Herald-Tribune*, August 10, 1942.

"Pete Reiser hopped...": op. cit., August 11, 1942.

"By the proverbial...": op. cit., August 13, 1942.

"Remember when...": op. cit., August 16, 1942.

"You'd better get him..." op. cit., August 26, 1942.

"I was seeing...": Heinz, *Rocky Road*, p. 244.

"Pete Reiser, removed...": *New York Herald-Tribune*, August 27, 1942.

"If Pete Reiser's injured...": op. cit., August 30, 1942.

"Nobody'll catch us...": op. cit., September 1, 1942.

"He should be as...": op. cit., September 2, 1942.

"I think we're in...": op. cit., September 13, 1942.

"Tipton was credited...": op. cit., September 14, 1942.

"That character...": Golenbock, p. 60.

15. Men of War

"Pete may have been...": *Los Angeles Herald-Examiner*, November 2, 1981.

"The Age of the Bottom...": Golenbock, p. 62–63.

"Is there a Harold ... supposed to do": Honig, 308–310.

"Considering what ... for Camp Lee": Heinz, *Rocky Road*, p. 246–247.

"By this time...": Honig, p. 310.

16. The Men Come Home

"Here was a man...": *New York Times*, April 27, 1964.

"Luke. Chapter Fifteen...": Durocher, *Nice Guys*, p. 188.

"I have only one ...": *New York Times*, February 20, 1946.

"a test of the lighting...": op. cit., March 25, 1946.

"There's too much...": op. cit., March 16, 1946.

"I don't know if...": op. cit., April 5, 1946.

"Pete Reiser brooding...": *The New York Post*, March 7, 1946.

"The big bat...": op. cit., March 12, 1946.

"It looks as though...": op. cit., March 16, 1946.

"Predictions are a dime...": op. cit., March 29, 1946.

"He may never..." op. cit., April 1, 1946.

"Most people are picking..." op. cit., April 8, 1946.

"I like the Dodgers...": op. cit., April 15, 1946.

"If Pete Reiser's arm...": op. cit., April 12, 1946.

17. Home Is for the Stealing

"Young man, you're...": Heinz, *Rocky Road*, p. 237.

"Mexican baseball...": *New York Herald-Tribune*, April 13, 1946.

"Which Reiser stole...": op. cit., April 19, 1946.

"My biggest scare...": op. cit., April 24, 1946.

"they might have snatched...": op. cit., May 4, 1946.

"The loss of Reiser...": ibid.

"titanic blast which...": op. cit., May 12, 1946.

"Reiser proved that he...": op. cit., May 16, 1946.

"We played a dirty trick...": op. cit., June 8, 1946.

"Baseball's steering committee...": op. cit., July 19, 1946.

"lost the services...": op. cit., May 20, 1946.

"Reiser may not play...": op. cit., June 1, 1946.

"Pete Reiser's ailing...": op. cit., June 4, 1946.

"He told me...": op. cit., June 13, 1946.

"Reiser's sore arm...": op. cit., June 20, 1946.

"The top third...": op. cit., June 21, 1946.

"Not that they're...": op. cit., June 22, 1946.

"Reiser is best ... up in Montreal": *New York Post*, July 6, 1946.

"You're out...": Honig, p. 311.

"An inside the park...": *New York Times*, July 30, 1946.

"Disaster dealt...": op. cit., August 2, 1946.

"Pistol Pete Reiser...": op. cit., August 9, 1946.

"It was Peter...": op. cit., August 11, 1946.

"The dangerous...": op. cit., August 13, 1946.

"Then the Dodgers...": op. cit., August 15, 1946.

"This optimism...": op. cit., August 20, 1946.

"The most heart-warming...": ibid.

"flooded every team ... about Lanier": op. cit., August 8, 1946.

"The Cards couldn't...": op. cit., August 28, 1946.

"Reiser withdrew...": *New York Herald Tribune*, September 1, 1946.

"Pete Reiser was in...": op. cit., September 2, 1946.

"Reiser, who plans...": op. cit., September 5, 1946.

"Before Pete Reiser...": *New York Times*, August 28, 1946.

"With Pete Reiser's...": *New York Post*, September 10, 1946.

"Whether Pete Reiser...": *New York Times*, September 25, 1946.

"was marred by the loss...": op. cit., September 27, 1946.

"The Pistol has now...": *New York Post*, September 27, 1946.

"It was a clean break...": ibid.

18. The Natural

"Reiser was proclaimed...": Michael Shapiro, *The Last Good Season* (Doubleday, 2003), p. 59.

"That's healed ... ball player this year": *New York Post*, Feburary 4, 1947.

"The Dodgers need...": ibid.

"The younger players ... all right, well": op. cit., February 18, 1947.

"Larry MacPhail offered...": Durocher, *The Dodgers*, p. 271.

"conduct detrimental...": *New York Times*, April 10, 1947.

"teamed up with...": Golenbock, p. 135.

"didn't think it...": *New York World Telegram*, November 1, 1945.

"Leo Durocher's suspension...": Golenbock, p. 161.

"Even Pete ... if necessary.": *New York Post*, April 11, 1947.

"You've got a great...": *New York Times*, April 12, 1947.

19. The Walls

"Pete Reiser just might...": *Los Angeles Times*, April 4, 1964.

"A solemn crowd...": *New York Herald-Tribune*, April 16, 1947.

"It was a typical...": ibid.

"Shotton watched...": Golenbock, p. 162.

"That one was...": ibid.

"The man just wasn't...": ibid.

"I don't think anybody...": *New York Daily News*, May 4, 1947.

"It sure is different...": *New York Herald-Tribune*, April 21, 1947.

"Shotton didn't like...": Patricia Reiser taped interview with Rick Tuber, circa 1985.

"For the first time...": *New York Daily News*, May 4, 1947.

"He does not...": *New York Herald-Tribune*, April 10, 1947.

"In case anyone...": op. cit., April 12, 1947.

"When I saw the commissioner...": *New York Daily News*, May 7, 1947.

"Walker is guarding Reiser...": *New York Herald-Tribune*, April 25, 1947.

"If it hadn't been for Reiser...": ibid.

"Reiser has not received...": *New York Times*, May 23, 1947.

"A fascinating, if painful, statistic...": *New York Herald-Tribune*, June 1, 1947.

"Hell, this is...": Honig, p. 313.

"The crowd, which...": *New York Herald-Tribune*, June 5, 1947.

'I knew I ...": Gene Hermanski taped interview with Rick Tuber, circa 1985.

"I almost died...": Golenbock, p. 246.

"Pete Reiser, who cracked...": *New York Herald-Tribune*, June 6, 1947.

"Pete Reiser, still recovering...": op. cit., June 8, 1947.

"I was out in...": Honig, p. 313.

"You're lucky...": Heinz, *Rocky Road*, p. 249.

"He was received...": *New York Herald-Tribune*, July 13, 1947.

"Pete Reiser started...": op. cit., July 16, 1947.

"The inherent recklessness...": op. cit., July 22, 1947.

"I always marveled...": Golenbock, p. 164.
"Reiser looks more...": *New York Herald-Tribune*, August 2, 1947.
"Pete Reiser still suffering...": op. cit., August 8, 1947.

20. End Game

"Durocher played him...": Golenbock, p. 60.
"I could feel myself..." Honig, p. 313.
"I want to play...": Heinz, *Rocky Road*, p. 249.
"It was a great thrill...": *New York Herald-Tribune*, September 27, 1947.
"Joe D started...": Golenbock, p. 168.
"I lost it...": *New York Herald-Tribune*, October 2, 1947.
"Pete Reiser had...": ibid.
"You've got a broken ankle...": Honig, p. 313.
"Aren't you going to...": Heinz, *Rocky Road*, p. 250.
"When the count got...": Golenbock, p. 169.
"I don't give a darn...": ibid.
"I had never faced...": op. cit., p. 171.
"I didn't get no butterflies...": op. cit., p. 172.
"For in one of...": *New York Times*, October 6, 1947.
"I'm positioned between ... with my butt": Golenbock, p. 173–174.
"Once Page entered...": *New York Times*, October 7, 1947.
"You're not doing...": op. cit., October 6, 1947.

21. The Image Fades

"Maybe Pete Reiser was..." Heinz, *Rocky Road*, p. 236.
"I was only nineteen...": Taped interview with Rick Tuber.
"He said he would pay...": Honig, p. 314.
"to keep him from...": Durocher, *Nice Guys*, p. 244–245.
"I got permission...": *Miami Daily News*, February 25, 1949.
"Reiser is the greatest...": *North American Newspaper Alliance*, February 26, 1949.

"They have tin...": *Miami Daily News*, February 25, 1949.
"I've found that Pete's...": *New York Daily News*, March 6, 1949.
"At one time...": *The Sporting News*, March 10, 1949.
"nine months of agony...": Taped interview with Rick Tuber.

22. Aftermath

"Pistol Pete Reiser...": McNeil, p. 92
"I asked him ... you think I'm worth": Glen Schaeffer taped interview with Rick Tuber, circa 1985.
"I couldn't buy ... thirty-seven years": Wills, Maury, *It Pays to Steal* (Prentice-Hall, 1963), p. 51–55.
"You had to give ... your ability": Carl Warwick taped interview with Rick Tuber, circa 1985.
"He can be more...": *Collier's Magazine*, May, 1942.
"found him moving ... have to drive": Heinz, *The Cheers*, p. 397.
"There was a big scrap...": op. cit., p. 404.
"He had a small...": op. cit., p. 402.

23. An Imperfect Appraisal

"Pete Reiser was the greatest...": Lonnie Frey telephone interview, March 12, 2002.
"I didn't see Hornsby...": ibid.
"There are competent...": *Collier's Magazine*, May, 1942.
"the Carey system...": *North American Newspaper Alliance*, July 31, 1942.
"If I had played...": Pete Reiser taped interview.

Bibliography

Durocher, Leo. *The Dodgers and Me*. New York: Ziff-Davis, 1948.

_____, with Lynn, Ed. *Nice Guys Finish Last*. New York: Simon & Schuster, 1975.

Golenbock, Peter. *Bums*. New York: Putnam, 1984.

Heinz, W.C. *Once They Heard the Cheers*. Garden City, N.Y.: Doubleday, 1979.

_____. "The Rocky Road of Pistol Pete." In *Best American Sports Writing of the Century*. Boston: Houghton Mifflin, 1999.

Honig, Donald. *Baseball When the Grass Was Real*. New York: Coward, McCann & Geoghegan, 1975.

Malamud, Bernard. *The Natural*. New York: Farrar, Straus & Giroux, 1952.

McNeil, William F. *The Dodgers Encyclopedia*. Champaign, Ill.: Sports Publishing, 1997.

Snyder-Grenier, Ellen M. *Brooklyn! An Illustrated History*. Philadelphia: Temple University Press, 1996.

Wills, Maury. *It Pays to Steal*. Englewood Cliffs, N.J.: Prentice Hall, 1963.

Index